Toscanini
and the
Art of Orchestral Performance

Toscanini
and the Art of
Orchestral Performance

by Robert Charles Marsh

J. B. LIPPINCOTT COMPANY
PHILADELPHIA   •   NEW YORK

20271

CONTENTS

Preface   7

I   The Man and His Audience   13

II   Toscanini's Musicianship   58

III   The Toscanini Recordings   97

IV   Toscanini's Repertory   193

Appendix One
The Toscanini Repertory   217

Appendix Two
A Note on Equipment   242

Appendix Three
Chronology of Toscanini's Life   244

Appendix Four
The Toscanini Recordings Listed by Composers   246

Preface

THIS STUDY is popular in the sense that it is written for intelligent persons who enjoy music rather than for specialists. It reflects the author's concern for the lack of communication between scholars and the educated citizenry and the evils that result on either side: the narrowing of viewpoint that follows when scholars become accustomed to speaking only to other scholars, and the difficulties the citizen may have in arriving at a well-balanced judgment when he is denied the opportunity of knowing what qualified persons have to say about subjects of interest to him.

Implicit in this work is the assumption that recordings possess a documentary value for the historian of music that is of equal (if not at times of greater) importance than that of manuscripts and printed music. I need not stress the limitations of notation and the value, for all musicians to follow, of the recordings we possess of great contemporary works (such as those of Stravinsky) as played under the direction of the composer himself. They establish a style and a tradition in an authoritative manner which cannot be ignored. In the case of Toscanini, recordings give us the achievements of a musician of unique powers, whose name will be remembered for generations to come, and whom persons now unborn will be able to hear with a clarity and force that is adequate to convey the magnitude of his achievements. The better Toscanini recordings are thus, in my eyes, among the most important "documents in sound" of contemporary music history.

This book could not have been written in any library, since much of the needed information lay in the files (and memories) of individuals. A great deal of the material in this book is here appearing in print for the first time. Let it be said at once that there is more to be gathered on this subject than is contained in these pages.

The contrast between the relative social positions of the celebrated personage and the young professor ought to make clear the difficulties involved. One consequence of this is that many of my statements cannot be attributed to their sources, since I am under a moral obligation to persons who spoke frankly with me and asked that I conceal their identity. In this group are several musicians of the highest reputation, more than one well-known critic, and a number of other individuals who have been associated with Toscanini for years and are familiar with his methods and point of view. It is my hope that I have escaped from the stereotypes which reappear in discussions of Toscanini from the public-relations viewpoint and have presented a picture of this great musician that is balanced, objective, and able to convey, in some degree, the force and vitality of the man.

A few specific words of thanks can be said, however. Mr. George R. Marek, Director of Artists and Repertoire for RCA Victor, promised assistance in advance and gave it fully and freely to the very end of the project. I feel my debt to him is very great, particularly since he had to bear with me in the difficult period toward the end of the study when I was living in Britain and recordings had to be shipped to me there. Mr. Alan Kayes, Manager of Red Seal Artists and Repertoire; Mr. Richard Mohr, Musical Director of Red Seal Recording, and the charming and helpful ladies who are their secretaries, must share in my gratitude for the patience and kindness shown me. For similar help I must thank Mr. J. D. Bicknell of The Gramophone Company and Mr. Owen Mase, Toscanini's British manager.

Mr. Walter Toscanini worked with me for several days collecting material which appears in the appendices and answering many questions, yielding information which is scattered throughout the text. For this assistance I am very grateful, but, to prevent any misunderstanding, it must be noted that the author is responsible for what has been done with this information, and the judgments contained in this study are his own. A well-known critic who examined the preliminary outline of this book and has, during a number of years, discussed many of the questions in it with me (so that it may reflect some of his views, just as a teacher's opinions may influence his students) has, in the light of our present relationship, requested that I thank him anonymously.

The Harvard College Library provided me with an agreeable place to work during the summer of 1954 when the MS was being drafted for the first time. No alumnus could ask for more. The Yale University Library allowed me to use the Max Smith papers, although some of the documents which I had been told were in this collection could not be found, and it was thought that they had been burned. It is my hope that the material in question (a collection of timings of Toscanini performances over a period of many years) has, in fact, escaped destruction, although I feel its loss for the purposes of my second chapter very keenly. The New York Public Library provided certain information on Toscanini's programs with the Philharmonic-Symphony Orchestra of New York which the orchestral management declined to supply. Because of these difficulties, there may be a few slips in Appendix One. I am in debt to the Socony-Vacuum Oil Company for tickets to the Toscanini broadcasts during his final season when the challenge of getting into Carnegie Hall on Sunday took on a really sporting character!

Portions of Chapters II and III appeared in *High Fidelity* magazine for December of 1954 and January and February of 1955. I must thank the editor, Mr. John M. Conly, the managing editor, Mr. Roy H. Hoopes, Jr., and the other members of the staff for the friendliness, consideration, and intelligence which have characterized my relations with them from the beginning. A similar relationship with Mr. Alan D. Williams of J. B. Lippincott Company has materially assisted the publication of this book.

R. C. M.

Trinity College
The University of Cambridge

Toscanini
and the
Art of Orchestral Performance

I

The Man and His Audience

1

THE CAREER of Arturo Toscanini contains all the elements of a successful novel except one: it is too fabulous to be plausible. That a poor boy should rise quickly to the top of his profession and remain there for over half a century, retiring with his skill virtually unimpaired and the devotion of his public at the highest pitch is the stuff of a film scenario. Our sensitivity to social realities causes us to doubt its possibility as an actual life pattern; but in this case the exceptional and the actual are the same.

Arturo Toscanini was born on the twenty-fifth of March, 1867, in Parma, which was then (as now) a reasonably good-sized city in northern Italy. Claudio Toscanini, his father, was a tailor, and he and his wife, Paola Montani, both represented working-class families that depended on agriculture or employment as craftsmen for subsistence. There were no musicians among them and no direct evidence of art in the blood, except perhaps Claudio Toscanini's dislike for the drudgery and routine of his craft which had led him to abandon his needle and cutting bench for a career in Garibaldi's army as a youth and made him vulnerable to shaky, if imaginative, ventures in later years. Arturo was the first of three children; two sisters were born during his early childhood.

Paola Toscanini was the strong member of the family. She too sewed, and she cared for her children as best she could, taught them to be honest, to work hard, and to stand up to their misfortunes rather than be overcome by them. Her handsome, cheerful, husband could not provide her with the way of life known to the rest of her family, but in spite of her difficulties she tried to meet her relatives as a peer, and demanded of her children that they

13

conceal their poverty and hunger. Apart from this she was too deeply involved in reviewing the unfortunate consequences of her situation to offer her children much affection or aid. Arturo had the ability to follow her guidance and better himself, but his sisters were unable to extract themselves from their environment, and their failure came to occupy her thoughts more than his success. There is good reason to think that Toscanini's short stature is due to malnutrition as a child.

Young Arturo was quick to learn to read and insatiable in his desire for books. The rapidity with which he could memorize things and the skill with which, when he finally got access to a piano in the home of one of his teachers, he played operatic airs of the day, led to the conclusion that he should become a musician. He was unsuccessful in obtaining a scholarship to the Royal School of Music at Parma but the family budget under the unusual strain yielded the fees, and at the age of nine he left his demanding, unaffectionate mother and indifferent father and took up a way of life with rigid discipline demanding complete dedication to music. Two years later, in 1878, he was granted a scholarship which he held to the end of his studies. His parents accepted his departure from the household and did not visit him at the conservatory. He worked unceasingly, winning honors for 'cello, piano, and composition on his graduation. The prescribed course did not take all his time, and when his assigned work was done he read scores.

The Toscanini that emerged from the Parma Conservatory in 1885 was a musician of recognized competence who had had the practical experience of conducting a small orchestra of his fellow students and playing in the pit orchestra of the Parma Opera House during five spring carnival seasons. (His zeal for Wagner goes back to a performance of *Lohengrin* in which he played in 1884.) He returned to his family as its head. His father gave in without a struggle; his mother accepted him in his new role, with pride probably mixed with meaner emotions.

He did not stay at home long. The impresario Claudio Rossi engaged him to play the 'cello and serve as assistant chorus master and vocal coach with an Italian opera company going to Brazil for the winter season.

The debut of the greatest Italian conductor of our times took place, therefore, not in Italy but in the Americas: in Rio de

Janeiro on June 25, 1886. He was nineteen, and the whole affair reads like fiction. The principal conductor of the company was a Brazilian, Leopoldo Miguez. After two months in São Paulo, where the performances had been bad, the company arrived in Rio, where they got no better. Miguez bet on the chauvinism of the audience to save himself and, sending a statement to the newspapers that placed the blame on the Italian singers (most of whom were well-established artists), walked out. When the assistant conductor appeared in the pit to lead *Aïda* on that memorable evening he was forced to retreat before the din from the house. So was the impresario, who tried to make a speech. The chorus master then attempted to start the performance, with the same lack of success. By then Toscanini, who had originally planned to stay away and avoid the uproar, had changed his mind and was in the theatre. He was the only remaining member of the company qualified to conduct, and under the persuasion of the singers and his fellows in the orchestra (somehow I feel that not a great deal of persuasion was necessary) he took up the stick, entered the pit, and led the opera from memory. The performance was a success, and his career as a conductor was ordained.

Before leaving Brazil he led eighteen operas from the repertory of the day (among them Gounod's *Faust* and the *Rigoletto* and *Il Trovatore* of his beloved Verdi). When he returned to Italy in the autumn the next step was not clearly marked out for him. The Italian public were indifferent to what had taken place in distant Rio, and there were no bids awaiting the young Maestro. The singers, however, knew what he had done, and through Nicola Figner, who had been the tenor of Rossi's troop, Toscanini was engaged to give Alfredo Catalani's *Edmea* at Turin. His Italian debut on November 4, 1886, in an opera house in which his reputation was to grow almost yearly during the twelve seasons to come, was a tame and orderly affair compared with his first Brazilian appearance, but it was a success, and Catalani (for whom he always retained the most sincere loyalty and affection) showed himself to be a good judge of musicians by predicting that Toscanini was on his way to an "extraordinary career."

At that moment, however, his position was none too secure, and he stayed on in Turin to coach the orchestra in the *Flying Dutchman* for another conductor. That job ended, he went to

Milan, and on the occasion of the first performance of Verdi's *Otello* on February 5, 1887, Toscanini was present as neither conductor nor spectator, but as the second desk 'cellist. La Scala was then, as it is today, the leading operatic theatre in Italy, and as Toscanini sat in the pit that first season it is possible he imagined that he would be able to make a career there, but he could hardly have conceived the nature of his relationship with the house in his various periods there, or the way that relationship would end in sixty-eight years.

His career as an orchestra player, however, was about over. The following season brought him engagements as a conductor, first in Casale Monferrato, which in those days could hardly be regarded as a center of the lyric stage, and then in Verona, a city of some importance. He was on his way through the theatres of the provinces and the smaller cities, broken by an occasional visit to a larger place such as Turin or the Teatro dal Verme in Milan, gaining the experience which these opera houses (and their counterparts in Central Europe) provided by way of practical training to nearly every great singer and conductor of our time. In the twelve seasons he spent acquiring a reputation, between 1886 and 1898, he appeared in twenty Italian cities and towns. (He left the Italian circuit briefly in 1890 to appear in Barcelona.) From 1892, when he gave three operas (including a première) at Rome, his apprenticeship can be regarded as definitely over. The fact that he achieved full professional stature while in his early twenties indicates a phenomenal natural aptitude for conducting which even a short period of experience could turn into mastery of the art. Of the operas he prepared in the years between his debut and 1898, only about half are known outside Italy, and of the seven world premières he gave only two, *Pagliacci* (Milan, 1892) and *La Bohème* (Turin, 1896), were of scores heard in many of the world's opera houses today. In the winter season of 1895-96 he applied himself to weightier matters, the first Italian performance of *Die Götterdämmerung*, in Turin, December 22, 1895.

The main stream of Italian music was opera; symphonic works came second, and it was a rare operatic conductor who was engaged to lead symphony concerts. It was, therefore, not until March 20, 1896, nearly ten years after his debut, that Toscanini, five days short of his twenty-ninth birthday, appeared on the stage of the opera house in Turin to lead a program that sounds much the same as those he offered throughout his later career: Brahms's *Tragic Overture,* the *Entry of the Gods into Valhalla* from *Das Rheingold,* a Wagnerian excerpt he did not play in any of his American concerts after 1921, the Tchaikovsky *Nutcracker Suite,* and the great *C Major Symphony, No. 9,* of Franz Schubert.° Later in the spring he gave four symphonic programs at La Scala in Milan. He played Haydn, Beethoven, Schubert, Brahms, Tchaikovsky, Wagner—all composers he continued to play until his retirement—plus some lesser music, a certain amount of which remained in his repertory along with the major compositions. During the following season he returned to operatic scores, but in 1898 he again turned to symphonic music and gave forty-three concerts (including the first Italian performance of the recent *Pathétique Symphony* of Tchaikovsky) during the International Exposition at Turin.

At thirty he was a man of position and recognized stature. In June, 1897, he married Carla de Martini, the daughter of a Milan banker. Their first child, Walter, was born in March of the following year. His family life, as his private life in the years before his marriage, was now completely divorced from that of his parents and sisters, with whom he had only the most tenuous links. They never attended his performances and were not present at his wedding.

It was possible to call Toscanini the foremost Italian conductor of the day, and it was natural that he should assume the musical direction of the leading Italian operatic theatre. This came to pass in 1898 when Giulio Gatti-Casazza was put in charge of the management of La Scala, Milan, and called Toscanini to be principal conductor. He was then thirty-one and, with twelve years of conducting behind him, had arrived at the highest position in the musical life of his country.

Toscanini's first period at La Scala ran five years. As had been the case in his previous engagements, he had a loyal and appreciative public, but there were also detractors and critics, musicians he drove too hard, singers he offended, and members of the audience who wanted encores and similar indulgences, on hand to speak against him. No selfless, hard-driving man is

___

° Previously he had given a short concert in Venice in 1895, but apparently not of the type one would regard today as a program of symphonic music.

ever completely popular, and those who did not share Toscanini's dedication to music found it somewhat oppressive at times.

In addition to Italian operas he offered a representative selection of Wagner; *Die Meistersinger* (with which he opened his first season), *Siegfried, Lohengrin,* and *Tristan und Isolde.* Among his other productions was the first Italian performance of another score of Tchaikovsky, *Eugene Onegin.*

It was customary to give four symphony concerts at the close of the opera season at La Scala, rather meagre fare by American or British standards, but to the Italian public music was primarily opera and ballet. In 1900, at the end of the season, Toscanini took the La Scala Orchestra on a short tour of northern Italy with considerable success. Parma welcomed him with enthusiasm.

There was a devoted audience for Italian opera in South America, and it was natural that Toscanini should want to appear there. The fact that the Argentine winter season ran from National Day (25 de Mayo) in May to late August or early September, a period in which there was little musical activity in the Italian opera houses, made it a particularly attractive opportunity to work the full season in both hemispheres. Toscanini accepted engagements at the Teatro de la Opera, Buenos Aires, in 1901, 1903, 1904, and 1906. In 1912 he returned, this time at the Teatro Colón. His next, and final, appearance in South America was twenty-eight years later with the National Broadcasting Company Symphony.

The spring symphonic programs at La Scala in 1902 contained the *Ninth Symphony* of Beethoven, which Toscanini conducted in full for the first time. (He did not prepare the *Missa Solemnis* until 1934, just before his sixty-seventh birthday.) The 1902-03 season began with a brilliant production of Berlioz's *Damnation of Faust* as an opera. There had been growing tension between Toscanini and segments of the La Scala audience, particularly with respect to encores during a performance. The 1901-02 season had ended with Toscanini storming out of the theatre in the midde of an opera because of such an outbreak, but when his passion subsided he had returned to complete the performance. On the final evening of the 1902-03 season there was another such demonstration, and this time Toscanini did not return. He sailed for Argentina.

The autumn of 1903 found him without a post in Italy. La

Scala had engaged Cleofonte Campanini for three years, and he was suffering (as others were to do) the exquisite misery of being a man of lesser powers following in the footsteps of a Toscanini. Moreover, La Scala wanted Toscanini to come back. He accepted only two offers that season, appearing in symphony concerts in Rome and leading two operas at Bologna. In May he returned to Buenos Aires. In the autumn of 1904 the same procedure was repeated. Toscanini remained at home in Milan and La Scala went its own way. The following April he conducted in Turin, and in June (he did not go to South America that summer) he brought the Turin Orchestra to La Scala for a pair of symphony concerts. It was a pointed lesson to the Milan audience that was no doubt understood. He even rewarded them for good behavior by playing an encore.

Early in the 1905-06 season Campanini departed from La Scala after a culminating battle with the orchestra. Toscanini was conspicuously active near by in Bologna and Turin, and at the close of the opera season he took the Turin Orchestra on another short tour of northern Italy, after which he again sailed to Argentina.

La Scala had had enough punishment. He was invited to return, and henceforth the program carried a notice that encores were forbidden. Toscanini found that everything had gone slack in his absence, and he went to work restoring order and discipline. The Milan audience, still not entirely pleased with the manner in which he had treated them, were none the less eager to have him back, and all went well. Among the works of the 1906-07 season was the first Italian production of Richard Strauss's *Salome*.

This period at La Scala lasted only two seasons. In the second, 1907-08, he again offered an important Italian première, Debussy's *Pelléas et Mélisande*, and a revival of Charpentier's *Louise*, in addition to staples of the national repertory and *Die Götterdämmerung*. One would think that a conductor who could offer such fare would have his public firmly behind him, but the limitations and boorishness of much of the Milan audience must be reckoned with. *Pelléas* nearly provoked a riot, and many of the finest passages were lost in the din created by yahoos who understood nothing more subtle than *"La donna è mobile."* When the opportunity for Gatti-Casazza and himself to go to the Metropolitan Opera House in New York arose, it was natural that Toscanini should accept it, just as it was natural that the chauvinistic elements of the public (which had never forgotten that he had been able to walk out on his adversaries and go to South America) should make his departure uncomfortable. He led two symphonic concerts at the end of the season, and split violently with the management of La Scala when they ordered him to include two specific works in his third program. Another conductor complied with their wishes, and Toscanini took his leave. This time he was not to return to La Scala for twelve years.

Toscanini arrived on the North American scene in the autumn of 1908. He was a man of forty-one who had been a conductor for twenty-two years. His great reputation in his own country was known, but he was by no means the conductor of universal renown he was to become in later years: indeed, his appearances had been limited virtually to northern Italy and two South American countries. His career in the United States falls into four sections, each of which ends with a full close: that is, the expectation that he would return to Italy and not be heard again in the United States for some time—if at all. The Metropolitan period is of seven years, 1908-15. There is then a gap of six years until Toscanini returns briefly to tour the United States with the La Scala Orchestra in 1920-21. Five years pass, and Toscanini comes back to be guest conductor of the New York Philharmonic, becomes its principal conductor in 1928, and appears with that orchestra during eleven seasons, until he leaves it in 1936. Nineteen months later he returns and assumes direction of the N.B.C. Symphony, which he leads for seventeen seasons, until his retirement in 1954. A number of New York musicians are willing to bet that the last of him is yet to be seen and heard.

Toscanini faced a New York audience for the first time on November 16, 1908. Five years before, when he had first turned his back on La Scala, the Metropolitan had been interested, but he had not wished to enter an unknown situation in an unknown city. When Gatti-Casazza, whom he trusted, also was approached, the situation became attractive to him and, to the degree he had been indifferent before, he now became enthusiastic. The presence of Gustav Mahler among the other conductors at the Metropolitan convinced Toscanini of the high standards of the house.

Reading the review of his American debut, one can easily imagine the performance that it describes: a performance no different from those which one later heard from the Old Man. It is doubtful that Toscanini was ever an immature musician, stylistically at a loss and unable to control his men. If I were told that his *Aïda* in 1886 was equal to the one I heard in 1949 I should be tempted to believe it. In any case, because the performances of his youth and middle life were experienced by few Americans, let us not suppose that they were any less miraculous than those of his later years.

Writing of that 1908 *Aïda* that opened the Metropolitan season and introduced Toscanini to New York, Richard Aldrich says:

"He is a strenuous force, a dominating power, a man of potent authority, a musician of infinite resource. He had the performance at every point firmly and directly under his hand. . . . He is a man that insists on a clear-cut outline, on abundant detail, on the strongest contrasts, on vivid color. In fortissimos the brasses could not blow loudly enough for him, nor could the crescendos be brought to climaxes fulminating enough. But there were other and finer points that could not have escaped the attention of the close observer; the fine modeling of phrases, the symmetry of musical outline in many places where mere brute force was not in question. And the pulsating, dramatic blood he sent coursing through the score was never allowed to stagnate. . . . This prevailing spirit influenced every member of the cast. . . . Caruso . . . sang with probably more power, with more insistent dwelling on the highest tones, with a more prodigal expenditure of his resources, than ever he has achieved before. . . ."[*]

This was probably the finest *Aïda* New York had ever heard, and it typified what was to come. He gave them Italian repertory, including *Falstaff,* and the first performance in the United States of *Le Villi,* Puccini's first opera—a work in one act that he paired with *Cavalleria Rusticana*—and, in remembrance of Catalani, *La Wally.* There was an abridged version of *Die Götterdämmerung,* a memorable *Carmen,* and a special concert program of the Verdi *Requiem* and the prelude to Boito's *Mefistofele* which he led four times. On his return to Italy he prepared a concert in Naples to honor the memory of his friend Martucci, who had died earlier that year.

[*] *Concert Life in New York* [New York: G. P. Putnam's Sons, 1941], pp. 234-35.

In the 1909-10 season he offered the Verdi *Requiem* twice and prepared both *Tristan und Isolde* and *Die Meistersinger* in addition to Italian operas and a revival of Gluck's *Orfeo*. In the spring the company went to Paris, and Toscanini found himself assigned to show Europeans the excellence of an American musical organization. (Twenty years later he was to repeat the demonstration with the New York Philharmonic.) He did his job well.

Toscanini's third New York season contained the world première of an opera on "an American subject"—Puccini's *The Girl of the Golden West*, a work that is musically completely Italian in idiom and American only in its setting and its absurd, melodramatic plot. None the less, it was taken as a compliment and was a success. A more important American première was Paul Dukas' opera *Ariane et Barbe-Bleu*, which received no comparable acclaim. For the rest, there were Toscanini performances of *Die Meistersinger, Tristan, Otello*, Gluck's *Armide*, in its first Metropolitan production (which held the stage for a single season), and a number of standard Italian scores. Much the same fare was offered in the 1911-12 season. Toscanini was working hard, but he was satisfied with his audience and his results. That summer in Buenos Aires he repeated the Dukas without great public recognition and led a demanding schedule of German and Italian works.

It was not until the 1912-13 season, his fifth at the Metropolitan, that New York heard him conduct a symphony concert. The high light of the opera that year had been the American première of Moussorgsky's *Boris Godunov*, in Italian(!), in March. Chaliapin, who had been given rough and unjustified treatment by the New York critics during the 1907-08 season, declined the offer to return, in spite of his admiration of Toscanini which resulted from their work together at La Scala. (He did not sing the role at the Metropolitan until 1921, long after Toscanini had left its pit.) On April 13 (and again on the eighteenth), 1913, Toscanini led the "somewhat augmented" Metropolitan Opera Orchestra in Wagner's *A Faust Overture*, Strauss's *Till Eulenspiegel* and the Beethoven *Ninth Symphony*, in which Frieda Hempel, Louise Homer, Karl Jörn, Putnam Griswold, and the chorus of the opera house were heard in the vocal parts.

Richard Aldrich wrote of the concert:

"The orchestra in the years that it has been under the control of Mr. Toscanini has gained greatly in suppleness and plasticity as well as in precision and perfection of ensemble. . . . He revealed in the fullest measure the qualities of the great symphonic conductor. In [the *Ninth Symphony*] Mr. Toscanini met in an unsual degree Wagner's criterion of the *melos*, of keeping unbroken the essentially melodic line that underlies it. The orchestra sang throughout, and in all the nuances of the performance the melodic line was not interrupted; nor in all the plastic shaping of the phrase was the symmetry of the larger proportion of the organic unit of the whole lost sight of. It was rhythmically of extraordinary vitality. It was a conservative reading without exaggerations or excesses. There were subtle and significant modulations of tempo, but never of a disturbing sort. It was devoted to the exposition of Beethoven and not of Mr. Toscanini, and it rose to heights of eloquence without the intrusion of the conductor's personality."*

The description matches what we have heard later, and there is no question that the *Ninth* given to New York in 1913 was equal in every way to the fine performances of 1927-52 with which we are more familiar.

During the 1913-14 season he worked harder than ever. Montemezzi's *L'Amore dei Tre Re* was given its American première, and he continued to offer *Boris, Tristan, Meistersinger,* and Italian repertory.

One might ask again why a man of these powers should not receive the full co-operation of management and sympathetic understanding from the public, but friction was developing again. During the 1914-15 season the situation built up to the threatening explosion. Although the company was not operating with a deficit, Otto H. Kahn, the most powerful member of the Metropolitan Opera Board, wanted to reduce costs and introduced a number of petty economies which served only to infuriate Toscanini, who was beginning to look upon the star system, the socialite boors in the audience, and some of the other aspects of the situation with increasing aversion. There was pressure on him to produce an American opera, with such works as

* *Ibid.*, pp. 395-97.

Walter Damrosch's *Cyrano* and *The Canterbury Pilgrims* of
Reginald de Koven as candidates. It took all the self-control he
had to keep Toscanini from giving his blunt verdict on their
quality. He managed to hold out until April, leading Wagner and
Weber, his Italian repertory, and even preparing special confec-
tions like Giordano's *Madame Sans-Gêne* for Farrar. Then the
pressure mounted as high as it could go; there was a scene with
Gatti-Casazza, and Giorgio Polacco, a *routinier* for whom Toscanini had only contempt, took over his scheduled performances
while the management announced Toscanini's indisposition. Ill-
disposition would have been better; so intense was his anger that
he had no qualms about appearing in public in New York while
Polacco filled in at the opera house for poor, sick Maestro
Toscanini. Although he led concerts in the Metropolitan Opera
House in later years, he never again appeared under the auspices
of the Opera Board, and New York did not hear him conduct an
operatic performance again for twenty-nine years, until he prepared *Fidelio* with the N.B.C. Symphony in 1944.*

At the end of the season he returned to an Italy which was on
the verge of war. He had appeared in his homeland on only three
occasions since his departure from La Scala in 1908: giving symphony concerts in Milan and Naples in 1909 and 1912 and preparing *Falstaff* and *La Traviata* at Busseto in 1913 to commemorate the hundredth anniversary of the birth of Verdi. Again
he rejected offers and voluntarily entered into a period of inactivity. He was now forty-eight and had been a conductor for nearly
thirty years. He led a few benefits, for which he accepted no fee,
spent his savings, sold his house, and played with the idea of
returning to the orchestra as a 'cellist, sparing himself the strain,
the responsibility, and the frustrations of directing opera under
the prevailing conditions.

After the tragic debacle which led to the internment of Karl
Muck (a Swiss national) as an alleged enemy agent (and real
victim of wartime demagoguery), the Boston Symphony Orchestra approached Toscanini, but so set was he in his reluctance to
take another position or leave Italy that he declined to consider
the offer, although chauvinistic elements of his own countrymen

* He offered the third act of *Rigoletto* in a concert performance in Madison
Square Garden in May, 1944, but I do not regard this as, properly speaking,
an operatic production.

were harassing him in his occasional appearances in charge of benefit concerts because of his insistence upon playing music of Beethoven and Wagner. The blind hatred of wartime madness could create difficulties, but there was no doubting his patriotism. His son, Walter, was in the Italian army as an artillery officer, and the Maestro was decorated for leading a military band under fire during the battle of Monte Santo.

In 1920, his fifty-third year behind him, he resumed work, leading symphony concerts in Rome and Padua. La Scala had been closed by the war, and its doors were still shut. The problem was to secure a financial basis for the operations of the house. Toscanini was interested only in artistic quality: impresarios with their eyes on the till, rich patrons with tendencies to give orders, these he had seen and wished to see no more. This time he got his way. The new organization of the house provided public funds to pay the bills and put artistic supervision in the hands of the musical director. There had to be a new orchestra, and after it had been engaged, it had to be given something to do until the house was ready. During the summer and autumn of 1920 Toscanini selected and rehearsed his men, and two tours were arranged, one in the United States and Canada and another in Italy.

A "tumult of welcome" awaited him in New York. The orchestra landed on the thirteenth of December, and on the eighteenth, twenty-first and twenty-fourth made recordings for the Victor Talking Machine Company in a church in Camden, New Jersey, where they were to hold seven further recording sessions prior to their return to Italy in March. On the twenty-eighth this initial battle with sound reproduction was forgotten and Toscanini returned to the stage of the Metropolitan Opera House to play to the Italian ambassador and an auditorium packed with persons who, as Richard Aldrich pointed out, hardly knew him as a symphony conductor. The program began with the national anthems of the United States and Italy and went on to the Vivaldi *Concerto No. 8 in A Minor* for strings, the Beethoven *Fifth, Iberia, The Fountains of Rome,* and the *Prelude* and *Liebestod* from *Tristan,* a typical Toscanini concert which he might have offered at any time between 1926 and 1954 without anyone remarking on the program. The opera auditorium did not do the orchestra justice, and the clean, transparent lines of sound which must have been produced in the Debussy and Respighi were not projected well. When he played his second concert, moving to Carnegie Hall (apparently his first appearance in the auditorium in which he was to lead so many triumphant performances) on January 3, 1921, the acoustics served him better. All in all he gave seven concerts in New York, five in the first series and a final pair in March. In a special concert at the New York Hippodrome on the sixteenth of January he played Dvořák's *New World Symphony*, the Beethoven *Seventh*, Brahms *Second*, Wagnerian excerpts, and contemporary Italian works were heard at other times.

The tour took him to twenty-five cities. He faced this circuit of North America with limited English and a defective geographic sense: it must have been mad. The public were dazzled, he was presented with a golden baton, Italian neighborhoods turned out in droves, he missed trains, tangled with well-wishers, and all was a most infuriating hubbub at times. Even with the family records at one's disposal, it is impossible to tell where all he went. (Some thirty years later when he made his second tour of the United States one of the running jokes was that often the Maestro could not recall whether he was visiting a place for the first or second time.)

Chicago heard him twice, February first and twenty-seventh. It was his first appearance there as a symphony conductor, although Chicagoans had heard him do opera with the Metropolitan in a tour some years before. On February first, he played the same program as he had at his opening concert in New York, and on his return offered the Brahms *Second, Don Juan,* the *William Tell Overture,* and Respighi's *Suite of Ancient Airs and Dances.* The drive to the west included stops in Des Moines, Omaha and Topeka where a Toscanini concert offered a musical experience that only the more widely traveled of the citizens could have encountered previously. On February twentieth Kansas City heard the overture to the *Barber of Seville,* the *New World Symphony, Juventus* and *Carnevale Piedmontese* by Victor de Sabata (better known today as a conductor), *William Tell,* the *Tristan Prelude* and *Liebestod,* "The Star-Spangled Banner," and "Garibaldi's War Hymn." Convention Hall was packed, as well it might have been for such a program. There has probably not been a concert to equal it in Kansas City since!

The De Sabata orchestration of "The Star-Spangled Banner" stunned the critic in Columbus, Ohio, who wrote that the national anthem was "played as no American orchestra has ever played it." His reaction to the program as a whole was one common among those who write about Toscanini: "never in a thousand years could we describe this. . . ." The St. Louis critic ventured that "such speed was never witnessed or heard" before. A loop through upper New York and New England brought the same praise, and Boston listeners had grounds for mingling with their enjoyment a sense of regret that he had not been persuaded to become director of their own orchestra. Having made a circuit that included Port- land, Maine, and the Canadian cities of Montreal and Toronto in the north, Tulsa in the west, Richmond in the south, and all major points in the center, Toscanini and his orchestra sailed home in April. In one respect they had made a miscalculation: several of the best players remained behind to lend their virtuosity to Amer- ican orchestras, just as an earlier tour of the band of the French Garde Républicaine provided the Boston Symphony with some brilliant instrumentalists. The Italian tour that followed could not have been anything but anti-climactic.

La Scala reopened in December, 1921, and the repertory for the first season contained *Meistersinger* and *Boris* as well as Italian works. The following year Toscanini prepared a revival of *The Magic Flute,* which the public accepted coolly (Mozart was not especially popular in Italy), and his symphonic series at the close of the season included the *Ninth Symphony* of Beethoven and the Verdi *Requiem.* The season 1923-24 contained new productions of *Tristan* and *Orfeo,* another work from Toscanini's Metropolitan repertory which he transferred to La Scala. All was going well; it was too good to last, and it didn't.

Mussolini was now in power and out to assert himself. Particu- larly he wanted the Fascist anthem *"Giovinezza"* played at La Scala on Empire Day, April twenty-first. In 1924 Toscanini refused, and in the two years following he arranged that the house should be closed for rehearsals on the holiday. None the less, trouble was afoot, and Toscanini was preparing to meet it. Early in 1925 he allowed it to be known that he would like to return to New York, and the management of the Philharmonic eagerly took him up. They were out to drive a hard bargain, and instructed their representative to keep Toscanini's fee as low as would satisfy him and avoid, if possible, a surcharge for his travel- ing expenses, indicating that Willem Mengelberg, the principal conductor of the orchestra, paid his own passage. At the close of the negotiations, Toscanini got the fee he had requested, plus an allowance to pay the United States income tax, plus an allowance for transportation.

The 1925-26 season was therefore the first of the eleven in which Toscanini appeared with the Philharmonic. The management had anticipated "a very extraordinary artistic success for Mr. Toscanini's concerts with the Philharmonic" and they lived up to expectations. He led the orchestra for the first time in a Carnegie Hall concert on January 14, 1926. The program was typical Toscanini fare: opening with Haydn's *Clock Symphony* and Respighi's *Pines of Rome*. *The Swan of Tuonella*, one of the few Sibelius works in his repertory, came after the interval and was followed by his concert version of *Siegfried's Death and Funeral Music* from *Götterdämmerung*, a Wagnerian excerpt that appeared frequently in his American programs, and the overture to Weber's opera *Euryanthe*. He was only a guest conductor that season, and at the completion of his series in February he returned to his duties at La Scala.

That year, back at La Scala, he prepared the première of *Turandot,* which had been left unfinished at Puccini's death and was performed in the form in which the composer had left it. The first Italian performance of Debussy's *Martyrdom of Saint Sebastian* was another innovation. Again there was a performance of *Falstaff* at Busseto to commemorate an anniversary of Verdi: in this case the passing of twenty-five years since his death. Another such date loomed: the hundredth anniversary of the death of Beethoven. Toscanini began his 1926-27 season by giving the nine symphonies in both Milan and Turin and introducing *Fidelio* into the repertory at La Scala. His series with the Philharmonic was cut short by illness in February, but he gave the *First, Third, Fifth,* and *Ninth* of the Beethoven symphonies, with Elisabeth Rethberg, Louise Homer, Richard Crooks, and Fraser Gange as his soloists in the latter work. In spite of his short stay, he took the orchestra out of town, and one of his four concerts was in the Academy of Music at Philadelphia.

The 1927-28 season marks his transition from a guest conductor to one of the principal conductors of the orchestra. The Philharmonic-Symphony Orchestra of New York, as it was called after its amalgamation with the New York Symphony, had too long and demanding a schedule for one conductor to lead, and the practice then, as today, was to rotate the concerts among a group of conductors, each being responsible for a portion of the season. The greater part of the season through this period was directed by Willem Mengelberg, who did not leave the Philharmonic until 1930. Toscanini began the season at La Scala and went to New York late in January, 1928. He led over forty concerts during the weeks remaining in the orchestral season, the largest number of appearances he had made with the Philharmonic up to that time. A short spring tour took the orchestra to Baltimore, Washington, Philadelphia, Buffalo and Pittsburgh.

The autumn of 1928 found him giving symphony concerts in Milan and preparing for the season at La Scala. On December 26 he celebrated the thirtieth anniversary of his first season as a regular conductor at the house with the same opera he had chosen in 1898—*Die Meistersinger*. It was a gloomy year, none the less. Mussolini was putting on pressure and it was a relief to get to New York in February. His series there was shorter than that of the previous year, twenty-five concerts, seven of them out of town. The spring tour this time included Philadelphia, Baltimore, Washington, Pittsburgh and Rochester.

On his return to La Scala he embarked on another tour in May, taking the company to Vienna and then to Berlin. There was a grim note underlying this triumphal procession, for Toscanini knew that it was the end of his association with the company. His third La Scala period, the one that had promised the fullest opportunities for the realization of opera in an atmosphere of artistic perfection, was about to close after eight seasons, the victim of fascism. He showed the Vienna and Berlin audiences what Italian opera could be, and then he took his leave. He had been with La Scala a total of fifteen seasons, and although he was to conduct there again, in triumph, in 1946, he never again was to enter the house as its musical director.

By the autumn of 1929 he belonged to New York, and Clarence H. Mackay and the Philharmonic Board eagerly awaited the opportunity to display their prized possession before the musical world. There was no longer any question over who was principal conductor of the orchestra, and Mengelberg was about to disappear for good. In future seasons the podium would be shared with men who were *persona grata* to Toscanini, as Mengelberg had ceased to be for some time. Toscanini was now entering his fifth season with the orchestra. They had prepared enough music together so that his programs became more flexible; rather than repeat a work several times, he might pick up a composition that had been given the season before, polish it briefly in rehearsal, and include it in a concert. Again one saw Toscanini at work as an orchestra builder. In 1954 one was to hear proof of his skill when his N.B.C. Symphony played brilliantly in concert without a conductor, but the same thing was happening with the Philharmonic. After the Maestro taught them a piece, he could re-create the performance in short order.

Toscanini conducted eighty-three concerts with the Philharmonic between his appearance on the opening night of the season, October 3, 1929, and its triumphant close in London, June 4, 1930. The European tour began on the third of May at the Paris Opera, and in the month to follow there were twenty-three concerts drawing upon a huge repertory for a touring orchestra—thirty-four compositions. From Paris the orchestra moved on south, to Zurich, and then into Italy where Toscanini returned to the La Scala stage with his American musicians and showed the Milan audience what they could do. In Turin there was a clash with the Fascists. The Princess of Piedmont attended the concert. Protocol demanded that the "Royal March" be played for her, but Mussolini's decree specified that *"Giovinezza"* must follow. Toscanini had fought that battle once and was not giving in, even if it meant no Turin concert. A compromise was reached. A local band (Winthrop Sargeant, who was a member of the orchestra at the time, writes in his *Geniuses, Goddesses and People* that it looked like a group of street cleaners) marched in and played the offensive airs while Toscanini stood on the podium with an unmerciful look fixed upon them. The Philharmonic went on to Rome, Florence, Munich, Vienna, Budapest, Prague, Leipzig, Dresden, Berlin, Brussels and finally to London. Everywhere the public and the press exhibited the familiar reaction: if one had not heard Toscanini one had never heard this music before. A Berlin critic wrote: "The Toscanini orchestra is a perfectly and thoroughly trained instrument that is absolutely mastered by one mind."

After fifteen cities and twenty-three concerts one would expect Toscanini to be tired. Not at all. He had given two concerts in

Paris, Milan, Rome, Vienna and Berlin, but for his first appearance before the British public he decided upon four programs, beginning in the Albert Hall on June 1 and closing in Queen's Hall, after four strenuous evenings of music, on the fourth. The opening night was an occasion. George the Fifth and his queen attended: so did Bernard Shaw and several thousand others. In properly solid prose the *Times* had its say the next morning:

"English musicians have been awaiting the opportunity of hearing Signor Toscanini in London for many years, and hopes held out from time to time that he might accept an engagement to conduct an orchestra here have remained unfulfilled. . . . [The concert was] an experience worth waiting for and a rich reward for patience. . . . There was no question about the absolute finish and clarity of yesterday's performances, a clarity which even the Albert Hall could not obscure, at any rate for long at a time. . . ."

Toscanini introduced himself to London by playing "God Save the King," "The Star-Spangled Banner," and the overture to Rossini's *The Italian Woman in Algiers* (the *Times* thought it trivial) in that order. Later there was the Brahms *Second,* and the concerts on the following evenings included the Moussorgsky-Ravel *Pictures at an Exhibition,* Debussy's *La Mer,* and Elgar's *Enigma Variations,* which was a more pronounced success with a British audience than the breathtaking Toscanini performance of Debussy's great score. The critic of the *Times* was not immune to the general feeling, ". . . the virtuosity of the players," he wrote, "and their extraordinary adaptability to their conductor's highly individual conceptions of the music completely carried the audience away. . . ." Indeed, after hearing the imprecise, underrehearsed performances of many British orchestras, it must have been quite an experience. The Elgar was not thought to be wholly satisfactory, although the *Times* conceded that ". . . probably never has the 'Troyte' variation been played with a more electric energy, or 'Nimrod' attained such an overwhelming final climax," but it was clear that no Italian conductor with an American orchestra was to be allowed to beat the British in their own music on their home ground, and the discussion went on to claim that Toscanini's ideas were "too definite for a satisfying reading of Elgar" whose "elusive quality" was lost in "this highly organized interpretation." To find that "elusive quality" all one had to do, I feel, was satisfy chauvinism by presenting a British orchestra, furiously sightreading under a beknighted conductor. I doubt if Toscanini took such criticism seriously.

Clarence H. Mackay, who had been sent regular reports on the tour (the satisfaction that it gave him was all the return he had for the more than two hundred thousand dollars it cost the backers of the orchestra), cabled congratulations and advice: ". . . overjoyed and frankly relieved that tour is at an end, and hope that . . . you will kick up your heels in a non-prohibition country . . . hurrah for the Philharmonic Orchestra born in 1842."

The question arose: "Why not tour the United States at the close of the 1930-31 season?" But Mackay did not support the idea. Like many upper-class Easterners he was oriented toward Europe rather than the hinterland of his own country. He wanted to send the Philharmonic to show Paris, Berlin and Vienna what a great orchestra New York could claim, but he had no desire to impress Des Moines, Iowa. The American radio audience that listened to Toscanini's Sunday broadcasts were therefore obliged to travel to New York if they wanted to hear him in a hall. Mackay argued that such an undertaking would be too hard on Toscanini, and that he wished "to avoid overtaxing this great and unique machine" since "at the end of season he is very tired and nervous and acts like an overtrained athlete. . . ." That was the end of the American tour.

If Toscanini needed a long rest, he didn't show it, or take it. He was off to Bayreuth to conduct at the sacred Festspielhaus for the first time. He whipped an indifferent pit orchestra into shape and produced *Tristan* and *Tannhäuser*. It was his second triumph of the year. Then he gave himself a vacation.

In the autumn he was back in Carnegie Hall for the 1930-31 season with the Philharmonic. Erich Kleiber and Bernardino Molinari were the other principal conductors, and for two weeks in late November and early December Leopold Stokowski conducted in New York while Toscanini led the Philadelphia Orchestra, his first guest appearance away from the Philharmonic in the six seasons he had been in New York. Everything considered, Toscanini's relations with Stokowski were good, and it was not until the 1943-44 season when they were both conducting the N.B.C. Symphony that the Maestro's regard for him declined. There were sixty-two Toscanini concerts, including the usual loops down to Washington in the winter and spring. During the months when the Philharmonic did not require him he divided his time between his home in Milan and a villa he has rented for many years which, with its grounds, occupies the whole of the Isolino di San Giovanni in Lago Maggiore at the foot of the Alps.

On the fifteenth of January, 1931, Winifred Wagner had cabled Toscanini: "*Parsifal* is yours. May I ask you to conduct *Tannhäuser* too because this opera wants your protection most of all? . . ." He agreed to return to Bayreuth. In May, after the close of the Philharmonic season, he went to Bologna to prepare a pair of concerts in memory of Martucci, but found that the Fascists were ready to put their maximum pressure upon him. A political gathering was scheduled for the same day as the first concert, followed by a banquet, and he was informed that when the officials took their places in the concert hall the "Royal March" and "Giovinezza" should be played. Toscanini refused. On his arrival at the theatre Toscanini encountered a mob that was out for trouble, and as he left his car he and his wife and elder daughter were attacked. Fortunately he was equal to the occasion, and they made their escape, first to a hotel, where they were abused verbally from the street. Respighi was sent to Toscanini with orders to leave town. (It must have been a painful meeting for them both.) During the night Toscanini and his family drove to Milan where he was held in house arrest for about three weeks before being permitted to leave the country. He did not attempt to conduct in Italy again until 1946, but was allowed to live there without further trouble until the war.

Bayreuth went well musically, but Toscanini found his health suddenly impaired by bursitis. He carried on in pain, leading *Tannhäuser* and *Parsifal* with his left arm at times, but the Philharmonic season was too much to face. He led fifteen concerts and returned to Italy to rest and recoup his health. In April he was feeling recovered somewhat and returned to New York for a post-season benefit which raised $26,000 for musicians unemployed because of the depression. In June he went up to Paris to lead a special concert in memory of Debussy.

Inactivity had its rewards. In October, 1932, he opened the Philharmonic season, and led sixty-five concerts before his return to Italy in the early summer. In the spring there was a Beethoven cycle, the first of several he was to offer in New York, and later in the year he accepted short engagements in Paris, Vienna, Copenhagen, and Stockholm. Bayreuth was now in Nazi hands, and Toscanini refused to go near it, although Hitler had personally appealed to him to return. The Nazi treatment of Jewish musicians offended Toscanini as if it had been intended as a personal affront. During the seasons 1931-34 he shared the podium of the Philharmonic with Bruno Walter, an old and respected friend who had suffered from the Nazi persecution.

In 1933-34 he returned to the orchestra a man of sixty-six, past the normal age for retirement in many professions. He cut down his schedule. Again there was a Beethoven cycle in the spring, which included this time the first Toscanini performances of the *Missa Solemnis,* but in all there were only forty-four Toscanini concerts that season. He was active in the summer, appearing in Paris and participating for the first time in the Salzburg Festival. In 1934-35 he shared the Philharmonic with five other conductors, among them Otto Klemperer, and Artur Rodzinski. His own appearances were down to thirty-five concerts, seventeen of which were given to his first Brahms cycle with the orchestra.

Toscanini returned to London in June of 1935 to lead a series of four concerts in Queen's Hall with the British Broadcasting Corporation Symphony. His British public had been eager to hear him again since his visit five years before, and welcomed him with the warmth and friendship he had known for so long in America. His programs included the *Enigma Variations,* still played *his* way, the Brahms *Fourth,* the Beethoven *Seventh, La Mer,* and familiar works by Mozart, Rossini, Mendelssohn, and Wagner. The B.B.C. Symphony was somewhat augmented for this series, and he found it a well-trained and responsive ensemble.

The summer of 1935 was a brilliant one at Salzburg. Toscanini prepared *Falstaff* and *Fidelio,* the latter with Lotte Lehmann who was then at the height of her powers, as well as symphonic programs with the Vienna Philharmonic. All seemed tranquil, but when he was unable to return to New York in time for the opening of the Philharmonic season the management, without asking his consent, engaged Sir Thomas Beecham to fill in for him and an explosion followed. Otto Klemperer, who was also

conducting the orchestra that year, was *persona grata* to Toscanini. Beecham, whom he viewed as a dilettante, was not. In an
angry mood he reviewed his various clashes with the orchestra
management and cabled that he would not return for the season
following—that of 1936-37—and in the spring of 1936, stubborn
and tired, he stuck to his decision.

There were thirty-three Toscanini concerts that year, including a special pair in Symphony Hall, Boston, in March when
the Philharmonic was sponsored by the Boston Symphony Orchestra. He played Beethoven, Brahms, Weber, Wagner, Verdi,
Debussy: composers he knew and felt deeply in mind and heart.
In all his years in America he was virtually the only conductor
of great reputation who never appeared with the Boston Symphony, and the tension which existed between himself and Koussevitzky had been a factor which deterred him from visiting
Boston with the Philharmonic, although he appeared regularly
in near-by Hartford, Connecticut. Even in 1950, after Koussevitzky had retired, he did not include Boston in his tour with
the N.B.C. Symphony.

In New York, in April, 1936, he ended his subscription series
with the same program he had played on his first appearance
with the Philharmonic more than a decade before, led a farewell
concert, and took his leave. He was sixty-nine and had been a
conductor for fifty years. When he left New York, few thought
that they would ever see him there again.

In the summer he returned to Salzburg once more, where his
principal offering was *Die Meistersinger,* and in December of
1936 he went to Palestine where he led the first concerts of
the orchestra which Bronislaw Hubermann had formed from
some of the many fine Jewish musicians displaced by Hitler's
racial decrees. (Afterwards the orchestra became the Palestine
Symphony.) Barnstorming around Europe appealed to him. He
visited Paris again, where he lectured to one of the violinists
in the orchestra for bowing his own way. The offender's name
was Charles Munch. In 1937 Toscanini made a second appearance in Stockholm and celebrated his seventieth birthday with
the Vienna Philharmonic. In late May he was back in London
for his second series with the B.B.C. Symphony. There were six
concerts and a trip up to Oxford, where he serenaded the university with the *Pastoral* and the Brahms *First* in a benefit concert

for the University of Oxford endowment fund. When offered the D. Mus. degree, *honoris causa,* he declined, as he customarily declined honors of this type. Being Dr. Toscanini meant nothing to him.

Again summer drew him to Salzburg, but this time there was Nazi Kultur in the air, and his production of Mozart's *The Magic Flute,* which drew a mixed reception, could well be taken as an act of homage and farewell to that composer's native city. Furtwängler was there to conduct the Beethoven *Ninth.* Toscanini resented his apparent capitulation to the Nazis and treated him with scorn. It was a painful situation, since only the year before Toscanini had suggested that Furtwängler be appointed to succeed him as conductor of the Philharmonic. The year 1937 was bringing political issues to a head, and after Furtwängler's performance of the *Ninth* Toscanini told him what he thought of it. There was never a reconciliation.

In November there was a Toscanini reading of the *Ninth* in London with the B.B.C., and in an earlier program he gave his British public the *German Requiem* of Brahms.

To the delight of his American audience, his next move was to return to New York, where those who had witnessed his departure, nineteen months before, with justifiable gloom were prepared to rejoice that he had changed his mind and decided to return and undertake further musical activity.

The idea of engaging Toscanini and creating a new symphony orchestra for his broadcast concerts apparently came from David Sarnoff, who was president of the Radio Corporation of America at that time, and early in 1937 Samuel Chotzinoff went to Europe to act as Sarnoff's emissary. Toscanini was in Italy, living in semi-retirement, and, although willing to discuss the matter, was hesitant about the labors involved. As he described the situation in his letter to Sarnoff in 1954 (when he indicated his intention to retire permanently), "You will remember how reluctant I was to accept your invitation because I felt at that time that I was too old to start a new venture. However, you persuaded me and all of my doubts were dispelled as soon as I began rehearsing for the first broadcast. . . ."

The offer was appealing. Artur Rodzinski, whom Toscanini had personally introduced to Salzburg in 1936 and 1937, accepted Toscanini's invitation to engage and train the ensemble and share it with him during the winter season. Taking a leave of absence from his own orchestra in Cleveland, Rodzinski spent two months auditioning players and put many hours into drilling them into shape before the Maestro began preparation for his opening concert. Toscanini's seventeen seasons with the N.B.C. Symphony proved to be his longest period of association with any musical organization. At the outset the situation looked ideal. In all his years with the Philharmonic, he could never feel that it belonged to him. Other conductors led it for much of the season, and the management was never out of sight. To make the break even stronger, he had not been consulted about the appointment of John Barbirolli as his successor. It was six years before he relented and, in honor of the orchestra's one hundredth anniversary, went back to conduct it again.

The seasons with the N.B.C. Symphony began with Vivaldi, the Mozart *Symphony No. 40,* and the *First Symphony* of Brahms on Christmas night, 1937, at ten o'clock. The audience, on entering a concert room known by the graceless name of Studio 8-H, Radio City, Rockefeller Center, New York (and presently to be called names that were worse than graceless by the serious musical public), read on their programs: "Since the modern microphone is extremely sensitive, your co-operation in maintaining silence during the music is urgently requested."

Sensitive or not, the change from the Philharmonic and Carnegie Hall to a new orchestra and a broadcasting studio was not brought about without a loss. It took more than a season of hard work to get the N.B.C. as responsive to his desires as the Philharmonic or the B.B.C. Orchestra had been, and what one heard in those early concerts was a fine, professional orchestra with which Rodzinski could secure excellent results, but which had not become sensitized through long association to Toscanini's desires and highly individual rehearsal methods. The only orchestra Toscanini ever trained from the very beginning was the La Scala ensemble he brought to America in 1920. There, of course, no language barrier existed. With his American orchestras Toscanini did not talk a great deal, they simply played for many minutes at a time, going over works again and again until the Maestro was satisfied. Rodzinski, who not only talked a great deal but was able to analyze difficulties and tell the men in detail how to cope with them, got his results much faster. The upshot of this was that Toscanini broke with Rodzinski before the end of the second season. Eventually the N.B.C. became an instrument reflecting Toscanini's musical ideas, but it was a prolonged and violent training period.

There were further losses. In theory, anyway, when the Philharmonic was playing in Carnegie Hall anyone who wanted to attend could buy a ticket and go. When Toscanini returned to lead the N.B.C. Symphony this came to an end. Studio 8-H, although ample as broadcasting studios go, was not a large hall, and since the tickets to the concerts were not for sale, only a few members of the public could count on getting in to hear the orchestra in a "live" performance. Even so, Studio 8-H was not a good place in which to listen to an orchestra because of the acoustical treatment which eliminated all resonance. For the same reason it was not an ideal place to record or to broadcast an orchestra, although heard from the air in the New York area the concerts were comparable with most commercial sound reproduction of the day. Chicago (say) was a different matter, for after the music had traveled through a thousand miles of telephone lines the limitations in frequency response and volume had turned it into a pale substitute for the original.

In the spring and summer following his first thirteen radio concerts he was again active in Europe. Again he gave a series of concerts in Palestine, without fee, as a gesture of friendship to the unfortunates who had been driven from their homes by Hitler and as a gesture of defiance to the dictator. In May he was in London with the B.B.C. Symphony for a series of six concerts extending into the middle of June. The major work was the Verdi *Requiem* and the shorter *Te Deum,* which he offered twice. There was Vaughan Williams' *Fantasia on a Theme of Thomas Tallis,* the Sibelius *Second Symphony,* the *Second Brandenburg Concerto* of Bach, a composer whose music he rarely played, and a generous offering of Beethoven, Brahms, Mozart, Schubert and Strauss. The Anschluss had taken place earlier in 1938, and "liberated" Salzburg was now intolerable to him. His first public concert with the N.B.C. Symphony in Carnegie Hall on March 4, 1938, had been intended as a benefit for the Salzburg Festival, but when he saw the way political currents were flowing, he directed that the proceeds should go to unemployed musicians in New York with a smaller portion to the Verdi Casa di Riposo in Milan, the great composer's home for retired musicians, a cause which had always been close to Toscanini's heart. He joined Adolf Busch, whose inability to stand Hitler was on a par with his own, and in the two summers remaining before war swept over the continent, they offered their own music festival in neutral Lucerne. The programs were distinguished, among them a special concert at near-by Triebschen where he played the *Siegfried Idyll* on the site of its original performance.

His 1938-39 season with the N.B.C. Symphony was somewhat longer, seventeen broadcasts and a short tour of six concerts as far west as Chicago, which had not seen Toscanini since 1921. London awaited him and a Beethoven festival of nine concerts, of which he led seven (playing the symphonies through in numerical order) and two programs made up largely of concerti which were conducted by Sir Adrian Boult. Both the *Ninth Symphony* and the *Missa Solemnis* were prepared, the latter work (given twice) serving to close the series and standing as Toscanini's farewell to London for twelve years. As the last days of peace ran to a close he was back in Lucerne, where he repeated the *Siegfried Idyll* with the original small orchestral forces in a private concert at Triebschen and filled the Jesuit Church in Lucerne with a special performance of the Verdi *Requiem*.

There were eighteen concerts in his 1939-40 series with the N.B.C. Symphony, and a nineteenth was added when Toscanini appeared at a benefit in New York with a special small orchestra with Heifetz as its concertmaster to play Mozart's *Musical Joke* (*K. 522*) and a romantic interlude by Gillet.

This year a major tour was planned, to Brazil, Uruguay and Argentina. The orchestra appeared in Providence, Rhode Island, for a pair of concerts in January and February and said *au revoir* to the United States at a concert in Washington on the fourteenth of May. The tour opened in Rio de Janeiro on June 13, scarcely two weeks before the fifty-fourth anniversary of Toscanini's debut there. After a pair of concerts they moved on to São Paulo, and then, on June 19, arrived in Buenos Aires where a series of eight programs was played. It was, undoubtedly, a happy reunion with the South American public that had supported him during difficult years at La Scala. In July there were two concerts in Montevideo, a return visit to São Paulo, and a final pair of concerts in Rio. As a gesture of inter-American friendship and support for the prestige of the United States in critical times it was an unquestioned success; but many North American cities could well envy Buenos Aires those eight concerts and wonder if the Maestro would ever come to play for them.

The 1940-41 season found him, for the first time, restricted to the United States, and so, for only the second time since his return to the United States, he left his own men momentarily and accepted an offer to be guest conductor of another orchestra. In addition to thirteen broadcasts, he went to Chicago and led its symphony for the first (and last) time in a special concert for the musicians' pension fund.

The summer of 1941 nearly saw the end of the N.B.C. Symphony. After a dispute over the competence of one of the guest conductors engaged for the summer series, Toscanini refused to lead the orchestra in the winter season, feeling that its quality had been impaired and, most of all, that it was no longer his but a property of the radio network. It was, therefore, with the Philadelphia Orchestra that he celebrated his seventy-fifth birthday, appearing in November for a pair of concerts and returning in January and February for six more, which included out-of-town dates in Washington and New York. He had traded orchestras with Stokowski eleven years before, and he still found the Philadelphia a responsive instrument of great beauty. In spite of his feelings about N.B.C. he consented to return for five special broadcast programs in support of the war bond drive.

Mussolini had plunged Italy into the conflict, and the Japanese attack on Pearl Harbor had caused the United States to enter the war in the previous December. Technically the Maestro was an enemy alien, although everyone knew that the Italian Fascists had no more intense foe. In the midst of war Toscanini made peace, first with the Philharmonic and then with the N.B.C. He closed the hundredth season of the Philharmonic with a six-concert Beethoven festival of all nine symphonies and the *Missa Solemnis*. In the summer he was asked to prepare the Shostakovich *Seventh Symphony* for its American première. The score, written during the fighting for Leningrad, appealed to him at the time. (Later he considered it bombastic and crude.) He studied the photographic prints of the pages with care (discovering in the process that the Russians had transmitted one of them upside down) and delivered a powerful reading.

In the spirit of the times, he wanted to have an orchestra with which he could hurl his own defiance at the Fascists, and he agreed to return to the N.B.C. for the 1942-43 season. He also consented to give an autumn series with the Philharmonic, repeating the Shostakovich three times in those concerts. His first program began, however, with "The Star-Spangled Banner" arranged for chorus, soloists, and orchestra and the dramatic symphony *Romeo and Juliet* of Berlioz, which was also given three performances. Later there was an all-Wagner concert, Toscanini's affirmation that great music belonged to the world and that Wagner was the property of neither the German state nor the Nazi party. In November he led a pair of concerts in Philadelphia and brought their orchestra to New York to repeat the program. December found him preparing a benefit for the Red Cross with the Philharmonic. The following February he again led a pension fund concert for another orchestra, this time the Cincinnati Symphony, and went from there to Philadelphia where illness prevented him from giving his final two programs. He never led the Philadelphia Orchestra again. There were fourteen broadcasts in his winter series and three of lighter music in the following summer.

The war continued. In the 1943-44 season there were two special concerts of which the most astonishing was in Madison Square Garden. Leading the combined N.B.C. and Philharmonic-Symphony orchestras in a program given entirely to "enemy alien" composers, Wagner and Verdi, he raised a sizable amount for the Red Cross. He repeated on this program Verdi's *Hymn of the Nations*, which he had revived in the previous season, with the phrase "Italy, my native land" replaced by "Italy, betrayed." When Mussolini finally was overthrown later that year, Toscanini was ready to commemorate the liberation of his homeland. On the ninth of September, with the Beethoven *Fifth*, the *William Tell Overture* and both "The Star-Spangled Banner" and the "Garibaldi's War Hymn" he jubilantly announced to the world the victory of freedom over the dictator whom he had long regarded as a personal adversary. Apart from these great events there were fourteen concerts in his winter series and four summer programs.

During 1944-45 he appeared with the Philharmonic for what proved to be the last time, preparing for the pension fund concert in January the same program of Haydn, Respighi, Sibelius, Weber, and Wagner that had introduced him to them in 1926 and with which he had closed his final series of subscription concerts a decade later. In April of 1945 he traveled to Los Angeles to give the pension fund concert of the Los Angeles Philharmonic Orchestra which Alfred Wallenstein, an old friend from the days in which Wallenstein had been first 'cellist of the Philharmonic, had conducted for a number of seasons. He made his first appearance on the West Coast a memorable one with a program of Rossini, Beethoven, Brahms, Weber, and Wagner specialties.

His N.B.C. series for the 1944-45 season ran for sixteen weeks, and there were six special concerts and two summer appearances. Notable was his production of Beethoven's *Fidelio* with its message of victory over tyranny. As the armies moved across Germany, Toscanini prepared for the victory concert to come, and when in the spring the end of Nazi domination was announced, he and his men played as they had rarely played before. When Japan surrendered he was ready again. For those who heard those concerts, even with the limited fidelity of radio, the effect, the passion, the intensity were unforgettable.

With the war over he wanted to return to Italy. He gave seventeen concerts with the N.B.C. in the 1945-46 season and went home in April. Somewhat to his surprise, he found himself a hero. Parma had named a street for him, and wherever he went he was viewed as a symbol of resistance to fascism. He conducted his second series of victory concerts, this time at La Scala, ending with the Beethoven *Ninth*. Back in the United States, he marked his eightieth birthday during the 1946-47 season with the N.B.C. He was cutting down his load now. There were only sixteen programs that winter and in the following seasons eighteen and seventeen respectively, but in October of 1947 he took a small ensemble from the N.B.C. Symphony and played a special benefit concert at Ridgefield, Connecticut, to show his friendly feeling for the community and repay the hospitality of the Chotzinoffs, who spent the summer there.

Two years later he repeated the gesture. After 1948 he began to make an occasional appearance in Italy again, but he wanted no heavy commitments.

None the less, when it was suggested that he tour the United States at the close of the 1949-50 season, he consented. For years thousands of persons had heard his broadcasts and bought his recordings without ever having an opportunity to experience his performances in terms of living sound in a concert hall. Now, in his twenty-fourth season in the United States since his return in 1926, he would go to them. Again there were seventeen programs in the winter series, and at their close (a public concert in Carnegie Hall) the special train pulled out of New York, bound southward to Baltimore, which knew him from his Philharmonic days, and on to Richmond (where the Frank Black arrangement of "Dixie" as an encore nearly caused a riot since Italian passion and Southern enthusiasm formed an explosive mixture), Atlanta, New Orleans, Houston, Austin, Dallas, Pasadena (where he played two programs), San Francisco, Portland, Seattle, and then eastward again via Denver, St. Louis, Chicago, Detroit, Cleveland, Pittsburgh, Washington and ending on familiar ground in Philadelphia. Everywhere he went he met houses sold out weeks in advance. It is difficult to imagine anyone who could have created more of a furor or commanded greater attention from the press and public on such a tour. In every city the requests for tickets came to a large multiple of the seats available in the hall.

So, his public had seen him at last, had feted him at banquets, observed him visiting the sights of their native cities, and tried (without success) to secure comments, interviews, autographs and the rest of the tokens of possession of a celebrity. In the end, he was tired, pleased and ready for an Italian vacation.

Those who had been asking, "How long can he go on?" now began to fear that the answer was at hand. An injury to his hip the following season reduced his broadcasts to four, and when he returned in 1951-52 there were only twelve concerts, although his hand seemed to be as strong as ever. That season ended with the Beethoven *Ninth*. There was a pair of summer concerts, the final pair it later proved to be, and in the autumn of 1952, before going to New York, he gave the four symphonies of Brahms, the *Haydn Variations*, and the *Tragic Overture* in the new Royal Festival Hall, London, with the Philharmonia Orchestra. Queen's Hall, like so many other things, had fallen to Hitler's offensive: but Toscanini took the new auditorium and new orchestra in stride, and the packed hall and thousands of radio listeners heard his brilliant and eloquent farewell to his British audience.

His N.B.C. season in 1952-53 came to fourteen programs, closing with the *Missa Solemnis*. He would have liked to stop, but his friends and family persuaded him to return once more. His powers seemed undiminished. The season 1953-54 got off to a bad start. He was ill and canceled the first two programs, but when he reappeared it was the same Toscanini as ever. In January he offered a concert production of Verdi's *A Masked Ball* that was brilliantly played and sung. Then, suddenly he seemed very tired. The *German Requiem* of Brahms, which had been planned for the final concert, was replaced by a Wagner program. He did not feel equal to preparing so large and demanding a work. Indeed, in his rehearsals and broadcasts there were moments when he was no longer able to sustain the intensity of earlier years, and the music would suddenly go slack, only to regain its former strength a moment later. He asked to be excused from one of the scheduled programs for a needed rest.

When he returned to prepare a group of Wagner excerpts early in April, 1954, his memory was plaguing him and his nerves were upset by the illness of his daughter-in-law. The rehearsals did not go well, and the dress rehearsal (with an invited audience) came the afternoon after she had suffered a serious relapse. (Before the end of summer he was to mourn her death.) After a calm start, a repeated, elementary error on the part of the tympanist precipitated an explosion. He left the stage with the program imperfectly prepared and retired into his mood of anxiety and choler. There was a question whether he would appear for the concert at all. The network had a stand-by conductor ready to take his place, but as the hour for the concert drew near he announced that he would be there. He had no heart for it. As in his debut, one heard the trooper, flinging himself into a bad situation rather than disappoint his audience. All went well enough until he neared the end of the *Tannhäuser Bacchanale,* and then the worst happened. He forgot the score:

under the pressure of the situation the fabulous memory failed. For a moment the baton stopped in its compelling arcs, the music faded, the orchestra and audience drew in their breath.* Then he began once more where he had stopped, picked up the line, and brought the work to a close. At once he plunged into the *Meistersinger Prelude,* which was virtually unrehearsed. He was angry and tense and the orchestra uncertain of his wishes. It was a rough performance. With the closing chord he let his baton fall and left the stage, oblivious of the applause. He did not return.

On his eighty-seventh birthday he had sent his letter of resignation to the network. ". . . Now the sad time has come when I must reluctantly lay aside my baton and say goodbye to my orchestra," he wrote. He had kept the news secret until after the concert. To many it did not come as a surprise. Neither did the action of the network, which dismissed the N.B.C. Symphony without further delay, indicating that without Toscanini it could not get a commercial sponsor for its concerts, and that the network could not maintain it otherwise. The destruction of the great orchestra he had trained with such pains came as a heavy blow. When he returned to lead them in a final recording session his feelings were tense, and at the farewell party he gave for them before his departure for Italy he was so saddened by the fact that his men were almost universally facing unemployment for the following season that he kept to his room and was unable to face them.

He returned to Italy, to his island in the Lago Maggiore, to his home in Milan. During the early summer he could find some pleasure in the way in which his men were successfully organizing themselves for existence independent of N.B.C., although when they cabled him in June, asking that he return to lead them again, he was obliged to send only his best wishes. With the memory of his final broadcast remaining to haunt him, he wrote: "my age and my present feeling do not allow me to make

---

* At Cantelli's insistence the broadcast was suddenly cut off and the unprepared listener plunged into the opening bars of the Toscanini recording of the Brahms *First,* part of a program of records that had been planned in case the Maestro failed to appear for the concert. It was a jarring, incongruous commentary on the tragic situation. When he lifted his baton Brahms suddenly gave way to Wagner again.

plans for the future." In the early autumn the reorganization was completed, and the orchestra (now rechristened "The Symphony of the Air") played a Carnegie Hall concert on October 27, 1954, that would have been distinguished in any season, but was particularly noteworthy because the sounds produced were the unique sounds of a Toscanini performance and the conductor's stand was empty.

In December Toscanini appeared at La Scala in the unaccustomed role of a spectator, when he attended the opening performance of the season (Spontini's *La Vestale*) in the box of the artistic director, Victor de Sabata. Earlier he announced that in the spring he would prepare *Falstaff* for the opening of a new, small theatre built in a former courtyard at La Scala (La Piccola Scala), but the curse that seemed to hang over his relations with the house continued to pursue him. His presence at rehearsals inspired some of the personnel to unexpected heights, but there were other rehearsals which he would not attend. Herbert von Karajan, whom he continued to consider (together with the late Wilhelm Furtwängler) a Nazi, had been invited to do *Carmen*, while Leonard Bernstein, whom he had once regarded in a friendly light, after some success in the previous season, produced a *Bohème* that the Italian critics panned without mercy. The score had been given its first performance under Toscanini nearly fifty years before and was sacred to him. In previous seasons, viewing La Scala from the distant vantage point of New York, he could retain his affection for it and for the artistic goals he had hoped to achieve there. Seeing it at close hand he realized that, as he is reported to have said, "It is just another Metropolitan." Friends report that he went to the house three days in succession, only to spit upon the door and turn away in frustration and rage. Finally he could contain himself in Milan no longer. He canceled the *Falstaff* and fled to New York in February, 1955. With the help of his son, Walter, he turned to editing the tapes of his broadcasts, so that as many of his performances as possible might be released on disks. Asked what he was doing, he replied that he was being "eighty-eight and hating it," probably no less because the sound of the music in the great house in which there were now only his son and his grandson could not but produce vivid recollections of other years.

2

Looking backward over his career we can begin to see Toscanini with some perspective. In his performances one heard the highest order of musicianship operating at a level of dedicated intensity, but for all his commanding appeal, he resisted the lures of a society which would willingly have lionized him had he allowed it to do so. He had succeeded because of his unique powers and because he was unsparing of himself in his labors. He had married well and made a handsome income, but he did not become an ostentatious socialite and again and again he gave large sums to causes he felt to be worthy. On the whole he moved within the world of music, and his three children shared that life. His daughter-in-law was Cia Fornaroli, who had been prima ballerina of La Scala; his younger daughter married Vladimir Horowitz, and his other son-in-law was Count Castelbarco.

Any person who achieves a great reputation is thrust into a dual role in which his public life and private life tend, sometimes, to merge. Toscanini avoided this with unparalleled success. He lived as he pleased with his family and friends. In later years he rarely appeared at social functions and was almost never seen in public places. He provided no news for the gossip columnists, attracted no attention to himself except through his art. Nor did he preside over a green-room reception after his concerts. It was not that he disliked people, but he was tired, in no mood for the flattery and gush that such relations with the public promote, and inclined to be short-tempered with those who spoke foolishly.

Adulation bothered him. The preliminary burst of applause that greeted his entrance to the stage seemed unjustified by anything he had done, and the applause after a work, although welcome, was usually excessive. When conducting opera he rarely took a bow; in symphony he did so reluctantly. "What do they expect me to do?" he once asked a friend. Bayreuth with its concealed orchestra pit suited him. There he wore no formal dress, came and went unnoticed, and did not need to acknowledge the audience. It was pure music. He wished a symphony concert could go the same way. He never read reviews, articles about himself, or troubled with scrapbooks, saving programs, or anything of the sort. He wanted no biography composed and offered no aid or support to anyone wishing to write about him. What was important was that he tried to be an honest musician, that he did his best, and that he was not a genius but performed the works of other men. To create music was the primary thing, to play it another.

At heart he was always an Italian, just as he never ceased to be an Italian national. Had the situation in Italy been different in his lifetime, he might have made his career at La Scala and appeared only rarely in other countries, but he could not make his career in Italy, and the United States offered him an obvious place to make a new start. The American people were friendly and receptive, the financial rewards were great, and his democratic principles were shared on all sides. No one expected him to lose interest in his homeland, and to say that he never became an American or participated intensely in American life is to suggest no criticism. He gave fully of himself and supported his adopted country whenever required; no more can be expected.

The sheer length of his career is so fabulous that one forgets that the United States knew him in only thirty-six of the sixty-eight seasons in which he appeared, since this period is itself the active life of most conductors. Koussevitzky made his debut in 1908 and led orchestras for forty-three seasons until his death in 1951. The United States knew him for twenty-seven years, a long time, certainly, but shorter than Toscanini's North American career by nearly a decade. Toscanini was a veteran conductor, entering middle life when he first came to New York, and this was eighteen years before the 1926 engagement with the Philharmonic which most young people tend to regard as the beginning of his career in the United States.

Actually when he first came to the Philharmonic he had been a conductor for nearly forty years. Our view of him is foreshortened and dominated by his final decades; we have lost the young Toscanini and see only the Old Man. Toscanini was a mature conductor in the 'nineties, years before he came to the Metropolitan, and because few of us have heard those performances does not mean that when he recalls them and says they were good they were not so good as the ones we were able to hear. The world has been very fortunate: this miraculous phenomenon, Toscanini's music, has been available for a long time.

Unfortunately it was a phenomenon that was known to only a small number of places. Toscanini has always disliked touring, and in his entire career there are really only four long tours, which coincidence placed just a decade apart: U.S.A., 1920-21; Europe, 1930; South America, 1940; U.S.A., 1950. He has had little interest in appearing as guest conductor; indeed, to hear him one must really have heard him with an orchestra that he had trained for a season or more and sensitized to his demands. Thus for years he was not known to the public in Northern Europe, and during his years in the United States, his activities were virtually restricted to New York with occasional visits to near-by eastern cities.

Further, in the twenty-eight seasons in which Toscanini was active in the United States after 1926, he probably gave fewer concerts and was heard in person by less people than any other conductor with a regular orchestral position. Forty appearances a season (including the repetition of programs) would be a round average for the period with the Philharmonic and less than half that number would be correct as an average for his years with the N.B.C. Since the Philharmonic audience was in large part those who had subscribed to a series of concerts, it is fair to suppose that actually he was playing to a large number of persons that remained unchanged week after week, while his N.B.C. Symphony concerts were not open to the public by way of a box-office.

Thus Koussevitzky's celebrated remark about Toscanini, "Dat poor old man, how hard dey make him vourk!" really applied better to himself. In the season in which he was seventy-five Koussevitzky played a heavy schedule of concerts with the Boston Symphony, toured as far west as Chicago, and appeared in a summer series at Tanglewood, where he also taught conducting and undertook further responsibilities for his Berkshire Music Center. In the 1941-42 season, in which he had celebrated his seventy-fifth birthday, it happened that Toscanini was savoring the self-indulgence of his break with N.B.C. and limited his appearances to six broadcasts of about one hour each and eight concerts with the Philadelphia Orchestra.

Koussevitzky was around giving concerts until a short time before his death. It required no great luck or ingenuity to get to hear him. In that sense, Toscanini never was around, and certainly a great deal of the frenzy that he produced whenever he appeared outside the East came from the fact that thousands of regular concert patrons had been supporting the musical life of their cities for years, had heard virtually every great musician of the day who was appearing in the United States, and yet had never seen or heard Toscanini. In a sense it was embarrassing to him. All one had to do to start the stampede was announce that he was coming at last and offer to sell tickets.

The tour in 1950 showed where Toscanini's great audience was to be found: in the thousands of persons who knew him from his broadcasts, who had followed his programs, season after season, in spite of the poor sound, in spite of the awkward hours, in spite of the intermission talks that caused the music to run overtime and be cut off, in spite of everything that American commercial broadcasting could do to make them uninviting. The New York public had the chance of hearing the real thing, the unique qualities of an orchestra under his baton. The unbelievable transparency of the lines of sound, the range of color and temperatures, from warm, dark hues to icy blue-white, the bite of the attack, the cutting power of the brass, the weight of the full ensemble, these things were merely suggested in the broadcasts. The limitations of the AM transmission, the losses on the long telephone lines between cities, the manipulations of the engineers, the low fidelity of most radio sets made it impossible to duplicate them in the ears of the listener. In spite of it all, one heard the things that made a Toscanini performance great. The engineer at the controls could upset the balance but not the tempo, flatten out the dynamics but not the accents. Toscanini educated his audience, showed them how music should be played, and when they turned on their sets and heard him they knew that this was the way it ought to go.

In later years there were FM transmissions in the New York area with good fidelity, and there were always the records. Even at their worst they were equal to the broadcasts, and as they improved they showed one the things that the radio did not reveal, so that one who had followed the Toscanini recordings would not find the sound of his living performances a new experience. (Similarly, after hearing him "live" for a time the records had more meaning.) If one considers the millions of persons who never had been to a concert hall to whom he brought symphonic music at the highest level of performance, weighing his contribution to the cultural life and artistic standards of people of the United States against the cost of the broadcasts, they seem to be the bargain of the century.

The private life of many artists is, in contrast to their public role, one of loneliness, of studied escape from bores and opportunists, of rejection of both trivial relationships with those who cannot understand their aims and inner compulsions and of more basic relationships which may be desired but cannot be achieved. The life of a celebrated artist may be one of severe discipline and great denial, and the achievement which the public applauds may be realized only through dedication and unceasing effort such as the public cannot share or understand. The great artist may, however, have many of the routine desires of ordinary men, and only through the greatest strength may he sacrifice them to goals which may be only dimly seen.

Toscanini has seemingly lived the life of a successful professional man, enjoying a degree of privacy unusual for one in his position and the affection and regard of his family, colleagues, and public. In a society of poseurs and pretentious mediocrities he has exhibited toward his art a degree of consistency of dedication that revealed an achievement in character as impressive as his power as a musician.

If one could merely say that Toscanini was a conductor of unique capabilities, sparing ourselves invidious comparison, one would still be faced with the necessity of recording his relations with the professional critics. As it is, Toscanini's partisans and detractors have been so conspicuous as to make it difficult to deal with this question objectively. Toscanini stimulated the public as well as professional musicians and critics to form strong opinions; to respect him carried the implication of membership in the cult, to criticize him allied one with the opposite faction. Actually, Toscanini's place as one of the great musicians of history is assured, and no critic can add or subtract from the height to which he has carried himself.

A perennial theme in Toscanini criticism was stated in the *American Mercury* for November of 1930 by Edward Robinson.

Toscanini, he maintained, "has the single, phenomenal capacity for maintaining a persistent tempo with the mechanical rigidity of a metronome . . ." This, the author held, was ruining the great orchestra created by Mengelberg, by forcing it into a strait jacket of precision in playing and eliminating all spontaneity and expression in performance, substituting for these desirable qualities only the demand that ". . . the notes must be clear, in tune, and observant of any expression marks that happen to be present. Beyond that [Toscanini] asks for nothing—and, I may add, gets it."

These remarks must be taken in context, for they came at a time when Mengelberg's public was irate about his displacement by Toscanini. The two men were opposite types. In the ten years he had been in New York, Mengelberg had made himself many friends, for his fine qualities as a musician were matched with an expansive, social nature. He came from Holland each year on a diplomatic passport with a cargo of liquor that made his parties unparalleled events in prohibition-ridden New York. Toscanini, in contrast, was aloof, frigid, and without interest in social success. Their opposite natures were reflected in their performances: Mengelberg's being romantic, lush, and expressive in the German (and Stokowskian) manner, which was undeniably better suited to much music than Toscanini's leaner and more ascetic approach. There was no question but that rivalry would not be tolerated by Toscanini, but similarly there seems to be no basis for holding that Toscanini ruined the orchestra, since the 1929 and 1936 Philharmonic recordings preserve the sound of a great ensemble.

Throughout Toscanini's American career there was always an element of criticism which came from skeptics, Teutons, professional highbrows, and others, who insisted that Toscanini was really an Italian vulgarian who played everything too fast, sacrificed beauty of tone to coarse brilliance and needless clarity, and felt at ease only in Italian music, or in any case could not play German, Russian, French, English, American, or eighteenth century works (or whatever other type of music the speaker championed) with understanding. This is partly nationalism, partly cross-cultural conflict, partly fabrication, and partly truth. Most of these points are discussed elsewhere in this study.

It is possible that Toscanini suffered less from bad criticism than from the adulation he received from other quarters. Toscanini's admirers quickly assumed the status of a cult in which the only approved attitude was that of worship. In its most violent form, the creed demanded of one the view that there was but one conductor, Toscanini, and that it was better to hear him play the *Dance of the Hours* than listen to an imperfect musician performing the Mozart *Linz Symphony* (to name but one great score which was not in the Toscanini repertory). To the cult, now that Toscanini has retired, infallibility has passed to Cantelli, who is to be regarded with the same uncritical attitudes previously reserved for the Old Man.

When Sir Adrian Boult introduced Toscanini to the B.B.C. Symphony for the first time he started to make a few remarks of welcome and appreciation, only to be cut off by the Maestro's insistence that this was not needed, that he was "only an honest musician." Such an attitude reflects the greatness of Toscanini, but apparently from time to time it underwent a certain alteration, and "only an honest musician" became "the only honest musician," which counts as quite a different thing. The fact has to be admitted that, although on the whole Toscanini's conduct in public has been in good taste, he has in private conversation expressed opinions of himself not greatly different from the views of his most fanatical admirers.

His relations with other musicians have reflected this attitude. Toscanini brooks no peers or critics, and the only role he will accept is a slightly paternalistic one in which there is no challenge to his dominant position. His statement that he does not want to be called a great conductor but, as Howard Taubman puts it, "a man and musician apart . . . in a class by himself" suggests his abhorrence of rivalry and any suggestion that there are other conductors who might be regarded as being of the same rank as himself. A great musician has told me of a day in which he found Toscanini brooding over a popular book about conductors which had recently been published. "Look at this!" Toscanini shouted, holding the volume open at the much-read and offensive passage. It was a statement that Weingartner was virtually unsurpassed as an interpreter of Beethoven, and no sooner had my informant read it than Toscanini hurled the book across the room. (I have few illusions about the fate of *this* book if he ever reads it!)

Needless to say, Toscanini's comments on his rivals, as repeated by friends, are lacking in charity. Koussevitzky's Boston Symphony, he is reported to have said, was a great orchestra because of the high quality of the men who composed it—not because Koussevitzky had provided them with training and leadership of a high order. In fact, although Koussevitzky was quite prepared at all times to play the role of Tsar, he treated Toscanini with respect and refused to conduct at La Scala in 1931 when the Fascists would not apologize to Toscanini for the Bologna episode. As for Beecham, Toscanini appears to have regarded him with mild contempt as no more than a rich man's son playing with orchestras and opera companies the way that other rich young men amuse themselves with chorus girls and horses. Only grudgingly would he concede that Beecham had achieved distinction on the basis of purely musical accomplishments.

Young conductors were able, under certain conditions, to make friends with the Maestro and enjoy a pleasant relationship with him until they became potential rivals, after which the friendship abruptly ceased. Thus in the mid-'thirties Toscanini favored Artur Rodzinski, whom he introduced to Salzburg in 1936 and 1937 and asked to engage and train the N.B.C. Symphony in 1937 and serve, with him, as its conductor. Rodzinski undertook the heavy duties of training the new orchestra (which came in addition to his responsibilities to the Cleveland Orchestra, which he then directed), without payment, out of affection and respect for Toscanini. Because of the abrupt cooling of Toscanini's regard for him, he never led the N.B.C. Symphony after its second season, and Toscanini has not spoken to him since 1939. When he sent his letter of resignation to General David Sarnoff on his retirement in 1954, Toscanini pointedly ignored Rodzinski's services to him (which were, after all, a matter of public record) and referred to the orchestra as "the group of fine musicians whom you had chosen." General Sarnoff deserves much credit for the greatness of the N.B.C. Symphony, but the injustice of that remark must have been clear to him.

In his enthusiasm for the Palestine Orchestra, in its early years Toscanini adopted one of its conductors, William Steinberg, and for several years held him in regard, although this friendship could no more withstand the increase in Steinberg's reputation than that for Rodzinski.

Toscanini has been friendly toward Charles Munch, but when the French conductor first appeared with the Philharmonic-Symphony Orchestra of New York, Toscanini managed, someway, to have a recording made of a part of Munch's performance of the *Symphony Fantastique* and subjected it to withering critical analysis before friends.

Erich Leinsdorf was for a time an intimate, and two young American conductors, Milton Katims who played the viola in the N.B.C. Symphony under the Maestro and Leonard Bernstein, have enjoyed Toscanini's favor. Several of the members of the Philharmonic of Toscanini's day have become conductors, one or two of them with the blessing of the Old Man. Alfred Wallenstein was Toscanini's first 'cello with the Philharmonic, and Leon Barzin was a violist in the orchestra at that time.

Every musician is human and, being human, has preferences.

In recent years Toscanini has reserved most of his praise for a young Italian conductor, Guido Cantelli. "He is the only one who plays music as I do," the Maestro is reported to have announced. Cantelli appears, indeed, to be a musician of unusual promise, although it can be questioned whether the effect of being named as heir-apparent to Toscanini has been entirely to the good. Cantelli's gift is essentially lyric, and he appeared at his best, in his first American appearances, when drawing a clean, expressive singing line from the orchestra in pieces such as Ravel's *Pavane for a Dead Princess.* In the seasons immediately after Toscanini's retirement his style appeared to change, together with his personality, and in attempting to combine with his melodic sensitivity the overpowering motor energy of Toscanini he seemed to this observer to be making an effort to play works on a larger scale than his understanding of them permitted without pretension and distortion. Because he is a fellow Italian, and because Toscanini has retired, there is a good chance of their relationship continuing to be close, and it is to be hoped that as he grows more mature Cantelli will benefit from the support and guidance Toscanini has given him and develop an approach of his own that is more in keeping with his powers.

The music produced by the major composers of even the past century in Europe involves a number of distinct styles and no musician can be expected to have equal degrees of sensitivity for all these varied media of expression in musical terms. The things Toscanini best understands are the music of his own country, Beethoven, the early romantics, Brahms, Wagner, and a group of romantic and post-romantic scores, especially the French impressionists. In these areas he is strong and secure and has given performances which surpass those of any other musician of his day. Similarly he is, on the whole, not partial to Slavic and Scandinavian music, has no great interest in English or American composers, and has no proper feeling for much Central European music, such as the Bohemian, the Viennese waltz, or the highly personal vocabulary of Mahler. Old music and modern music leave him cold.

We do not condemn a pianist because he cannot play the *Goldberg Variations,* the *Hammerklavier Sonata,* the Chopin *Études,* and *Estamps* with equal skill and understanding. The uncritical adoration of Toscanini has tended to suggest that he could do no wrong, and that any way he chose to play a work was not *a* right way but *THE* right way. The more obvious truth is that Toscanini has special gifts in relation to music of certain types, that his performances of this music have been exceptional, and that when he has played music for which he had no comparable degree of feeling his performances have been, on occasion, indifferent or even downright bad. This subtracts nothing from his great achievements; it merely takes away the blindness of idolatry and sets the record straight.

The opinion that Toscanini was "really" the only conductor worth hearing was made absurd by the fact that even during Toscanini's most brilliant period other musicians played works deserving of one's most serious attention which Toscanini either never programed or could not play as well as they. Indeed, since the living work of music is the thing to which Toscanini has been dedicated, and since his own changing manner of performance has shown that he has not regarded even his own conception of many works to be taken as final, balanced musical intelligence would appear to demand that one regard with respectful attention any conductor who appeared to be able to give effective and justifiable statements of important scores. It is not a sign of intelligence to wish to escape from the complexity of a situation by offering a set of simplified and imperfectly qualified answers and then closing one's mind to the inadequacies of such a conceptual scheme. There is no one performance which reveals all the inherent characteristics of a great work of music, although certain Toscanini performances (such as that of *La Mer*) appear to have come as close as humanly possible to doing this. The size and scope of the true masterpiece is always larger than a single, consistent interpretation of it can convey. In many instances the Toscanini performances of a given score were clearly among the finest and best conceived one had ever experienced, but only a person with the outlook of an ignorant dogmatist could suggest that one should not listen to other statements of these same works, realizing that the music is greater than the musician.

Toscanini first came to America in 1908, in an era when the United States still looked to Europe as the source of the arts and sciences and could be aptly characterized as a rich, powerful, and productive nation that sought to buy and enjoy the culture which application to other than materialistic ends had produced in older and poorer countries. Toscanini saw the native arts in the United States when they were still, on the whole, second-rate imitations of European models, when few Americans made efforts to compete with the imported European artist (and practically no American artists were to be found in Europe), and the fashionable attitude, well preserved in the autobiographical writings of Santayana and Van Wyck Brooks, was one of unconcealed disparagement of American culture (an aggressive compensation for any feeling of inferiority) and a certain masochistic delight in being put in one's place by the culturally secure European. This has all changed. American artists have made world reputations in nearly every field, and with the growing power of the United States in the international scene, American cultural imperialism, which has met with universal success on the mass level, has made itself felt in more elevated forms as well. In this process Toscanini stood apart. His attitude toward American music was patronizing and hostile at first, mildly curious later, but never strong or enthusiastic. Toward the fine American musicians with whom he worked in his orchestras he was warm and even affectionate. He appreciated their skills and did much to develop them. But Toscanini himself was always the visitor, the representative of European musical culture, and in the history of music by American composers, it is unfortunate in a way, what a small role Toscanini has played.

II

Toscanini's Musicianship

1

To EXPLAIN the ways in which Toscanini was superior to other conductors of his times we must appreciate the fundamental qualities of his mind and character which have produced performances which were not merely those of a musician of extraordinary technical accomplishment, but which seemed at times to reflect a perfection of concept and execution which might exist in the mind of the composer but almost never is realized by means of human resources in a concert hall.

One of his most quoted statements is his insistence that it is the composer who is great, not the performer. "I am no genius. I have created nothing. I play the music of other men. I am just a musician." The achievements of Beethoven and Verdi (for example) as performing artists are now matters of merely historic interest, and the many triumphs before the public of Mahler and Richard Strauss, who knew extraordinary success as conductors, are, in Toscanini's eyes, minor when compared to their achievements as composers. In fact, Toscanini has attempted composition. His youthful efforts use the familiar materials of Italian operatic style, just as Koussevitzky's somewhat later essays at writing music drew upon the conventions of the nineteenth century Russian school, and Furtwängler's scores reflect neo-Wagnerian romanticism. These men were not creative in this sense. The power to draw a great work of music from their inner resources was not there, but present in its place was the power to re-create, from printed notes, the original concept (or something very close to it) of composers with whom they were in special rapport. On an absolute scale this is a secondary talent, but in terms of the distribution of gifts in the population as a whole, it is a capacity almost as rare as the highest levels of artistic genius.

Many efforts have been made to explain Toscanini's unique capabilities, and many of them, I feel, have failed through superficiality in analysis. Explanation of a phenomenon as distinct as Toscanini's music is certain to be difficult, and excessively simple, misleading answers are easier to give than complex, accurate ones. If we are to avoid being naïve or incorrect, we must look deeper into this matter than has commonly been done.

Toscanini is a fanatic. In a work of fiction only an author with the powers of Dostoevsky could create him or make him convincing. His concentration while conducting has to be considered in the same terms as the behavior of a mystic in contemplation or a poet in the throes of inspired creativity. Richard Mohr, who made all of the Maestro's high fidelity recordings, described it briefly with: "He gets transfixed. A look comes over his face." The distinguished English critic W. J. Turner said of the same phenomenon that he was sure Toscanini suffered, in the literal sense, as he conducted. The difference between Toscanini giving himself to the music with intensity of this order and a *routinier* beating time in a relaxed and indifferent manner is the difference between St. Francis in ecstasy and a sleepy vicar stumbling through the order of morning prayer.

For Toscanini the ideal musical experience probably comes when he reads a score and hears it in his mind, for there seems no doubt that he can "hear" printed music before him with the sense of immediacy that ordinary men and women know only in actual performance. What he must do is match this ideal experience with the playing of an imperfect and fallible group of men, and since Toscanini's concept of many works seems to have been formed without any concern for human limitations, so long as string players must bow, brass and woodwind players breathe, and singers produce tones from a human larynx, Toscanini will never achieve exactly what he desires in every case. There are limits to virtuosity, and his concept of certain scores far exceeds them. He knows this. When the musicians with whom he is working share his desire to achieve the best performance possible, work as hard, as conscientiously, and unstintingly as he, putting forth their best effort at all times, he can be patient, compassionate, even affectionate. Because of these qualities he has accepted some poor playing and singing and allowed recordings containing flaws of this sort to be issued. The musicians who failed him were still, in his eyes, doing their best. Toscanini's rages are a response to the other aspect of the situation, that in which he feels he is giving his maximum in physical and nervous energy, concentration, and intensity of feeling, and others are holding back and making things easy for themselves. The person who suggests he is unconcerned about whether or not he is operating at his highest level of skill can drive Toscanini into paroxysms of fury going far beyond the normal indignation of a conductor and approaching frenzy.

These tantrums have been one of the few aspects of his personality which the popular press could exploit, although his rehearsals were always closed to reporters and the public (with the exception of close friends) and when his "dress rehearsals" with the N.B.C. Symphony were opened to a small, invited audience, Toscanini treated them as concerts, forbidding the spectators to applaud or make any sound, but never stopping the orchestra except for major errors and (with a few exceptions) controlling his outbursts with the same Stoic self-discipline he invariably displayed in public. During concerts he would restrain himself, even if a player made a catastrophic blunder. The tantrums, in other words, were for the orchestra, not publicity, and it was not Toscanini's intention that anyone should know of them, although no phenomenon in which so many persons were involved could be kept secret in an age of celebrity-worship. In the past, under provocation, he exchanged remarks with his Italian audiences, but in the United States and Britain, where Stokowski and Beecham had no inhibitions about lecturing concertgoers, Toscanini remained silent, feeling that it was inappropriate for him to step out of his role as a musician and speak.

Sir Adrian Boult, who was associated with Toscanini through several seasons of London concerts with the B.B.C. Symphony, has described Toscanini's rehearsals as models of economy and reasonableness, stressing that he never required the players to do more than was necessary for the preparation of the work, even if there was further time at his disposal. "Nothing that I have ever heard or seen of the Maestro and his work is out of line with a perfectly consistent pursuit of the ideal in music and an absolute horror of personal publicity and showmanship," he has written.*

B. H. Haggin, who followed Toscanini's American career from the very beginning, has written that Toscanini's rages are a natural outgrowth of the internal state of "a man obsessed and possessed" rather than self-indulgence, "and such a man is not rational or reasonable—not in music nor in anything else."** Toscanini is primarily a creature of his emotions, and his emotions are unpredictable and likely to run to extremes. In the full eighteenth century sense he is governed by the passions of the soul. The proper attitude toward such a person, Haggin suggests, is not a patronizing air of superiority based upon one's sense of greater emotional stability, but gratitude that the artist is willing to suffer in order to provide his audience with musical experiences which happy, well-adjusted musicians of lesser sensitivity cannot duplicate.

For Toscanini the music is all. To create the performance he conceives he will spare no one, least of all himself, from the utmost expenditure of every physical and emotional resource. To the hardened professional musician, out to earn his pay with as little work as possible, Toscanini is a horror—and the feeling is mutual. Toscanini knows few psychological subtleties. His method is simple: to drive, assault, and flay his players until he breaks their wills and forces them to yield the performance he demands. Artur Rodzinski has insisted on many occasions that the horrid aspect of conducting that takes it out of the realm of art and makes it in some ways analogous to lion taming comes from the fact that orchestras are made up largely of frustrated men who feel they can do a better job than the conductor and yearn unceasingly for a chance to assert their wills. To unify them into a well-integrated ensemble which co-operates with its leader and plays well together, as much psychology as musicianship is necessary, together with an appreciation that orchestral playing is as boring an occupation as a musician can be asked to follow. Rodzinski's many successes in orchestra training and his good relations with his men (no demanding conductor is ever, strictly speaking, popular) support his judgment. Tos-

* *The Listener,* June 16, 1937, pp. 1177-78.
** *The Nation,* August 29, 1953, p. 179.

canini's approach was more impersonal and reserved. He wanted obedience and veneration, and to get it he could be anything from the stern father to an avenging deity.

The relationship of conductor and ensemble here described is largely a product of the nineteenth century. There have been instrumental groups and virtuoso performers since the beginning of music, but the symphony orchestra under a conductor with a baton and absolute authority is a product of the mid-nineteenth century, and its development into the virtuoso orchestra is almost an event of our own times. Indeed, the emergence of the large, virtuoso orchestra, although anticipated in the music of Berlioz, can best be dated by the production of music scored for such a group, such as Strauss's *Don Juan* (1888). There is every reason to believe that the great orchestras of this century are the finest there have ever been.

Much of this development took place in the United States, where the conditions of orchestral performance were ideal for the creation of virtuoso ensembles. *First,* the great American orchestras play long seasons. The Boston Symphony, for example, gives at least two concerts a week—very likely five to seven—forty-eight weeks a year. The month without work is not a period of unemployment but a necessary holiday at the close of the summer season. The Philadelphia Orchestra has a thirty-eight-week schedule, somewhat more typical, during which it plays more than a hundred and seventy-five concerts. *Second,* the musicians are on contract, are paid weekly throughout the season, and are financially secure. Although a few teach, extra-musical activities are not necessary for a comfortable standard of living, nor is there need to divide one's interest between the orchestra and other engagements. The minimum salary (paid to about half the ensemble) is roughly $140 (£50) a week in the great orchestras, rising to $250-$300 (£84-£107) paid to the concertmaster (leader) and the principals of the various sections. Recording sessions and broadcasts provide extra income which may amount to $900 (£315) a year or more for each player. With salaries of this level, an orchestra of extremely able personnel can be secured and maintained. *Third,* the season in most American cities is sold out, in advance, on subscription, the purchaser accepting as many as twenty-eight weekly concerts in a series at a price as high as $6 (£2/2) each. "Friends" and "guarantors" of the orchestra agree to pay whatever deficit is left at the close of the season.

The pattern, then, is one of generous financial support, combined with the demand that the music be of the highest quality. The conductor has at his disposal resources that are unequaled virtually anywhere else in the world, but he also has a critical and demanding audience, and if he fails to maintain the standards American audiences have come to expect, he will probably not last beyond his first contract—although he may be able to pursue his career successfully in Europe.

The virtuoso orchestra is the product of the virtuoso conductor, who is both coach and teacher as well as musical director. The measure of his ensemble is a measure of what he has made of the orchestra. The first of the great virtuoso combinations in the United States was undoubtedly the Boston Symphony Orchestra in its seasons under Karl Muck,* and next in order I would place the Philadelphia Orchestra as trained by Leopold Stokowski and the Boston Symphony as brilliantly transformed from a "German" to a "French" orchestra by Serge Koussevitzky. A peer of these great ensembles was the New York Philharmonic Orchestra of the mid-'twenties under Willem Mengelberg, to which Toscanini came as guest conductor in 1926 and the season following. He had under him a fine orchestra, for Mengelberg was a strict disciplinarian and had trained it well, and although it always responded to Toscanini with sensitivity and fine playing, the Philharmonic apparently did not begin to take on all of the characteristics it was to exhibit under him in later seasons until 1927-28, when he led it for a longer period.

As the Boston and Philadelphia ensembles were polished to unbelievable brilliance they acquired a keen sense of pride, so that even under conductors of less ability than Koussevitzky and Stokowski they never fell below a high standard of excellence. The Philharmonic-Symphony of New York never seemed to have this esprit, and even when Toscanini was its principal conductor was capable of wretched performances when led by musicians of lesser stature. In the hands of John Barbirolli, who could maintain neither the discipline nor the high standards Toscanini had established, the quality of playing quickly de-

* Perhaps the Boston Symphony reached this level at an earlier date under Arthur Nikisch, but there seems to be good reason to question it.

clined as the incorrigible elements in the personnel whom only Toscanini could control were free to assert themselves. The cry was raised that Toscanini had ruined the orchestra—"burned it out" was a common phrase—when in fact it had not forgotten how to play as it had under his direction, but simply had been able to get by without doing so. When Toscanini returned at the end of the 1941-42 season it reverted to its former self within the first few minutes of his first rehearsal because it knew its man.*

The orchestral performances produced in Boston after Koussevitzky's arrival in 1924, in New York from the beginning of Mengelberg's tenure, and in Philadelphia as Stokowski perfected his distinctive style, together with contemporary performances (which I know less about) by Beecham (when he had the opportunity to prepare things adequately), by Furtwängler in Berlin and Vienna, by Mengelberg in Amsterdam, and so on can be said to make up the period of the highest development of orchestral playing since the emergence of the large orchestra in the late eighteenth century.

By 1939, of the three American orchestras named, only the Boston remained under the same direction it had had in the preceding decade; Stokowski was gone from Philadelphia and first Mengelberg and then Toscanini had left the Philharmonic, which was only to regain its former glory in later seasons under Rodzinski. In Europe political troubles were providing serious obstacles to the arts, although the great orchestras of Amsterdam, Berlin, and Vienna survived the conflict and in Palestine an orchestra of distinctive qualities appeared to have been formed.

My own feeling is that the Boston Symphony as Koussevitzky had polished it in 1945 was the finest orchestra the world had ever heard, especially in French music.

Koussevitzky's orchestra had the transparency which came from precision. The strings bowed in unison. (I remember him saying in rehearsal again and again, "Gentlemen, you are not together. It is no use if you are not together!") He had a variety of colors at his disposal, rich, glowing tones (that in Mozart were a little too gorgeous, although impressive none the less), richer hues (such as appeared in Russian scores), and weight of ensemble for German works. Unlike most "French" orchestras

* Or so Haggin maintains. *Music in the Nation,* New York, 1949, p. 253.

Koussevitzky could play Wagner in a manner that, although different from Bayreuth, was effective and convincing. About the only music that the Boston orchestra could not play well was Mahler; the style was too alien to them.

At the peak of its development the Boston Symphony had carried the cultivation of refinement and virtuosity about as far as it could be expected to go, and the resultant orchestral sound was something which had to be heard to be believed, but might not be believed even when heard. If conductors were to be judged solely on the basis of the quality of the sound they could produce from an orchestra, Koussevitzky would be an almost unbeatable candidate for the title of greatest conductor of all time. There are, however, other factors, and the New York critic Virgil Thomson (who is also, of course, a composer of importance) correctly stated that after a number of years these beautiful performances had become over-refined and no longer were "about anything" except how beautifully the Boston Symphony could play. This came from long rehearsals, season after season, of the group of works which Koussevitzky had made the heart of the repertory, so when he remarked in one of his later seasons that he had worked seventeen years on a certain effect in *La Mer*, he was talking about a passage that he had played with the orchestra hundreds of times if the concerts and rehearsals were all counted.

Stokowski's orchestra was also capable of the highest level of virtuosity and produced sounds of spectacular beauty, but within a more limited range. The tonal qualities that Stokowski desired above all others were the darker, the more exotic, the openly voluptuous and erotic, and the flowing rhythmic inflection of music as he produced it, with brilliance mixed with Oriental languor and sensuality (particularly in his unconventional phrasing), could only be achieved in scores which permitted interpretation on these lines. Thus Stokowski was in his element with *Scheherazade* and at a loss in a Mozart symphony—with the result that he didn't play much Mozart. For a time he abolished the office of concertmaster (leader) and had the players bow as they pleased, so that instead of breaks he would have a smooth, viscous stream of tone moving through the string parts. The Stokowski approach was effective and musically justifiable only in a very small number of works; beyond that it was an unjustifiable distortion of works in terms of a set of mannerisms of interpretation, although taken for their own sake, if one didn't care about what was being done to the music, the effects were sensational.

Toscanini's orchestra sacrificed some beauty to his demand for absolute clarity. His ideas of orchestral sound were based entirely on how the orchestra sounded to him, *on the stage,* thus his perverse affection for studio 8-H, which from his vantage point didn't seem too unsatisfactory. (One of the difficulties with Toscanini recordings is that people often don't realize that some of their faults are simply slightly imperfect reproduction of characteristics which Toscanini looked upon as virtues.) Toscanini's strings were transparent. Every line of the instrumentation stood out, because he wanted his men to play so that every strand had a little "edge" to it. He wanted the lines to stand apart, as if in relief, rather than blend. If one wanted a beautifully integrated section producing a magnificent sound of massed string tone one went to Boston. Toscanini did not regard this as "correct." Unlike the elegance and beauty of the Boston brass, Toscanini's ensemble had a decided "burr" and often he had his horns conspicuously "forward" in the over-all sound of the ensemble, blowing rather hard and producing the rather coarse, brassy tone that the F horn yields when blown hard. It was exactly what he wanted. (Heard on a recording of limited range the quality could be most disturbing.) His ideal was transparency to the point that one could listen with the score in one's lap and *hear* everything he saw in the printed music. (Even modified, this made recording a nightmare. He was insensitive to the low fidelity and poor quality of the sound of many of his disks. He passed them because they were "correct," i.e., the men were together and the sound was reasonably transparent. Toscanini probably does not regard his 1951 Beethoven *Fourth* as a bad recording.)

When one compares the Toscanini and Koussevitzky performances of such works as the *Italian* and *Classical* symphonies, *La Mer, Pictures at an Exhibition,* and the second *Daphnis and Chloe Suite,* one finds that Toscanini offered more sensitive and exact rhythm with an impressive feeling for the unity of the work and a spectacular level of transparency and virtuosity in the ensemble. In the Koussevitzky version the virtuosity was of equal, perhaps on occasion even greater skill, and the lines of sound were blended to provide a glowing whole. In the Koussevitzky performance one could not hear everything, because certain lines, regarded as accompaniments, had been made secondary, so as to focus attention on the principal themes. In a work such as *Daphnis* this always seemed to me to be more effective than Toscanini's method, which, in fact, was the more difficult, since keeping the many strands of the orchestration transparent and in balance was a task of titanic difficulty. Both performances were beautiful and both were right, if one means by that faithful replicas of the intentions of the composer as shown in the score. Which one preferred is a more subjective matter than most questions of criticism. Unfortunately, comparison today on the basis of recordings is difficult, because the Koussevitzky versions are to be heard only on old and defective disks.

The virtuoso orchestra emphasized and dramatized the role of the conductor to an extraordinary degree, and it is natural that as attention was centered upon the eminent conductors of the day, composers and orchestral musicians might well come to feel that their contributions to the total performance had been slighted, particularly when one reads Koussevitzky's pronouncements, in which the "interpreter" appears to have a role only slightly inferior to that of the composer, or when one notes the many instances in which the conductor is given credit for the fine performance of an instrumentalist, who has every right to be regarded as a virtuoso in his own right. Chief of the conductor-hating composers has been Paul Hindemith, himself a conductor of not inconsiderable merit.

In *A Composer's World** he writes with obvious feeling:

"There was a time when leading an orchestra was the exclusive task of men with a universal musical wisdom, when outstanding musicianship and great musical and human idealism were the foremost requirements. Granted that today we have many conductors with these old-time qualities, we nevertheless cannot overlook the fact that with the many times greater number of orchestras and hence the multi-production and consumption of conductors, their musical wisdom is frequently anything but

* Cambridge [Mass.]: Harvard University Press, 1953. Pp. 137-38. Quoted with permission.

universal, their musicianship doubtful, and their idealism replaced by an insatiable vanity and a deadly fight against any other being who happens also to wield a baton."

The veneration in which conductors are held, Hindemith feels, is "disproportionate" to the actual skills they possess, but reflects a musical embodiment of a social-psychological phenomenon:

"In an era that leaves little opportunity in the individual's life for the application and display of overt despotism, the demonstration of some refined and stylized form of oppression seems to be imperative. The listener in the audience who in his normal behavior has to suppress, thousands of times, his most natural human desire of governing, ordering, dictating to, and even torturing his fellow men, projects himself into the conductor's personality. Here he sees a man who with the consent of human society exercises a power which we would look upon as cruelty if applied to dogs or horses. Identifying himself with these activities the listener enjoys the perfect abreaction of his own suppressed feelings: he now swings the teacher's cane, the dignitary's mace, the general's sword, the king's scepter, the sorcerer's wand, and the slave driver's whip over his subjects, and quite contrary to the effects such dictatorial manners have in real life, the result seems to be pleasant to all concerned."

Can it be that a part of Toscanini's popular success has been the result of publicity resulting from the exploitation of his own uncompromising autocracy and unyielding will? A London critic, on the occasion of Toscanini's two concerts in 1952, remarked that many of "the wrong people" were present for "the wrong reasons"—and that their hope of a tantrum (reflecting ignorance of Toscanini's self-control in public) and their desire to see British musicians under the control of the baton of steel, introduced into two distinguished musical events a subcurrent more appropriate to the Roman arena. Could a part of the incredible success of the 1950 Toscanini tour of the United States have come from the purely theatrical desire to see the most celebrated martinet of our times?

Whatever extra-musical aspects Toscanini's reputation may have had, his career was based on his musicianship and the unique qualities which it exhibited. There are certain obvious features of this musicianship which have been advanced as the explanation of its general excellence, and it is well to consider these, although explanations in such limited terms are faulty through being incomplete.

We are told, for example, that the impact of a Toscanini performance derives from absolute fidelity to the score. This is misleading. In the first place, in many scores there is no possible standard of "absolute fidelity" since the composer's markings permit alternative interpretations which, within certain limits, appear to be equally faithful to his desires. Music is a living art because it is possible for two performances of a work to be "faithful" or "correct" or "effective and artistically justifiable" without being identical. In freeing himself from metronomic rigidity in execution, and other such limitations, within limits, Toscanini is simply doing what every musician does, this representing artistic virtues rather than faults. Again, Toscanini's performances are not always faithful in even the sense indicated above. He introduces not merely slight changes in pace, for expressive purposes, but major departures from composers' markings of tempo and the like. Toscanini's most consistent departure from the printed music has been in the matter of tempo, and as he has grown older, almost nothing has ever really been played slowly, no matter how it was marked. His versions of the slow movements of certain symphonies have thus been as mannered as those of any other musician, and his preference for fast tempi has given to many works a character which appears foreign to the composer's wishes. A part of this has been excess intensity, and a part has been a fear that at a slower pace the music will lose continuity. Toscanini would rather rush a work than run the risk of its going slack for even a moment.

There is another category of Toscanini changes relevant to the issue of fidelity to the score. Toscanini is a musical scholar of great perception. He has insisted upon playing works with the instrumentation desired by the composer, and he has not allowed extra instruments to be added. For example, he will not play Italian music in German editions (in which extra brass parts are sometimes inserted by editors), and in the Tchaikovsky *Pathétique Symphony* he follows the original score and plays the slowly descending scale leading to the crashing chord midway in the first movement (bar 160) with the clarinet taking the passage down to the bottom of its range and the bassoon entering to complete it, rather than add a bass clarinet, as other conductors do, so as to retain the same tone color through this important phrase. Further, Toscanini has (when possible) read autograph scores, consulted early editions, and inserted corrections in the printed text of many of the works he has played. In his last recording session he corrected Herva Nelli's high B in *Ritorna Vincitor!* insisting from his knowledge of the original that the printed edition was wrong and the note Verdi had written was B-flat. Toscanini stands, therefore, for purity and accuracy in the text.

He does not, however, stand for a literal duplication of that text in performance, and when he feels, as a performing musician, that the composer has made a miscalculation, he undertakes the responsibility of correcting it so as to realize the objective which he perceives the composer desired. I have looked at some of the scores on his shelves and found them full of the sort of markings one would expect to find in a scholar's library. When the same passage is written in an inconsistent style in two places, Toscanini makes it consistent, if that is the composer's evident intention. If a bad disposition of parts obscures a harmonic progression, buries a melodic line under the weight of the orchestration, or conceals an important feature of the counterpoint, Toscanini alters the voicing to make this detail clear. If Brahms gives the horn a low note that does not sound well, Toscanini reserves the right to cut it out. If Debussy writes an important phrase which cannot be heard without doubling and reinforcing the part, Toscanini subtly applies what extra tonal power is needed to make it audible. In all of this he is merely fulfilling his duties as a conductor, and in most instances it is impossible, even following with a score, to tell when changes have taken place, for they are never alterations in the substance or effect of the music.* One simply

* A somewhat extreme example of this is the second big orchestral passage (following the introductory statement of the theme and the *p* statement of the counter theme) at number 107 in the "Great Gate of Kiev" section of *Pictures at an Exhibition.* On the ground that this passage (17 bars to number 109) was not orchestrated by Ravel, Toscanini writes in trumpets and scalewise passages for the 'cello section and raises the level from *f* to *ff*. This is undeniably more of an effect, although I am not sure the movement needs as much *ff* as Toscanini gives it. The reader may compare the Toscanini revision with any of the excellent recordings of the unaltered Ravel scoring and decide for himself. At number 115 in the same score,

knows, hearing flute tone standing out bold against the other sounds, for instance, that more than one instrument must be playing, even though the score reads, "First flute, solo."

There is a final way in which fidelity to the score plays an important role in Toscanini's musicianship. He has come to loathe the word "interpretation" and what is done in its name, and thus is scrupulous in making no unwarranted changes in the music he plays. The operations of Stock, who rewrote a portion of Chausson's symphony to provide an organ solo, and added a few bars of his own to the Schumann *Fourth,* or the more conspicuous activities of Stokowski in subjecting Wagner to "symphonic synthesis" and eliminating the coda to Tchaikovsky's *Romeo and Juliet,* so as to conclude the work with a feeling of Hollywood-transfiguration, although not alien to a nineteenth century tradition of "arrangement" and transcription, were repellent to Toscanini. However, he, himself, appeared to be insensitive to the faults of certain traditional Wagner excerpts which he played repeatedly.

Greatly as one respects Toscanini's insistence upon adhering to the intentions of the composer, this alone is not a sufficient explanation of his powers. His competence in the scholarly aspect of reading eighteenth century music and knowing how to grasp the proper dynamic levels in a score that the composer had only partly marked in this respect, or his careful editing of the score of *La Mer,* which provided a great performance with a solid foundation in a perfectly calculated text, reflect musicianship of a high order, but I feel that other conductors possess equal dedication to fidelity to the composer without being peers of Toscanini. This factor is but a part of a complex of skills which makes Toscanini unique.

In another example of incomplete explanation, we are told that Toscanini is a master of the orchestra, that he is familiar with the technique of all the instruments, and that as a result of years of experience he is able to use their resources to maximum effect. This is all true, but many conductors, some of them in no way comparable to Toscanini in their musicianship, can be said to have mastered the orchestra to this degree. Taking effects for their own sake, a considerable body of candidates

---

Toscanini rewrites the trumpet parts, and there are probably other changes which my ear cannot fully detect.

could produce effects just as beautiful and striking in their own way as any effects Toscanini could command. One can agree, then, that Toscanini knows the orchestra forward and backward, but this is not the reason for his primacy among conductors.

The same must be said of his supposedly evocative power. He has no difficulty in projecting his intensity. Under his direction artists have repeatedly given themselves to the music without holding any emotional energy in reserve, offering performances which, by themselves, they could not achieve. This is a rare quality, but I do not think that Toscanini is the only conductor of our day to possess it, and it is not the thing which, of itself, sets him apart from his contemporaries.

$\vee$ Another explanation tells us that Toscanini is a master of styles, that he always plays music in the manner best suited to it, thereby stating it in the most effective way. This is not even a partial truth. Toscanini is the master of only one style, his own. Music which is not well suited to this approach he plays with a loss of effect or does not play at all. His own style, a purified and hyper-sensitized version of *bel canto* singing in orchestral terms, is well suited to a great deal of the finest music, but works which require a different sort of feeling, he cannot transmit effectively except in unusual reinterpretations in *bel canto* terms. Such a score is the *Moldau,* which Toscanini plays beautifully but appears to transform into a piece of Italian music.

Certain other generalizations of a critical nature about Toscanini are not merely incomplete but faulty in a much more obvious manner. Some tell us that Toscanini's tempi for a given work are always faster than what is usual among other conductors. This is exaggerated. (It is nearly always absurd to say always, since the world is not such a clean-cut proposition.) For instance his frequently repeated reading of *La Mer*, represents one of the slowest performances to be heard today, while some of his readings of Wagner are slower than the "traditional" German versions recorded by Muck. Toscanini has a preference for tempi faster than those regarded as the conventional pace in many scores, but beyond this one cannot generalize.

Nor is there any basis for the contention that Toscanini's performances of a given work never changed—a thesis I shall contest in detail later in this chapter. Suffice it to say at this point that Toscanini's performances seem to be continually in a process of change, but that some have changed more rapidly than others, and that some of the alterations were conspicuous and others were slight. Those who have followed him closely have been able to hear for themselves that he would play a Brahms symphony (say) one way in the spring and another way the following autumn. His performances are living things, produced from the heart and mind of an intense and perceptive musician, and it is inevitable that—at different times and under different conditions—they should change.

Two skills contributing to Toscanini's success which have received less attention than they might are his ear and his baton technique. So called "absolute pitch" is often overestimated by conservatory professors. It is not a prerequisite for a brilliant musical career (Koussevitzky, for example, lacked it), or, of itself, evidence of particular musical gifts. Toscanini, however, has a remarkable sense of pitch (so acute, in fact, that the high 445 tuning of A in the Boston Symphony made him uncomfortable while listening to its playing, Walter Toscanini reports) and this has undoubtedly played an important role in his performances.

Whatever he may have had to do with the creation of the scoreless type of conductor, Toscanini was in no way responsible for the batonless species. He always used a stick. In later years these were made for him by his physician (as a hobby, rather than a professional service). Dr. Hubert Howe, working to the Maestro's specifications, produced a baton twenty inches long, four and three quarter inches of its length being a cylindrical cork and plastic grip about one half inch in diameter. Toscanini held his baton firmly with his three middle fingers (his little finger sticking out at right angles to the shaft). His beat was not of the textbook variety, although eloquent to an astonishing degree and (except for an occasional slip) completely unambiguous. He preferred circular motions (in common time he seemed to be stirring in a large, vertically positioned tub) in which the pattern of the beats flowed into a single, continuous rhythmic pulse. He never sat while conducting, never appeared to do anything showy, and never ceased giving the impression that he was aware of what each individual player was about. His degree of command, therefore, was phenomenal.

The truth of the matter, it seems to me, is that Toscanini's unique qualities come from a synthesis of the factors given above in combination with an unparalleled understanding of the nature of music and an ethic of honest musicianship in which it is not the great maestro but the great composer who speaks through the orchestra. For him the task of the conductor is to master the score and combine intelligence with musical skill in giving voice to what the composer has written. The gap between Toscanini and the "interpreter-conductor" who places himself above the composer and uses the music and the orchestra as vehicles for the assertion of his own will and the enlargement of his ego cannot be bridged; and because so many conductors have allowed themselves to be affected in this way the selfless musicianship of Toscanini is sufficient to place him in a very small and distinguished group of artists.

It is not straining an analogy to speak of music as a language. In a word-language used expressively, as in poetry, we have the elements of the meaning of words, accent, rhythm, and tempo; the combination of these things as we read a poem giving us our feeling of coherence, continuity, and form. A poem is an artistic unity. If we change words, drop out or rearrange lines, or read with accents other than those the poet expected the words to have, we destroy the integrity of the work and substitute an artless muddle.

In music the units are not words but combinations of sounds of short or extended duration, and just as words must have a certain order to make sense, so certain combinations of sounds when followed by certain other combinations of sounds have a significance they would not otherwise possess. It is this fundamental thing about tonality—that a given sound appears to lead naturally into only a limited number of other sounds—that gives us a basis for harmony and allows us to create feelings of tension and repose which, in a rhythmic pattern, constitute the fundamental elements of musical structure.

This combination of rhythmic stress and suspension, the sustained alternation of strong beats and weak beats, with their ability to convey the sense of a rising and falling melodic line combined with the pattern of tension and repose, the "moving" unresolved tone and the "stationary" tone that offers momentary resolution, provides the basis for harmonic rhythm, that is, the integral union of the two basic elements of music, rhythm and tonality. In a Toscanini performance one hears what is surely the highest possible development of harmonic rhythm as a key to the exposition of music, since invariably he places rhythmic stress on what is harmonically strong and makes the unresolved harmony the weak beat.

It may be that it is the lack of these unities of rhythm and harmony which make contemporary music uncongenial to Toscanini, so that he can find some understanding for *Petrouchka,* which retains some of the conventions of tonic-dominant harmony (without adhering to it), but none for *Sacre du printemps,* where rhythm is not clearly an outgrowth of harmonic patterns. It is to be noted that Toscanini appears to have played a certain amount of inferior modern music simply because it is comprehensible in terms of older harmonic-rhythmic unities. These facts constitute a reply to those who insist that "everyone" puts rhythmic stress on consonant harmonies. In many works one cannot escape from doing so, but this need not make harmonic rhythm as central to one's manner of performance as it appears to be to Toscanini.

The foundation of a Toscanini performance is the rhythmic pattern he has selected as best fitted to the expressive content of the music. His choice of tempi appears to reflect two drives, first his emotional response to a given work, a response that apparently is heightened by fast tempi, and secondly, as was noted earlier, his desire to preserve continuity at all cost and avoid any strain upon the themes or the successions of intervals which compose and accompany them and, taken together in a time series, make up the musical structure. The rhythmic foundation does not change except when the composer has indicated that it should. There is consequently a line to the performance, a steady propulsive force which is always felt and which is never sacrificed to a special effect, but remains and through its presence gives the work coherence and cumulative power. Toscanini's preference, even in rehearsals, for playing on to the end of a work, or the end of a part of a work, before stopping to go back and make such corrections as are necessary, reflects this insistence upon continuity. He must experience works as unfolding unities, not as bits and pieces strung together in a series. The wonderful plastic qualities of a Toscanini performance come from the fact that within the limits of the rhythmic pattern he can pass from the softest to the loudest dynamic levels and through a score of changes in expression or orchestral color without losing the integral drive of the harmonic rhythm. The nature of a work of music is such that it must be revealed as a sequence in time, but the composer and the performer must see it as a structural whole in which all parts are properly balanced in terms of the entire composition. The unique quality of Toscanini's performances comes, essentially, from his awareness of form and his magnificent capacity to reveal it.

Toscanini's way of playing music, I have said, is an orchestral interpretation of song in the *bel canto* manner. Undoubtedly this has always been a part of his artistry, since it is the ideal style for Italian music such as has been in his heart and on his lips since childhood. It is not a traditional style for the performance of German music, nor is the Toscanini orchestral sound that of a German orchestra. The tone of a German ensemble rests upon a solid bass provided by the 'cello, contrabass, percussion, and the lower woodwind and brass instruments. If these registers are not well developed and forcefully present a German work will probably lack the body and strength of tone which is required. (In earlier years Toscanini often played German works with too little bass. As he has grown older he appears to have seen the need for firmer registration and has strengthened these lines.) In a German orchestra violas and violins add to the bass strands of lighter substance and, especially in the case of the first violins, great brilliance in the upper octaves, but the parts falling in the higher voices never detach themselves from the unified sound of the whole ensemble and the firm bass it provides. Their brilliance is subordinated to the whole. Similarly the wind and brass (which may include somewhat coarser but more powerful instruments than the lighter B-flat trumpet and F horn—such monsters as the F trumpet, for example), although not without virtuosity, seemed to be in their element blowing chords that struck one like hammer blows and carried a weight that Koussevitzky's Boston Symphony, for example, could not duplicate. A well-integrated ensemble of the German type could have great beauty of tone, offering in place of the luminescence and overall brilliance of the Boston a mellow "old wine" quality such as I knew in the Chicago Symphony of my youth under such capable German musicians as Frederick Stock and Hans Lange, and which I heard that orchestra revive, for concerts of over-powering beauty, in later seasons under Bruno Walter. The Berlin and Vienna Philharmonic orchestras and to a large degree the Amsterdam Concertgebouw Orchestra (which has certain "French" influences as well) are of this character.*

The German orchestra of the nineteenth century developed in an atmosphere of idealism and romanticism in which the overt expression of certain types of feeling was cultivated and approved and warmth, spontaneity, and an almost improvisatory sense of flowing emotions was desired. This style of performance is virtually dead—at least outside a few remote parts of Germany—and Toscanini deserves as much credit as any individual for killing it off, although I have been told by reliable musical sources that not even he could get the Vienna Philharmonic to play with the characteristic integration and ensemble tone he secured from other orchestras. To achieve "expression" in the romantic style the tempo was adjusted at will (whether or not the composer had authorized such a departure), pauses were inserted before especially dramatic or impassioned outbursts, sighs, retardations, heaving and panting were slipped into passages *ad libitum,* rubatto ceased to be an indulgence, and rhetorical emphasis, which made the most conventional series of cadential chords on a tonic-dominant pattern into a world-shaking *dah DUM dah,* became the staple elements of performance. The emasculation of much great music by the imposition of these mannerisms has often been defended in the name of authentic Viennese style, sanctioned by the masters themselves. This is absurd. The style is Viennese, but it is a creation of the nineteenth century.

Some of these characteristics, qualified by genuine poetic feeling, are to be found in the conducting of the late Wilhelm Furtwängler. The Furtwängler method was to allow the music

* If one did not object to being unkind one would have to say that British orchestras have no national character except the sloppy and perfunctory playing which is the inevitable result of almost never having enough rehearsal. A conductor of great skill and inspiration as well as musical power can, however, get beautiful sounds from them under even these conditions, and when well prepared some are equal to the best ensembles of Central Europe. There is a distinctive quality, however, in the story about the well-known player who remarked to a friend, "We did — the other night." "Really? Who was conducting?" "I don't know. I never looked."

to fall into deceptively natural phrases (or groups of phrases) and a succession of simple, but carefully molded statements of this type, spun out in a series, made up the work. In such music as the *Tristan Prelude,* where Furtwängler's feeling and understanding provided close affinity to the score, such a performance could be eloquent, moving, and beautiful, lacking the intensity, cohesion, and cumulative power of Toscanini, but in its place offering a degree of communication and a sense of shared emotion which the cool perfection of Toscanini never approached. It is difficult to find a Furtwängler performance that does not contain moments of great beauty and strength, however mannered the whole may be. Unfortunately, Furtwängler did not limit himself to music for which he had special feeling or which was best revealed in his type of performance, and in less congenial works one sensed a desire to create effects for their own sake, without any spontaneous feeling for them. Since these performances lacked firm rhythmic continuity, the obvious means of increasing tension was to increase speed, so that constant acceleration and retardation, together with the distention of phrases (often to the point at which they seemed to become parodies of themselves), were, together with other crude or insensitive manipulations, imposed upon a basic rhythmic pulse that rushed or dawdled. The effect of this was to destroy any sense of unity in the composition and reduce it to a series of episodes in sequence. Furtwängler's defects came from lapses in understanding and taste combined with an exhibitionist tendency that was insufficiently restrained.

The defects of Toscanini come from characteristics desirable in the mean being carried to excess. His rhythmic accuracy is splendid, but at times it has been metronomic rather than musical and the performance has revealed mechanical exactitude rather than a feeling of creativity and spontaneity. His intensity is magnificent, but on occasion it has gone beyond reasonable limits and the music has been driven so hard that its power, eloquence, and natural melodic flow were impaired or diminished. The strength of his style is the way in which he allows music to sing; the weakness is his personal tension which often dominates and prevents this. Another of Toscanini's weaknesses is a tendency, like Koussevitzky's, to over-refine music which he plays too frequently. As one works over a score season after season there is always the tendency for it to go stale, and the mechanism of "going stale" in Toscanini operates by the performance becoming fast, slick, mechanically perfect, and cool, a succession of beautiful, highly polished surfaces, none colored too deeply, and all practically without meaning. The musician must always balance himself between seemingly opposite poles: the achievement of near-perfection in polish and form at the cost of losing communicative and expressive power. With Toscanini the first extreme—near-perfection—was the reef on which lay the shattered hulks of several of his most-performed works and toward which, at the end of his career, much else of his repertory seemed to be moving in a steady breeze.

The metamorphosis of a Toscanini performance appears to be roughly as follows. In his early years he played Italian music in the *bel canto* manner which is correct and which, without significant deviation, he followed throughout his life. In German scores, however, he followed the practice of German conductors, and one heard the broader phrasing, slower tempi, and a certain number of the rhetorical inflections of the usual German style. It is clear that he adopted German practices to different degrees in different works, that whatever he adopted was absorbed within his own artistic personality and thus was never literally German but Toscanini-German, and that his concept of orchestral sound, which one cannot say never varied (because it did, becoming richer and more robust in his later years), remained his own and never duplicated German practice. Three "performances" can be distinguished. First, the "ancestral" performance, that is, the earliest Toscanini performance of a German work, based upon his assimilation of the reading of German conductors; secondly, the "transitional" performance, in which Toscanini's *bel canto* manner has replaced some of the German style and rhetorical devices have been subdued; third, the "singing" performance, in which German influences have disappeared and Toscanini has reconceived the work in terms of little or no rhetoric.

Toscanini's performances are based upon years of analytic study of scores with the determination to play them honestly and effectively. His style and tempi are the outgrowth of the application of a musical intelligence of extraordinary sensitivity to the music he has examined with attention to the slightest detail. His tempi, in particular, grow out of his sense of the plastic continuity of thematic material, from his sense that a written melody actually contains its tempo inside itself, if one can only sense the pulse at which its intervals are linked with the greatest lyricism and freedom of movement.

Haggin's contention that ". . . any pace that Toscanini adopts is one in which he can make the music effective,"* is true or false depending on how one takes the word "effective." Toscanini could make music thrilling at any pace, but often the effect was alien to the character of the music and violated the "natural" tempo of the material, suggested above. Toscanini's playing of the slow movement of the Mozart *Jupiter Symphony* may be effective, but it is not remotely what I can conceive as Mozart's intention, and I cannot regard it as other than a departure, through an excess of intensity, from Toscanini's normally great powers. In *La Mer*, on the other hand, I can accept his reading as a perfect statement of Debussy's concept of the work.

The elements of Toscanini's style, particularly in recent years, are so consistent that it is possible to imagine the general outline of a Toscanini performance of works which, in fact, he never played. Winthrop Sargeant, one of Toscanini's musicians in the Philharmonic period, thus (involuntarily) gave his readers in *The New Yorker* a fine account of the Toscanini performance of the Tchaikovsky *Fifth*. I agree that the Toscanini reading of the score would be exactly as Sargeant describes it. The fact that Toscanini never played the work is quite irrelevant, and Sargeant's graceful apology was not really necessary. If anyone desires I shall be happy to describe the Toscanini performance of the Berlioz *Fantastic Symphony*, the Toscanini *Spring Symphony* of Schumann, and a number of other works which, for one reason or another, he never played. The only limitation on this exercise of musical imagination that I can see, is that sometimes when I have conceived Toscanini performances *a priori* I have been disturbed to find, not merely that the treatment of detail in the actual reading was different from that in my mental one (I was prepared for that) but that, inevitable human limitations being a factor, a particularly grand Toscanini-effect I had heard in my mind failed to appear. A good example of this is the Brahms *Third Symphony*, for which I have conceived a Toscanini

---

* *Music in the Nation*, New York, 1949, p. 128.

performance (based on what I have heard him achieve in the other three of that composer) far superior to any I have actually heard him conduct. Others who have followed his career for many years ought to have experienced a similar feeling at one time or another.

If we are to indicate Toscanini's influence upon orchestral playing and the standards of musical performance, omitting irrelevant matters (such as Toscanini's memorization of scores, necessitated by an eye defect which made it impossible to read music except at very short distances and produced—by accident— a crop of scoreless conductors) it centers about three points: (1) Toscanini was of primary influence in killing off the fashion of "expressive" performance, lingering from the nineteenth century, and substituting criteria based upon mastery of form, rhythmic and plastic continuity, and unity of concept. (2) Toscanini revealed new and hitherto unknown possibilities of virtuosity and clarity in orchestral playing, setting standards which no conductor has surpassed and which few have equaled in these areas. (3) Toscanini's continual attitude of honesty, dedication, and humility toward great music, the antithesis of the celebrated personage who sets himself above the works he plays, not only reaffirmed the highest standard of artistic morality, but resulted in the achievement of performances which exhibited an astonishing degree of penetration into the innermost and hitherto unrevealed aspects of many great works. Toscanini continued to show us new and unexpected things about great music which, in the hands of other conductors, we thought we knew fully and completely. In his performances one enjoyed, again and again, unique musical experiences, and until there is another Toscanini, we shall never hear them again.

2

Toscanini's long career provided him with an unusual opportunity for artistic development, but we seem doomed to suggest the lines along which it took place rather than describe it in detail. In writing about music there comes a time, sooner or later, when words are no longer sufficient to convey one's ideas and it is necessary to turn to music itself. Were this a lecture rather than a book, I should make that move now. As it is, I must refer to recordings and suggest to the reader that he supply his own illustrations. I should like to talk here about a few recordings which are by no means the best, or even the most interesting, Toscanini has made, but which are of value for purposes of illustration.

In the discography that follows I list only recordings which were made and distributed with Toscanini's knowledge, omitting all private recordings from broadcasts, although some broadcast performances otherwise unobtainable have been sold in "pirated" editions at one time or another. Walter Toscanini has a basement full of tapes and disks, but it is still an open question how many of them the world is ever going to hear. I have heard only a small number of them. Because of recording contracts and union rules it is impossible for recordings of broadcasts to be made available for study purposes, and the network has no facilities for allowing interested persons to hear their acetates of broadcast concerts. All in all, with the loss of the Max Smith notes and difficulty of hearing a series of Toscanini recordings of a given work, I have become increasingly skeptical as to whether it is possible to write of his changes in style without indulging in a certain amount of speculation.

Worst of all is the lack of material from the Philharmonic years. I am becoming more and more convinced that the vintage period of Toscanini's career was the decade with the Philharmonic, and here there are very few recordings. I would gladly trade a couple of dozen Toscanini disks of the past few years for just three or four more Toscanini recordings from about 1936. As it is, there is an early electrical series—which is too old to be more than ghostly echoes of great things—and the splendid 1936 group that is so well known. Unfortunately a number of problems are not solved by those disks. I would give a great deal to hear how Toscanini played the *Eroica* in 1936, but I doubt if I shall ever know.

Progress in recording techniques has been so rapid that we tend to forget that to record symphonic music from the air in the 'thirties one had to have two expensive disk cutters and keep switching back and forth as one changed recording blanks. None of the Toscanini air checks of this period that I have seen were made this way. Amateur jobs, they represent the efforts of men with a single cutter who were resigned to losing some of the music while switching blanks. They made use of the longest playing surface available at the time, 16-inch, .025-inch groove, 33⅓ rpm acetates. Most of these disks exist in the one copy, and that often is in poor condition. With a strong imagination, one can sense the original.

None the less, it is on the basis of what material exists that the question of Toscanini's changing manner of interpretation must be discussed. It seems clear that the least changes have occurred in his performances of Italian music. There is a 1921 recording of the *Don Pasquale Overture*. We can put it on one turntable, place the 1951 version on another, and proceed right through the work, alternating passages between the two, without producing anything inconsistent or artistically disturbing. The *style* of both performances is the same, and thus they can be spliced into one another without violent injury to the music. The *detail*, however, differs somewhat, the earlier performance being somewhat more relaxed and containing some *tempo rubato* that the version of thirty years later lacks. (Such a composite recording was actually played during a talk I made on this subject for the B.B.C. Third Program.) There is variation *in detail*, but limits are imposed on the range of variation by the over-all consistency in *style*. The lesson seems obvious. The *bel canto* style which is correct for Italian music has been thoroughly ingrained in Toscanini from his earliest years, as I have noted earlier, and in the works in which it can be adopted he has felt stylistically secure from the start of his musical life and, quite properly, seen no reason for altering his performances. I am therefore not at all surprised that the two *Don Pasquales* sound so much alike; what would shock me would be that they did not.

In German music a different situation prevailed. The "ancestral" performances I spoke of earlier were, of course, sincerely felt, since they could not have been honest and musically convincing if Toscanini did not find the medium sympathetic, but none the less they appear to have required him to accept tempi and traditions of performance which were different from those he would have adopted in Italian works, and which he could regard as sufficiently different from his natural stylistic inclinations to permit him to think that there was another, freer, way in which he might play this music if it were correct to do so. Eventually he came to feel that it *was* "correct." The result of this was the late, or "singing" performance in the Italian manner, and the development of this reading often produced one or more "transitional" performances, as I indicated in the earlier discussion.

A classic example of this, for me, is an air check recording in Walter Toscanini's collection which preserves the Maestro's 1935 performance of the great slow movement of the Bruckner *Seventh Symphony*. So far as I know there is only the one copy of that disk in the world, and the reader may well curse me for whetting his appetite only to frustrate him, but those who heard the performance or have been lucky enough to hear the record, may recall that although the sound—imperfect as it is on the disk—is obviously that of a Toscanini ensemble, transparent and glowing, the tempi are those of German tradition, and the long phrases, in which the tensile strength of the line of sound seems enormous and the firm but slow rhythmic pulse allows amazing effects of spaciousness and splendor, follow one after another like a succession of miraculous invocations. When I heard that record I realized, as never before, the difference between the Toscanini of the Philharmonic days and the Old Man.

We can hear something similar to this in the 1939 recording of the slow movement of the *Eroica,* in the final pages of that titanic Funeral March where Beethoven (as he sometimes does) appears to bid his theme a lingering farewell. The effect is lost in the 1949 recording because the tempo is faster and the feeling is different. There is little to recommend anyone's looking up that 1939 *Eroica* recording, long since withdrawn from the catalog, but there are things in the slow movement which repay the search for a copy.

It is a "transitional" performance. If a recording of 1930 existed, although I have no reason to think that one does, it would be a quite different reading of the score, I am convinced, particularly in the first and final movements. The opening *Allegro con brio* is taken here at a furious pace which accounts for the 691 bars (it is the second longest movement in all the Beethoven symphonies, even if—as Toscanini does—one follows the usual modern practice and eliminates the repeat) in 13:30. To offer a basis for comparison, Bruno Walter takes 14:50 for the same material, while the late Wilhelm Furtwängler required 15:57 in his recording.

In the 1939 performance Toscanini seems unsure of himself, and the pacing of the first movement reveals to an unusual degree his habit of speeding up contrapuntal material without authorization from the composer. For example, at bar 65 he increases the pace and whips through the "second group" (Tovey's term) at a much faster tempo than that adopted for the earlier portion of the movement. Bar 85 marks the end of this section and there is a jolt as the brake is applied, but Toscanini proceeds on this speed-up, slow-down basis through the movement, giving me the effect of riding with a cowboy driver in a hot rod. By 1949, when he recorded the work again, he had decided on another set of tempi, and in the final two hundred bars or so there are none of the unexpected thrills of the 1939 version, but there is greater unity in style and much closer adherence to Beethoven's intentions.

If we compare three recordings made around 1949, the second Toscanini version and the Walter and Furtwängler sets mentioned above, we find that it is not Toscanini but Walter who follows Beethoven's directions with the greatest fidelity, and although there are moments of poor ensemble and an occasional tendency to insert unneeded rhetorical pauses that only arrest the natural flow of the music, Walter's version, on the whole, is reserved and without mannerisms to a much greater degree than either the Toscanini or Furtwängler performances. That the Furtwängler should contain interpretive liberties and faulty execution is more or less to be expected; he played music as he felt it, and he tolerated slips that perfectionists such as Toscanini could never have passed. For all that he achieves better playing in the opening bars of the final movement than Walter, and he produces a number of beautiful things (for example the clarinet solo in bar 258 of the movement cited) which the other conductors cannot match.

In the 1949 *Eroica* Toscanini starts off at a more relaxed tempo than that of ten years before, and one begins to expect a somewhat different version of the score than, in fact, one is going to hear. At bar 65 the pace increases, and from there on the two performances run very close together *with respect to time,* although the tempi of the 1949 set are much more consistent. Purely in terms of time, there is not much difference between the two Toscanini versions of the Funeral March (the 1939 set is 15:55,

18 seconds longer), but when one hears them the difference becomes clear: the 1939 set appearing not merely a bit slower, but also more eloquent, powerfully shaped, and deeply felt. The 1949 version is thrilling, particularly in the climax that the fugal development provides in terms of the "singing style"—but it is another approach to the music, and it is this view of the symphony that was developed even further in the 1953 broadcast performance which we may eventually get on a disk.

In terms of orchestral sound the two Toscanini performances appear to be very much alike. In both the weight of tone is not as great as that of the German conductors, and the basic color is brilliant and light rather than dark or burnished. Toscanini's brass has a tendency to cut through the orchestral texture with a rather uninteresting *dum, dum, dum, Dum Dum DUM* cadential pattern which I don't think needs so much emphasis, and it is here that one questions the point of transparency. Compared to some of the heavy, even sloppy, playing in the Furtwängler recording, the extraordinary lightness and virtuosity of the Toscanini is amazing to hear, but there are places where I feel Furtwängler is right and Toscanini wrong. Take the horn solo in the trio of the *Scherzo:* for one thing Beethoven doesn't indicate that the trio should be slower than the opening section, but everyone slows down for it, simply because the usual practice is to play the first part of the movement so fast that no horn player (and Toscanini has some fine ones) could possibly navigate his part at that speed. Furtwängler, however, takes a slower tempo and his alteration of pace for the trio is less evident. (He also makes more of the final pages of the *Scherzo.*) Toscanini reads the phrase in bars 232/9 and 243/8 as running from the B to the A (concert notes), and he takes the two final quarter notes as detached sounds, thus giving the whole passage a clipped effect which I dislike. Both Furtwängler and Walter take the phrase in the German tradition as running from the B to the F, and in the Furtwängler recording one hears it properly—and beautifully—played.

The final movement presents no interpretive problems. The 1939 Toscanini version is often nothing short of a massacre—possibly due to the need to rush to finish the broadcast on time. It is ruthlessly hard driving and clipped off short in the places where a lighter hand would produce melody and charm. Even the most superficial comparison with the 1949 version shows the improvement which relaxation has produced in the later performance. The German versions are both satisfactory. The Furtwängler suffers from a rather crude and tasteless retard just after the introduction, but it has its moments later on, and the Walter again offers a faithful statement of Beethoven's desires as indicated in the score.

Since the *Eroica* was the symphony Toscanini played more than any other during his American career, it is worth noting these things, for they show not only that his performance was always, to some degree, in a state of change, but they indicate that at times the performance suffered from the fact that Toscanini was stylistically insecure. A 1935 *Eroica*, I feel, would be a consistent reading in the "ancestral" manner, just as the 1953 *Eroica* was a perfect restatement of the score in the "singing" style. The 1939 set contains too many Italian elements that don't belong in Beethoven, fugues whipped up like the long, accelerating climaxes of Rossini overtures, chords like falling blows, violent and unexpected compression and expansion of phrases. These theatrical devices cheapen and vulgarize the *Eroica,* and having tried them, Toscanini was right in removing them, for the most part, from his reading of the score.

A similar change from an "ancestral" to a "singing" performance, although in this case characterized simply by increased intensification and faster tempi, is documented in the 1936 and 1949 versions of the *Dawn Music* and *Siegfried's Rhine Journey,* another Toscanini specialty that has gone through the full metamorphosis. If we play the 1936 version we hear the dawn arriving at an appropriate speed, and the first climax, beginning in the strings with the theme of Brunhilde as a mortal woman and ending with that of Siegfried as hero, although slightly quickened for effect, is followed by a return to a slower tempo and a gradual and powerful development of the material through the "Freedom" motif to the tremendous climax in the brass on "Siegfried as hero" at the close of the introductory pages. The *Rhine Journey* proper then begins, and this performance has changed relatively slightly since 1936, except to become faster and very lightly inflected indeed.

The 1936 recording we can imagine as part of an operatic performance in which, to quote Wagner's stage directions, "the red glow of dawn" gradually becomes brighter, and "full daylight" finally bursts upon us at the first climax, but as Toscanini plays it in 1949 it is no longer related to dawn (unless it is the fastest sunrise in history) or to the opera house, but has become a concert work. The Brunhilde material is therefore not merely given an increase in tempo for effect, but the fast tempo is retained after the climax, and the conclusion of the introduction with the big climax on "Siegfried as hero" becomes a frenzied outburst. No better contrast between the Toscanini of 1936 and the Toscanini of the last years can be found than that passage, which comes just at the start of the second side of the 1936 records. The early version is slower, more powerful, and musically justifiable; the second is a triumph of virtuosity, but unless this is enough to satisfy one, it must be added that in purely musical terms the effect has been diminished. Those who wish to contrast the two performances in terms of modern sound may play the 1949 Toscanini against a Furtwängler performance of about the same date on LHMV-1049 or ALP-1016. The timings of the Furtwängler are to within a second or two of the 1936 Toscanini at each common point (Furtwängler makes use of Humperdinck's text), and there is no question for me but that his approach is more in keeping with Wagner's intentions.

None the less, speed was what Toscanini wanted, and even at his final rehearsal when playing this score after preparation the day before and eleven past performances, the brass could not navigate the "Siegfried as hero" motif without errors (there are minor slips in the 1949 recording) and an outburst of hoarse shouts of "*Ignoranti!*" from the Maestro, and the strings, falling into a reasonable tempo in the Brunhilde material, provoked another outburst with much pounding on the score and shouts of "*Subito! Subito!*" ("Hurry up! Hurry up!"), when in fact they were playing at a tempo which musicianship and intelligence would specify.

In his later seasons there must have been many times when the only thing that saved Toscanini from disaster in some performances was the phenomenal virtuosity of his orchestra, which could play anything at virtually any tempo, even though his demands required them at times to rush, simply to get all the notes in, without an opportunity to shape the phrases or accent them in the manner which one had previously expected to find in a Toscanini reading.

In the case of the *Haffner, Clock,* and Beethoven *Fourth* symphonies the newer Toscanini recordings give us performances that have tightened up in a consistent manner, and the contrast is therefore the obvious one between a relaxed and naturally-flowing melodic line and one that is artificially hastened and intensified. There are also cases where the opposite effect has taken place, in the contrast between a tight 1929 *Sorcerer's Apprentice* and a relaxed 1950 version, or a poor Mozart *G Minor Symphony* from 1938-39 and a fine one, again, from 1950. (1950 was a good year for Toscanini; it is a pity he did not make more records then.) The two *Leonore No. 3*'s offer a more interesting contrast. In the 1939 version the opening pages are played with the breadth and nobility implied in Beethoven's specification that the tempo should be *Adagio.* The more rapid performance of 1945 does not capture this so well. With the second of the two famed trumpet calls the 1939 recording picks up speed and proceeds to the finish in a faster and more brilliant style. In spite of its quicker opening, after the second trumpet call the 1945 recording adopts a trifle slower tempo than that of 1939. Both are "transitional" performances. In time (1939, 13:04 vs. 1945, 12:49) the faster pace of the opening pages of the 1945 version compensates for a few seconds' difference in the final ones. The 1945 set covers the material of the first side of the 1939 recording in seventeen seconds less time, which is a fair difference in three and a half minutes of *Adagio* comprising only thirty-six bars of music. The "ancestral" performance was probably more like that of 1939, only perhaps a bit slower in the final portion of the score. The faster opening of 1945 is distinctly in keeping with the accustomed style of Toscanini's later years. I suspect that to get the "ancestral" performance unaltered by his later tendencies to increase tempi a recording of 1930 would have been necessary, and I doubt if an air check of this period exists.

In the case of the Brahms *Third Symphony,* Toscanini apparently has never found a performance which satisfied him as an adequate statement of the score. There are basically two approaches we have heard from him, the first a tight, hard-driving version in which lyricism was sacrificed to intensity; the second, a slower, relaxed statement of the score that was even a little loose and slack on occasion. The second version, when held well in hand, always appeared to me to be the more enjoyable and Brahmsian, but when, before making the recording, Toscanini pieced together an "ideal" performance for himself it was of the former type. Ironically the recording is a mongrel. It certainly is not the "ideal" performance he had in mind, and it is an inferior statement of the relaxed version compared with those I have heard on other occasions. I find it a very interesting disk, largely because I look upon it as a failure, and in analyzing its weaknesses we learn something about Toscanini's customary strong points.

"The first movement of the *Third*," a great conductor has told me, "contains more problems than all the rest of the four Brahms symphonies put together." The opening bars clearly are to be taken two beats to the measure and at a reasonably brisk pace which gives a firm rhythmic feeling to the phrases, but Toscanini's tempo is actually too slow to provide this. A problem arises over the semi-staccato notes which close bars 4, 6, 8, and 10. The proper feeling for them is of a lighter, i.e., "up" beat, but Toscanini gives the passages in question a choppy, irregular rhythmic quality by taking the semi-staccato notes lightly accented but at their full written value and allowing the first note of the bar following to be heavily accented in bar 5 by the supporting harmonies in the trombones and tympani. The question of scanning this figure is not made easier by Brahms' deviations in the notation. For example, in bar 10 these notes are marked staccato; but to give a most troublesome instance, in bar 129 the notes are written semi-staccato, although two bars later in bar 131 they are staccato once more. (References are to the Eulenberg edition of the score.) Koussevitzky's solution was to take these notes as if they were staccato in every case, thus the shorter, more accented playing of them in his performance.

In this recording the intensity and clean, brilliant attacks one expects from Toscanini are missing, together with his accustomed rapid tempi and strong rhythmic feeling. In bars 60-63 the first note of each phrase must be given the slightest accent and the final one the slightest prolongation beyond its written value if the interweaving of the voices is to be smooth and the sense of forward movement secure, but Toscanini's listless execution of the passage lacks these desired qualities. His response to the points at which Brahms asks for a slight retardation (such as bar 109) and his interpretation of the *Un poco sostenuto* marking in bar 112 involve excesses, which in the former case almost halt the forward progress of the music. Repeatedly he fails to set a strong, rhythmic pulse when it is required, and in bars 187-94 where the cross-rhythm demands an absolutely solid and reliable feeling for accent and scansion, Toscanini fails utterly, with the result that the playing is meaningless confusion. While the "ideal" version was forceful and consistent in style, this is insecure and tentative.

The second movement is easy and goes well, and the third, which has given Toscanini difficulty in the past, is here stated effectively, if one has no objection to the slow tempo. The final movement again calls for intensity and strength, and here Toscanini simply throws away his opportunities and fails to make the score yield up more than a fraction of its glories. The opening phrases are slack, although the same material is better stated later in the movement (perhaps a splice from another take?). It must not be thought that this was a recording from one of Toscanini's final concerts. Within a week of this session he made his powerful and characteristic Beethoven *Eighth,* and many excellent disks followed. I suggest that he had over-prepared the score, like a schoolboy who studies too hard for an examination, although the weaknesses exhibited here anticipate features of a few performances the year following, in his final season with the orchestra, in which old age was clearly responsible for a decline in his powers. Meanwhile, it would be a good thing if the "ideal" version were released for general circulation.

If the Brahms *Third* gave Toscanini troubles, the final passacaglia of the *Fourth,* which the majority of conductors do not play correctly, was perfectly grasped and achieved in a manner all but unequaled by any of his contemporaries. The basis of a passacaglia is an eight-bar phrase, usually in the bass (although Brahms does not always keep it there) which provides a vertebrate foundation for a series of variations in the upper voices. In the final movement there are exactly thirty variations after the statement of the theme, and it is on bar 249 that the final variation ends and the transition into the coda begins. The form, then, is a strict one, and it demands strict respect in the execution of the work. Specifically, since the eight-bar phrase is the link which holds the variations together, it must always be stated at the same tempo so that the cumulative effect of the thirty-one varied repetitions will come with the full weight the composer intended. It is therefore a great pleasure to hear the movement played with the careful attention to plastic continuity which Toscanini provides, and especially to find that the fourth variation is not speeded up, nor the twelfth retarded beyond the indicated change in the time signature, and that the many other things, such as the surging power of variation 25, which are lost through the insensitivity of other conductors to the form of the work, Toscanini does exactly right. In this recording, therefore, we have from him a model for all others to follow in performing this great score.

Ironically two of Toscanini's finest performances have not been generally recognized as such and have provoked a considerable amount of criticism, usually from those whose opinions are based upon misplaced respect for faulty traditions of style, or whose judgments of music are based entirely on its emotional effect, in other words persons who fail to see that the critic is not simply an individual who for one reason or another is allowed to circulate his opinions and impressions in print, but rather one who (at least ideally) is competent to study a score, secure a justifiable, musicianlike concept of how it should be played, and appraise whether or not a given performance appears to be a satisfactory statement of the composer's intentions. This is particularly important in this case, since a musically honest version of some scores is emotionally less stimulating than a grossly exaggerated one, and if the degree of stimulation is, in fact, the criterion invoked, debased musical values are asserted.

The critiques of Toscanini's performance of the great *C Major Symphony* of Schubert reflect a lack of study of the score and the instructions the composer clearly provided in the music. At the best one can concede that a slightly slower tempo might be appropriate for the *Andante,* but the most rudimentary comprehension of the score justifies Toscanini's practice and rebuts the standard of the insensitive "traditional" performance which is invoked against him. The Tchaikovsky *Pathétique Symphony* is another case of the same type, but worth fuller discussion. Here the criticisms are three in number: that Toscanini does not know

the proper "Russian" style or Tchaikovsky style; that his performance is completely unsympathetic; that his performance diminishes the content and value of the music. Let us consider these in
order.

Actually, Tchaikovsky was regarded by his hyper-nationalist
contemporaries of the Moussorgsky–Borodin–Rimsky-Korsakov
school as a German, that is, as a composer who rejected distinctive national idiom of musical expression. Certainly the demand that as pure and universal a work as the *Pathétique* be
played with heavy, overdone "Russian" style is an absurdity.
Toscanini's approach is musically justifiable beyond any doubt.

The orchestral sound of the Toscanini performance is clear,
bright and transparent, an unfamiliar effect in Tchaikovsky,
where conductors tend to run the lines of instrumentation into
a thicker, darker tone. None the less, Toscanini uses the same
type of sound (it is his standard approach) in *Manfred, Romeo
and Juliet,* the *Nutcracker,* etc., without any comparable chorus
of discontent. The answer is, I suppose, that although scored with
wonderful transparency, the *Pathétique* is *supposed* to sound
dark and murky and suggest the limp, hooded figures Victor
placed on the album cover.

The *Pathétique* is apparently thought by some to be unadul-
terated purple passion from start to finish, and they want it
played that way. The orchestral sound must not only be dark
and mellow, but the phrasing, accents, tempi, etc., must depart
from the composer's printed instructions and turn the work
into a traumatic field day. The demand for such falsification is
an insult to the emotionally mature listener.

To appreciate this performance one must follow it, at least
once, with the score, noting the splendid transparency and balance and the skill with which every detail is stated clearly
and effectively, and yet as a part of a whole. The beginning is
really the marked *Adagio,* but without excess. There is no fussing
with the solos in the woodwind here, or anywhere else, the
ritenuto in bar 17 is that, and no emotional upheaval, and the
following *Allegro non troppo* is just that, with the figures clean
and well defined, consistent, rhythmically accurate, and firm in
their propulsive force.

When one has experienced such things as the middle section
of the slow movement with the strings and woodwind blending

in lovely, controlled motion as the composer intended, followed by the march as a thing of lightning and fire, moving forward with increasing brilliance, and heard the final pages of the score as the quiet chant of low voices, each singing clearly and well to the very end, one will, I think, appreciate that this is the way it ought to be, that this is a beautiful and effective performance of a magnificent score, and that anyone who tries to tell him different is talking nonsense.

Another such model is Toscanini's performance of *La Mer,* which, although played in fifty-three concerts during his American career, miraculously escaped over-refinement and remained fresh and brilliant, probably because it is not a German work and the style appropriate to it was based upon clarity and song, the two basic elements of his musicianship. Here again the appreciation of his performance demands that we hear it, at least once, with the score and discover for ourselves the manner in which he does, literally, give our ears everything which the printed music presents to our eyes.

Debussy's instructions are that the first part of *La Mer (From Dawn to Noon on the Sea)* should begin very slowly with the sustained low note of the contrabasses and tympani suggesting the darkness covering the water just before the first appearance of light. The rising theme in the 'cellos, which moves to the violas and finally the violins, suggests the gradually increasing luminosity as the dawn begins to break, and the sustained countertheme in the woodwind and trumpet conveys the sensation of air moving over the now visible water. Toscanini achieves these effects splendidly, and at number 2 in the score,* where Debussy asks for a gradual increase in the movement of the voices to prepare for the change in the time signature from 6/4 to 6/8 at 9 bars after 2, Toscanini produces the desired effect subtly and establishes the moderate and very supple rhythm requested with consummate understanding of the composer's desires.

As I have mentioned before, music is the one art in which the creator of the work cannot speak directly to the public but must employ the services of an intermediary. Were musical notation perfect, it might be possible for the composer to indi-

---

* References are to the numbering of the sections in the copyright score published by Durand & Cie, Paris.

cate exactly how he intends his music to be played; but musical notation is not perfect, and a good performance demands of the performer that he be able to read into the printed notes the elements of style and execution which lie beyond the limits of the notation itself.

The middle section of the first of these symphonic sketches is given to a series of vigorous passages which suggests the movement of the water as the sun gradually climbs higher in the sky and casts changing patterns of light on its surface through the clouds. This material comes to an end 5 bars after 8 in three massive chords for full orchestra, and a quieter mood follows. At 2 bars before 9 there is an unusually imaginative passage in which the strings depict a sudden upward swell in the waves and the tympani and horns in turn echo the sound. During the remaining pages of the movement the scene tends to be more subdued than before, until suddenly, from the peak of its arc, the noonday sun bursts through the overcast sky and casts a blazing shaft of light down upon the water.

The second part of *La Mer (The Play of the Waves)* is the most difficult work Debussy wrote for orchestra, since its climax depends on a faultless execution of one of the most demanding passages ever scored for strings. The tempo of the music is fast, but again Debussy insists upon a supple rhythm, and it is clear that he wants a flexible, sensitive beat rather than metronomic accuracy. In the very first bars we hear the rise and fall of the water, and, high above, the graceful soaring flight of a bird. (It is a part of Debussy's genius that his pictures are always vivid but never crudely explicit.) This interplay of water and air continues for a few minutes, a violin solo suggesting the foam flying before the breeze, and out of this image a climactic passage for full orchestra is developed. At 33 the true climax of the movement begins, and if Toscanini has not produced marvels enough up to this point, he now surpasses himself in the manner in which he keeps his orchestra integrated and holds the groups of notes in a firm, singing line, so that no detail intrudes upon the complete form of the whole, ending with a breathtaking statement of the four supremely difficult bars before 38. It is an amazing vision of air, water, and light in motion.

The Dialogue of the Wind and the Sea which concludes the three sketches is a somewhat grimmer picture than those which precede it. Over a hushed bass note we hear the splash of angry waves, to which the wind replies with a faraway call from vast spaces ruled by no man. This is developed, and at 46 we hear the song of this wilderness of air sung over the steady slap and fall of the earth-bound water, and out of this grows a climactic passage. Quiet follows, and then, over the unworldly sound of a sustained harmonic in the violins, the wind, soft and with great expression, sings once more. A short, climactic passage follows, full of moving water, and this leads to the final pages, a magnificent vision of swirling air and choppy water mounting to the intensity of the final blast of flying spray that breaks and brings the work to a close.

La Mer is a difficult and complicated score. When we realize that in 1860 Tristan und Isolde was regarded by presumably competent persons as being so difficult as to be impossible to produce, the mere fact that La Mer could be written in 1905 with the thought of a performance shows the great advances in the technique of orchestral playing in the final decades of the nineteenth century; and the fact that a Toscanini could achieve a performance of this level, not merely in 1950, but by all reports in 1926 when he first played the score in New York, and probably soon after he first played the work in Europe,* shows the level of mastery which he introduced into the art of orchestral conducting. Perfection in art is the rarest of all things, especially in an art with as many difficulties as conducting. Toscanini's La Mer is an example of such perfection. It is, to begin, one of the greatest pieces of music ever written. His conception of it shows complete understanding, sympathy, and mastery at every point, not merely in the things given in the written notation, but in the elements of style, color, texture, etc., which the notation can never give. Finally it is a performance polished to the highest limits of virtuosity by an orchestra completely familiar with his methods, demands, and artistic creed. The result is something which will stand indefinitely as a triumph of orchestral playing and which sets a standard for the performance of this work which few conductors will ever meet and none is likely to surpass: for here surely, one feels, is the very image that lay in the composer's mind.

* Toscanini gave La Mer some time in the period 1905-18, since he prepared it during Debussy's lifetime, but only he can give the exact date.

III

The Toscanini Recordings

ON DECEMBER 18, 1920, Toscanini gathered the La Scala Orchestra into a compact group before the horns of the acoustical recording apparatus in an ecclesiastical structure that, in this secular role, was known as the Trinity Church Studio of the Victor Talking Machine Company in Camden, New Jersey. In that setting he made his first records, a minuet from a Mozart symphony and a Respighi transcription of a work by the father of Galileo.

Toscanini was at the mid-point of his career. A man of fifty-three, he had been conducting for thirty-four years, and thirty-four more years were to pass before he retired from the direction of his last, and greatest orchestra. In the decades between 1920 and 1954 Toscanini made and approved for commercial release over two hundred recordings (in addition to authorizing a non-commercial series for the American armed forces). Thus preserved are Toscanini performances of one hundred and eighty compositions, seventy-two of which have been recorded more than once, the champion being the *Scherzo* from Mendelssohn's *Incidental Music to "A Midsummer Night's Dream"* which has been released in five versions: 1921, 1926, 1929, 1946, and 1947. In the list which follows on p. 108, there are two hundred and fifty-two Toscanini recordings of complete compositions or portions of larger works capable of independent existence. By 1954 over twenty million copies of Toscanini recordings had been sold for more than thirty-three million dollars. In every way it is a fabulous achievement. Few conductors have been active so long, have recorded so much of their repertory, or have been accepted so universally by the musical public.

This chapter contains a full list of those records, but more than that, it is an appraisal of the documents in sound which Toscanini has left for the generations who will never hear him in a concert hall and must rely (as many of his contemporaries were obliged to do) upon recordings for an understanding of the principles of honesty in musicianship for which he has always stood and an appreciation of his contribution to orchestral playing.

Recording is not a new thing, but faithful reproduction of anything as complex as the sound of a symphony orchestra is a recent phenomenon. The acoustical method was adequate for preserving human voices, and recordings of singers made even fifty years ago give an accurate impression of the artist. Pre-electrical recordings of symphony orchestras, on the other hand, are poor as a group, and although some early electrical recordings have life in them in spite of limited fidelity, really faithful reproduction of orchestral sound is less than twenty years old, with the work of the past five years greatly superior to that of the preceding fifteen and complete verisimilitude still to be achieved, especially with the sound equipment available in the average home. Because of this it is still possible to view recordings with a certain amount of patronizing indifference. The truth is, modern electroacoustical techniques are adding a new dimension to the history of music and making the re-creation of past experiences an actual possibility.

If one were to document the sixty-eight years of Toscanini's career with records, it would first be necessary to have adequate disks from his early period, and, secondly, widely spaced re-recordings of a number of works, so that important changes in his manner of performing them could be noted. The recordings necessary for such documentation do not exist, although acetate recordings of the N.B.C. Symphony broadcasts, recordings taken from the air of his broadcasts with the Philharmonic-Symphony Orchestra of New York, and similar materials extend the available recordings considerably beyond the list of commercially released disks given here. The greater part of this supplementary material is in the collection of the Maestro's son, Mr. Walter Toscanini. Unfortunately, technicalities prevent the circulation of recordings of broadcasts, rehearsals, and the like, even for study purposes. One hopes, however, that at some time the range of available Toscanini material will be extended (with permission of the American Federation of Musicians and the Maestro) to include some of the great broadcast performances that have up to now been neglected. My own feeling is that a Toscanini Society Series is in order to preserve, in limited editions for students and musicians, Toscanini performances that may be flawed in one way or another, but still contain miracles.

For half of his career Toscanini made no records. In middle life we have a brief acoustical series from 1920-21 and early electrical recordings from 1926 and 1929. As acoustical records go, the Toscanini disks are good, and the 1926 and 1929 records are technically adequate for their day. One would have thought that in eleven seasons with the Philharmonic-Symphony Orchestra of New York there would have been recording sessions at regular intervals, but in fact all that are documented are his first concerts with the orchestra as a guest conductor, the period in which he left La Scala to become the principal conductor of the Philharmonic, and his final season. (Victor's great 1936 series is the lasting demonstration of what the Philharmonic had become in his hands.) There were three good reasons for this apparent neglect of a unique opportunity: (1) The country was in a state of depression and the record business was supposedly finished because radio could provide limitless "free" music in the home. The natural reply to this was Victor's famous advertising slogan, "The music you want when you want it." (2) Toscanini didn't care whether he made any records or not, since he could not see how anyone could obtain musical satisfaction from listening to them. (3) An experiment at taking recordings from a broadcast on April 9, 1933, using optical sound recording (an early technique to get around the limitations of disks and secure some of the technical advantages later obtained with tape) together with continuous disk transcription had produced versions of the *Fifth* and *Pastoral* symphonies of Beethoven which were unsatisfactory to the Maestro. This meant the only way to get records was to invest money in an expensive recording session with the hope that something could be obtained which, when released, would pay for the job. The 1936 investment seems to have liquidated itself nicely.

Toscanini hated to stop at the end of a four minute "take" and then try to begin a new one with the same tempo and rhythmic drive he had established previously. The whole point of a Toscanini performance is plastic continuity, and the way to secure this was by recording continuously, without pauses. Therefore in 1936 the engineers set up their recording machines so that they could switch from one to another at predetermined points in the score, without the orchestra having to stop, and for this reason the sides do not always begin and end as neatly as they might. Often the cutters were running for several seconds before the break was made and the sound fed to them. None the less, the three days of recording that took place on February 8 and April 9 and 10, 1936, produced the finest series of disks then available in the Victor catalog and preserved a group of brilliant performances which Toscanini has never been able to duplicate.

Toscanini went to Britain in October, 1937, and made two excellent sets for the His Master's Voice Company with the symphony orchestra of the British Broadcasting Corporation. Their first efforts to record him had been unsuccessful, but the 1937 series was an unqualified triumph. Returning to the United States in December, he made his first records with his new N.B.C. orchestra the following March. They marked the beginning of the seven lean and dreadful years of Toscanini's American recording. The orchestra was not then as responsive an ensemble as the Philharmonic or the B.B.C. had been, and the recording was done in the notorious Studio 8-H.

It was in this studio that Toscanini played and recorded for about thirteen years, an appropriate interval of time, everything considered. The main thing wrong with 8-H was that it was heavily treated acoustically to eliminate the natural reverberation which, it was thought, would be bad for broadcasting, and the sound took on a dead, wooden quality even in the brief interval that it lived before being absorbed by the walls or ceiling. One had the sense, therefore, that one was listening to an orchestra play in a soundproof box, and it was this distorted and unnatural sound, made worse by low fidelity reproduction, that one heard on a Toscanini broadcast and in Toscanini recordings of the period. Indeed, in 1954 these disks were being used for research in the addition of resonance to music, since they were practically the only available recordings of an orchestra playing in an almost completely dead room. Unfortunately this quality was not what one wanted in records for home listening. One bad consequence of this is that it set up a form of conditioning in some people, a few of them critics, that Toscanini recordings could always be expected to be technically inferior to those of other conductors. The facts do not support this. Although unsatisfactory by present-day criteria of fidelity, Victor gave Toscanini excellent acoustical recording in 1920-21 and electrical recording in the 1929 and 1936 series. The sudden decline in quality was a departure from their previously high standards. In recent years the level of excellence has been restored.

In 1938 and 1939 Toscanini was alternately making superior recordings for HMV in England and technically poor ones for Victor in the United States. After the outbreak of war the British engineers had no further opportunities to work with him, and from 1940 to the beginning of the recording ban by the American Federation of Musicians in 1942 Victor could do their worst, without competition offering any basis for invidious comparison. After recording resumed in 1944 their work was uneven, with startling improvements followed by temporary relapses into earlier ways.

In 1940 Victor responded to the criticism of its Studio 8-H recordings by moving to Carnegie Hall for the Brahms *Piano Concerto No. 2,* producing a set that, on the good machines of the period, sounded full and beautiful, and conveyed a reasonable likeness of an exciting Toscanini-Horowitz performance. On the high fidelity equipment of today the set is limited and coarse, but this is not a fair test of the effect it produced when it first appeared.

Unfortunately Victor did not keep their work at this level. One of the big problems of the time was the rapid wear of the bass cut in shellac records, due mainly to the heavy pick-ups and "permanent" or "multiple play" steel needles that were then the standard equipment in home-type machines. Victor tried to reduce bass wear by emphasizing treble and reducing bass (in some records one could actually hear the volume being turned up for the passages with important low notes and turned down immediately after they had sounded), a practice which could only distort and coarsen the sound of Toscanini performances. Most of the 1941-42 recordings bear the scars of this, the worst one being the *Traviata Preludes,* made with the nearest thing to no bass at all.

For the two years following, due to the union edict, there was no recording, except sixteen works taken from broadcast acetates for V-Disks. A single item from these years has recently been revived for release on longplay. When Victor resumed work, after an abortive start with still another broadcast recording, the quality of the sound had improved remarkably. Bass was back, the middle registers, supported now from below, had solidity, and the highs were not distorted by overemphasis. There was still a certain amount of coarseness, due mainly to limited frequency response that gave us the hard, fundamental tone of an instrument without the overtones which make the live performance brilliant and agreeable to the ear, and at times the sound was confined or flattened out by excessive monitoring, but the greater part of the 1944-47 recordings can be played on high fidelity equipment and reveal themselves to be competent, medium fidelity, disks which can still be heard with satisfaction.

In the early 'forties Toscanini finally became interested in making records. It was now possible for recorded sound to approximate the actual sound of an orchestra. Always before, the drastic reduction of the relative levels of volume, the lack of presence, and the loss of tonal values, together with the generally artificial quality of the sound, had prevented him from securing any pleasure from listening to records, and he found it difficult to understand how others could enjoy them. "That must be a flute," Walter Toscanini recalls his father remarking as something was being played, "because the violin cannot do that. But [pause for growing exasperation] it does not *sound* like a flute!"

At that time he was listening to his own recordings on a large and handsome RCA Victor machine, supplied him by the company. It was typical of the best home-type phonographs of the period. The public demanded record changers, and, indeed, with four-minute 78 rpm disks they were a great convenience, so the playing unit was a changer mechanism with a small motor driving a table that might carry the weight of a dozen records or that of a single disk, with the speed changing as the weight increased. The pick-up had to be heavy, since the record-changing cycle subjected it to a certain amount of abuse, and the needle was of the quasi-permanent metallic sort. A high-output crystal head fed into a low-gain amplifier with a functional top limit at about 3,800 cps, a weak middle range, and distortion up to fifty per cent in some frequencies at high volume settings. The speaker was a large, single cone type hung on the front of the cabinet without an adequate baffle. There is no question but that the sound produced by such machines was poor, but the public as a whole did not know that there was, in fact, much better sound on their records, and that with adequate reproducing equipment it could be heard.

The irony was that Toscanini never really heard his records and rejected a number of things that, played today, seem much better than those that were approved. Victor wanted a Beethoven *Ninth* from him very badly, and, judging from the test records, made a very tolerable one in 1938 at the close of his first season with the N.B.C. Symphony. It was not approved for release, although inferior recordings of the *Eroica Symphony, Egmont,* and two of the *Leonore Overtures* from his first Beethoven cycle with the orchestra during the season following were given his approval. In this case the issue was largely dynamics. A 1938 recording could not capture the climaxes of the Toscanini Beethoven *Ninth;* they had to be monitored in order to keep them on the record, just as the softest passages had to be raised in volume to keep the level of the sound above the surface noise of the shellac records. This did not suit the Maestro. "That is NOT my *fortissimo,*" he would shout as the record was played, just as a moment later he would insist, "That is NOT my *pianissimo.* That is not even *pianissimo.* That is *PIANO!*" Everything considered, it is probably miraculous that he gave his consent to the release of as many records as he did.

Recording was always something of an ordeal for Toscanini. Even if the disk was low in fidelity, it preserved something, and if it said Toscanini on it, it had to meet his criteria of perfection. From the very beginning he has recorded only on the condition that he have the right to reject any disk which failed to meet his standards. In 1920-21 he lavished the greatest concentration of energy and skill on ten recording sessions from which emerged sixteen sides of acceptable music (six of them only ten inch) which, at best, could reproduce only a small part of the over-all effect of the performance. The 1926 and 1929 records, even the great 1936 series, left him unsatisfied.

In recent years the tension has not vanished from his recording sessions. When cutting a 78 rpm master a single slip could ruin a take and four minutes of tense and otherwise perfect work.

A series of minor slips could ruin an entire album and prevent its release. Stopping and starting were unwelcome requirements which persisted for a time, even after the substitution of tape for wax master disks, since Victor wanted to record in seven-minute takes to fit 45 rpm "standard" and extended play surfaces. Tape did, however, make splicing and correction relatively easy. Improvements of this sort made it easier to convince the Maestro that his agonies were for a worthy cause.

The most celebrated instance of a long and expensive series of recording sessions producing nothing for commercial release is the Maestro's work with the Philadelphia Orchestra in 1942. Two symphonies, the *Pathétique* and the Schubert *Ninth, La Mer, Iberia,* the *Midsummer Night's Dream* music, *Roman Festivals, Death and Transfiguration,* and Berlioz's *Queen Mab Scherzo* were recorded in brilliant performances, but the level was too low, there were occasional flaws (such as an oboe that could not be heard properly at the beginning of the second movement of *La Mer*) and in some instances no duplicate masters were cut, which means there was only one wax blank of the take. When the whole lot was damaged in the process of electro-plating the wax blanks, there was no way of salvaging the recordings, since the level of the surface noise was as high as that of the quieter parts of the music. It is doubtful if any of these disks will ever be available to the public, splendid as the performances were. Toscanini would not allow his name to be used to sell a defective record—although emotional drives (and what is probably capriciousness due to temperament) have caused him to give his approval to recordings which are as bad as some of the Philadelphia series.

Early in the 'forties Walter Toscanini had a high fidelity system built for his father's use. Sixteen speakers were wired in parallel and mounted around a large room in groups of four, giving the sense of non-directional sound emerging from a wide source. With a high quality amplifier which could provide a great deal of volume without distortion, some feeling of orchestral presence could be secured, and at once the Maestro became more interested in his recordings and in preserving his performances on disks. He was finally coming to think that the result was worth the effort it demanded. Toscanini's house in Riverdale, a northern extension of New York City, now contains a profusion of recording and playback equipment, and the sixteen speakers have given way to a large, corner-type baffle with supplementary speakers located in the same and near-by rooms. The principle of non-directional sound, low distortion, and volume levels equal to the concert hall original are still maintained, however. The Maestro wants a record to sound exactly as the music sounded to him on the podium, which makes for a certain amount of harshness and clarity at the expense of the resonance and diffusion of sound experienced by a person in the middle of the floor of the hall.

Of all conductors, Toscanini most needed high fidelity. The brilliance of the sound he produced with an orchestra, the transparency of the texture, the clarity of the lines of the instrumentation, all required recording which gave one the effect of the strings, brasses, winds, and percussion, without any loss of definition or overtones, properly balanced, and placed in resonant space. Anything less than this was not merely poor recording but a gross distortion of the sound of the original, since something which was blazing and beautiful in the hall might well, when cut down to 3,800 cps on top and confined by a low volume level, come out coarse, blatant, and wooden.

Starting in December, 1944, with a respectable Studio 8-H version of the Beethoven *Prometheus Overture,* Toscanini's records could be compared favorably with those being made by other conductors at the time. The following May, again in Studio 8-H, he recorded Gershwin's *An American in Paris,* and the sound was so good that when the record was released in the 'fifties (for some reason it never appeared on 78 disks) in a long-play transfer, most critics accepted it as recent work.

A part of this improvement could be laid to a "new technique" being used for recording in the studio. The orchestra was taken off the rather shallow stage and set up on the floor, which had been cleared of the seats normally occupied by the audience. In this way fuller use could be made of the natural resonance of what was, all in all, a reasonably large concert room. Unfortunately Victor moved Toscanini into another, smaller studio, 3-A, for two recording sessions in 1946 and one in 1947, and here they reached the low point of their work in the 1944-47 period.

None the less, the majority of Toscanini recordings were then being made in Carnegie Hall, and although the uneven quality of the engineering of the period can be found in the contrast between the poor sound of the Carnegie Hall recording of the Mozart *Jupiter Symphony* and the excellence of *An American in Paris* or the Mozart *Divertimento K.287*, both made in Studio 8-H, on the whole the technical side was doing well by the Old Man. With a few elementary adjustments in equalization, filtering, and the like, nearly all of the records of 1944-47 can be heard on high fidelity equipment with pleasure. Fundamentally the sound that is there is an accurate replica of the playing of a great orchestra.

Medium fidelity gave way to high fidelity with the sudden upheaval of the American recording industry caused by the introduction by the Columbia company of the modern long-playing record in the early summer of 1948. Because of these disturbed conditions, Toscanini made no records for fifteen months, and when he resumed, everything was changed. He no longer cut wax disks which became more or less direct copies of themselves in shellac, but recorded tapes of five to seven minutes' duration which eventually appeared as 45 or 33⅓ rpm disks.

His first work in the new period was a complete recording of *Aïda,* made during broadcasts in March and April of 1949. This set is still to be released, although it was corrected and approved in 1954. There were no formal recording sessions until November when somewhat disappointing versions of the Beethoven *Second Symphony, Daphnis and Chloe,* and the *Eroica* were done in Carnegie Hall. After that, improvement was rapid. A group of recordings made in Carnegie Hall in December, 1949, are all excellent, high fidelity disks, and two groups of recordings made in Carnegie Hall and Studio 8-H (the last, in fact, to be done in that inglorious place) in March and June, 1950, immediately before and after the Maestro's American tour with the N.B.C. Symphony, are highly acceptable. There is then a gap until January, when he made the first of the three recordings which represent the 1950-51 season—two of them takes from the broadcast line.

The seasons 1951-52 and 1952-53 were Toscanini's period of intense, high fidelity recording. Forty-three compositions were recorded in the 1951-52 season and the summer following, and twenty were done in 1952-53. In his final season with the orchestra he canceled the recording sessions which had been arranged, as well as the Brahms *German Requiem* which he had been asked to prepare for his final concert of the spring series. A number of recordings were made during broadcasts, six of which have been released, and in June he returned briefly to make a few corrections for insertion in his broadcast performances of *Aïda* and *Un Ballo in Maschera*. With that he stepped down.

As we survey the thirty-four years in which Toscanini made records, we must be thankful for the length of his career and the opportunity given us to preserve his unique powers on high fidelity disks. If, like Koussevitzky, he had retired at seventy-five, there would have been no Toscanini recordings later than 1942, and his position would be similar to that of Weingartner, whose excellence is still universally acknowledged but is suggested rather than retained in the recordings he left us. The great Stokowski-Philadelphia Orchestra combination never was preserved with adequate recordings, and only at the end was the great Koussevitzky-Boston Symphony sound approximated by Victor engineers. Of the distinguished conductors of the generation before (some of them Toscanini's contemporaries) very little remains for us to hear. Mahler—only seven years senior to Toscanini—would have remained active, in all probability, until the 'thirties, had he not died prematurely. He made no recordings. Nikisch, whose recording career was limited to a few, historic oddities, we have lost, while Muck's ancient-sounding disks offer only imperfect replicas of great playing. Toscanini we have in full blood. However much recording improves, the best of the Toscanini records will show the future what he could do.

None the less, what we have on modern disks comes from the final years of a very long career. Toscanini, the musician, has been before the public and the critics since 1886, but it was the septuagenarian Toscanini who recorded after 1937, and it is the octogenarian Maestro who comes to us with high fidelity. The 1951-53 series is the supreme achievement of the Old Man. In the past he has said that he would conduct until he was ninety, and there are many among us still who hope that that promise will be redeemed.

List of the Toscanini Recordings

A star [★] before the number of a record indicates that it has been dropped from the catalog and thus is not available from the manufacturer. It is to be hoped that some of these disks will be issued again.

Since many of these recordings have been pressed under more than one number (for example in both manual and automatic couplings), I do not attempt to give *all* the numbers which have been assigned to these masters. Those who wish full details of this sort, plus convenient listings of what is on the reverse of some double-faced records, and similar data, should consult the *World's Encyclopedia of Recorded Music,* edited by Francis F. Clough and G. J. Cuming, together with its supplementary volumes. This splendid work is to discography what the Oxford English Dictionary is to philology. Since it does not cover the acoustical period, I have given full details for Toscanini's acoustical recordings.

In these listings the "name" of a recording will be the master number under which it *first* appeared in the RCA Victor and His Master's Voice catalogs. Thus, the "name" of all sets will be their *manual* sequence designation, with the exception of certain sets which appeared *only* in automatic sequence. For each record I give, *first,* the RCA Victor number, *second,* the HMV number, and *third,* the number of the longplay or 45 rpm transfer (if the original is a 78 rpm record that has been so treated). If there is only one number, the recording in question was issued by only the one company. Unless otherwise noted, the records are twelve-inch disks.

D, DB, and DA are HMV series designations for shellac records. Victor numbers carry no letter prefixes, although in the later period 11- and 12- were used. M and DM (automatic) designate Victor album sets. LM and LRY prefixes indicate Victor twelve-inch, longplay "albums," i.e., records in a cardboard "sleeve." The LM-*nn* series is ten inch, as is the lower-priced

LRM series. ALP is the HMV twelve-inch, longplay series; BLP the ten-inch series. The Victor LCT series is made up of longplay transfers from 78 rpm masters which are felt to retain their interest for the collector in spite of their older date. There is no equivalent HMV series at this time. *I list 45 rpm recordings only when the performance is not available on a longplay disk, or when there seems to be other justification. Normally 45 rpm duplications are ignored.* 49- is the Victor 45 rpm "normal play" prefix, with various special prefixes for album sets. ERA is the common prefix of Victor "extended play" records; 7R and 7ER are the equivalent HMV prefixes. This information should be sufficient to allow the reader to interpret the designations in the text; fuller information can be found in the *World's Encyclopedia of Recorded Music* cited above.

Acoustical Recordings

Recordings with the La Scala Orchestra of Milan, made in the Trinity Church Studio of the Victor Talking Machine Company, Camden, New Jersey, U.S.A. Numbers are of the Victor and HMV acoustical series.

1920

GALILEI *(Orch.* Respighi *as No. 2 of Respighi's Suite No. 1 of Ancient Dances and Airs)*
Gagliarda
  Recorded December 18.
  ★74672, later recoupled with *Fête Bohème* as ★6301 and ★DB-418
  (The DB and DA numbers are those of the HMV editions.)

Mozart

Symphony No. 39: Minuetto
  Recorded December 18.
  ★74668, later recoupled with *Finale* as ★6303 and ★DB-419

Symphony No. 39: Finale [Allegro]
  Recorded December 21.
  ★74669, later recoupled with *Minuetto* as ★6303 and ★DB-419

PIZZETTI

La Pisanelle: Le quai du port de Famagouste
  Recorded December 21.
  ★64952, later recoupled with *Suzanne* as ★840 and ★DA-375
  (10″)

BEETHOVEN

Symphony No. 5: Finale
  Recorded December 24.
  ★74769/70, later recoupled as ★6304 and ★DB-420

BERLIOZ

The Damnation of Faust: Scene 3, Rákóczy March
  Recorded December 24.
  ★74695, later recoupled with Beethoven *Symphony No. 1:
  Finale* as ★6300 and ★DB-3417

1921

MASSENET

Suite No. 4 [Scènes pittoresques]: No. 4 Fête Bohème
  Recorded March 3.
  ★74725, later recoupled with *Gagliarda* as ★6301 and ★DB-418

MENDELSSOHN

*Incidental Music to "A Midsummer Night's Dream": No. 1
Scherzo*
  Recorded March 9.
  ★74779, later recoupled with *Wedding March* as ★6302 and
  ★DB-191

WOLF-FERRARI

The Secret of Suzanne: Overture
  Recorded March 10.
  ★66081, later recoupled with *Le quai du port* as ★840 and
  ★DA-375 (10″)

BIZET

L'Arlésienne Suite No. 2: No. 4 Farandole
  Recorded March 11.
  ★64986, later recoupled with *Carmen* as ★839 and ★DA-374
  (10″)

MENDELSSOHN

Incidental Music to "A Midsummer Night's Dream": No. 10 Wedding March
Recorded March 11.
★74745, later recoupled with *Scherzo* as ★6302 and ★DB-191

DONIZETTI

Don Pasquale: Overture
The recording of part two, which was released, was made March 29, but a successful recording of part one was not made until March 30.
★66030/31, later recoupled as ★841 and ★DA-376 (10″)

BEETHOVEN

Symphony No. 1: Finale [Adagio, Allegro molto e vivace]
Recorded March 30.
★74690, later recoupled with *Rákóczy March* as ★6300 and ★DB-3417

BIZET

Carmen: Prelude to Act IV [Aragonaise]
Recorded March 31.
★64999, later recoupled with *L'Arlésienne* as ★839 and ★DA-374 (10″)

For acoustical recording of a symphony orchestra this series is really quite acceptable. The sound is, of course, greatly limited, distorted, and lacking in presence, but it has life and a great deal of vitality. There is no doubt that one is listening to a fine ensemble under a powerful musician. Given ample volume and the benefit of modern electronic filters to remove the surface noise, some really astonishing results can be obtained, not greatly inferior to those possible with early electrical disks.

The ten recording sessions listed here represent a prolonged effort on the part of Toscanini and his orchestra and undoubtedly had much to do with forming his long-standing dislike of making records. The acoustical process was not sensitive enough to capture *p* or *pp* with accuracy, so dynamics had to be adjusted artificially, and what comes off the record as a soft passage had, in fact, gone into the apparatus as a fairly loud one. This was difficult for Toscanini, who demanded perfection then as much as now, and there were many retakes.

Originally sixteen single-faced disks were released, but in the mid-'twenties Victor recoupled them as double-faced records.

The HMV editions were all in the double-faced form. All of these items were withdrawn after the introduction of electrical recordings; most of them have been out of print for close to thirty years.

It is unfortunate that we have no complete recording of a major symphonic work in this series, but the feeling at the time was that the public wanted short pieces, indeed an average symphony on ten, single-faced records would have been quite expensive, so the aria, the instrumental solo, and the four-minute orchestral work dominated the catalogs.

Seven of the fourteen items in the series are available in new recordings of high fidelity standards. The *Don Pasquale* is virtually the same in the two versions, although separated by thirty years. (Apparently Toscanini's performances of Italian music have changed less through the years than his performances of works by German composers.) The Mendelssohn *Scherzo* is essentially the same as the 1929 and 1946 versions. The Beethoven *Fifth* is similar to the 1939 set, broader and more inflected than the 1951 recording, although the *First* is closer to the 1951 performance than the 1937 one. The *Minuetto* of the Mozart is a little slow, although the *Finale* is obviously the way the Maestro wants it to go, very fast indeed, and is quite similar to the 1948 broadcast performance, which, incidentally, is the only time Toscanini played this work in the United States or Britain between 1925 and 1954.

A society reissue of some of these things would provide a basis for further and wider comparisons. As things now stand the series is known merely to those who collect old records.

ELECTRICAL RECORDINGS

Including all RCA Victor releases through April, 1956, and all HMV numbers through December, 1955.

1926

MENDELSSOHN

Incidental Music to "A Midsummer Night's Dream": No. 1 Scherzo, No. 7 Nocturne
The New York Philharmonic Orchestra

Recorded in Carnegie Hall, New York, probably toward the end of January or early in February.

Brunswick ★50074 [A second and somewhat more common form couples the *Scherzo* with the *Ride of the Valkyries* (under Mengelberg) as ★50161] European edition as Polydor ★595008

Toscanini was guest conductor of the Philharmonic for the first time during the 1925-26 season and this recording was made during those few weeks. The works appear in his programs for January 17 and February 1; presumably the recording was made close to one of those dates.

The Maestro has never liked this disk. The performance of the *Scherzo* seems slow and is inferior to other versions, such as that of 1929. A well-known critic, who heard the original at the time, says that this is the way Toscanini played the score in 1926 and that it sounded magical then, growing dull only in later years when the Toscanini performance had been carried to higher levels of incandescence.

This is the only record Toscanini ever made for a company other than Victor (or its affiliate HMV). It is an early example of the electrical method, and although superior to the acoustical series, is still quite ancient in sound. I would classify it as a collector's item of no great interest.

1929

Henceforth the manual sequence numbers of the RCA Victor and HMV electrical series are given for each disk.

Dukas

The Sorcerer's Apprentice
    Recorded March 18.
    ★7021 and D-1689

Verdi

La Traviata: Preludes to Acts I and III
    Recorded March 18 and 29.
    ★6994 and ★D-1672

Haydn

Symphony No. 101 [Clock]
    Recorded March 29 and 30.
    ★M-57 and ★D-1668/71

MENDELSSOHN

Incidental Music to "A Midsummer Night's Dream": No. 1 Scherzo
Recorded March 30.
★7080 (in ★M-57) and ★D-1671

MOZART

Symphony No. 35 [Haffner]
Recorded March 30 and April 4.
★M-65 and ★D-1782/84

GLUCK

Orfeo: Dance of the Spirits
Recorded November 21.
★7138 (in ★M-65) and ★D-1784

ROSSINI

Barber of Seville: Overture
Recorded November 21.
★7255 and D-1835

The Philharmonic-Symphony Orchestra of New York
Recorded in Carnegie Hall, New York.

Played on modern equipment which can eliminate surface noise with electronic filters, these old disks have a pleasant, if greatly limited, sound which reproduces the fundamental elements of a Toscanini performance. In every case there is a later recording of the same work. The Dukas is less intense, more enjoyable, and infinitely superior in sound in the 1950 version. (On this 1929 disk the Maestro might well have been rushing to finish within the limits of the 78 rpm surface.) The 1945 version of the Rossini is preferable to this, and the Verdi is best heard in the 1946 recording of the entire opera. This is a fine performance of the Mendelssohn, but nothing to touch the 1947 one. The Gluck is not satisfactory in the 1946 version, but the entire act is now available.

Two items resist classification as uninteresting, antique duplications. The Haydn and Mozart are both played with a relaxed lyricism and beauty that is not found in the more intense versions of 1947 and 1946. Here the delicacy and effortless singing of the clock episode in the opening of Haydn's slow movement is breathtaking, and everything seems exactly right as the line of sound moves with just enough inflection to give it force and a sense of continuing motion. The *Haffner* sings with equal freedom, and the lovely melodic line flows without urgency. Toscanini is not afraid to pause for natural expression (as in the opening bars) and is under no demoniac compulsion to drive the music any faster than seems appropriate to its content. (The *Finale* of the *Haffner* is hardly retarded!) Perhaps the fast movements of the Haydn are better done in the 1947 version, but certainly the slow movement does not get the magnificent statement it received here.

1936

WAGNER

Die Götterdämmerung: Dawn and *Siegfried's Rhine Journey*
[concert version by Toscanini]
★14007/08 (in ★M-308) and DB-2860/61

Lohengrin: Preludes to Acts I and III
★14006/07 (in ★M-308) and ★DB-2904 and DB-2861

Siegfried Idyll
★14009/10 (in ★M-308) and ★DB-2920/21

The Philharmonic-Symphony Orchestra of New York
Recorded February 8 and April 9 in Carnegie Hall.

All of these works are available in later versions. The 1951 recordings of the two *Lohengrin* preludes are technically of another era and preserve the identical performance given here, while the 1946 *Siegfried Idyll* gives one this 1936 performance, with its warmth and expressive lyricism, enhanced with more modern sound. We can say of these works, then, that adequate re-recordings are available.

The *Götterdämmerung* is a slightly different matter, since what is preserved here is a slower performance of the Dawn music than is heard on later records. To be exact, the Dawn music through the statement of the Valkyrie theme (just before the heavy brass passage based largely upon the "Siegfried as Hero" material) lasts 4:51 here, as opposed to 4:31 in the 1949 recording, the times for the two performances being: 1936: 11:10; 1949: 10:51 in all.

The use of timings in criticism is limited, but here we can see evidence for the argument I offered in Chapter II, that as Toscanini has grown older (a) he has speeded up the performances of almost all the works he has played frequently—indeed, in some cases one can give the actual performance in which the speed up first appeared, (b) he has almost stopped playing things slowly, regardless of how they are marked, and this has become his most conspicuous departure from the printed instructions of composers which, otherwise, he has followed scrupulously.

My feeling is that in 1936 he had the right tempi for the Dawn music, and that in later years he played the opening section of the work at too accelerated a pace, seriously diminishing its dramatic impact. The 1936 recording is thus the best statement of this great performance.

Technically this series is entirely adequate, even when played on high fidelity equipment of the most modern type. It has good solid bass and firm middle registers, so the sound has plenty of body, and the limitations on the highs of the strings and brass, although unfortunate, are not sufficient to distort the over-all effect.

BEETHOVEN

Symphony No. 7
The Philharmonic-Symphony Orchestra of New York
Recorded April 9 and 10 in Carnegie Hall.
★M-317 and ★DB-2986/90 and LCT-1013

This symphony is one of the core works in the Maestro's repertory, and without any question he gives it a reading that is breathtaking from beginning to end. The process of increasing tempi through the years has affected this work as well. The best statement of Toscanini's performance is this 1936 set *as originally issued,* that is, with the opening pages taken slowly and majestically. Unfortunately the master of the first side became worn, probably due to the process of making stampers, and a second master from the same recording session but with more rapid tempi was substituted with Toscanini's approval. It is in this form that the set was transferred to long play. I think the slower version was right, although undoubtedly the slightly faster one is tremendously effective as well.

Quite apart from this, in the 1936 performance Toscanini achieves a finer climax in the slow movement and better control of the movement of the lines of sound, particularly the tricky, sustained harmonies in the wind instruments during the final pages of the score. Toscanini at sixty-nine had a firmer hand on the performance than Toscanini at eighty-four, and although the 1951 version is fine, this is finer still.

The volume level of the recording was unusually high, and although the sound does not always have the most pleasant quality, it is good, and everything important can be heard without difficulty. The LCT transfer is not a success. The engineers tried to refine away some of the ruggedness that gives the set its formidable vitality, and the third movement in particular is washed out in consequence.

BRAHMS

Variations on a Theme of Haydn
  The Philharmonic-Symphony Orchestra of New York
  Recorded April 10 in Carnegie Hall.
  ★M-355 and ★DB-3031/32 and LCT-1023

These variations are another basic item in Toscanini's repertory, and his performance is excellent. In this case the 1952 version is virtually identical except for a couple of expressive changes of pace which I find appropriate. (Toscanini's Brahms is best when he is relaxed; he seems inclined to drive this music a little too hard.) Although this set preserves the beautiful sound of the Philharmonic after eleven seasons under the Maestro, it can be considered superseded by the new recording.

ROSSINI

The Italian Woman in Algiers: Overture
  ★14161 and DB-2943

Semiramide: Overture
  ★M-408 and DB-3079/80

  The Philharmonic-Symphony Orchestra of New York
  Recorded April 10 in Carnegie Hall.

Both of these recordings were smashers in their day, and they still sound remarkably good. In the case of the *Italian Woman* (which through a mistranslation on the label became *The Italians in Algiers* for a great many people) this is something to be grateful for since there has never been another Toscanini recording. *Semiramide* was originally not even scheduled for the April 10 session, but things went well that day (all in all, it was probably the greatest recording session of the century!), so it was played with white-hot heat while the fires were still raging from the Beethoven and the Brahms. The 1951 version is not so delicate or quite so hair-raising as this, but it is very good. In both overtures the beauty of the Philharmonic's sound and the manner in which, in complete sympathy to Toscanini's wishes, it can build up and sustain a rhythmic line are marvels to hear.

1937

BEETHOVEN

Symphony No. 6 [Pastoral]
    Recorded October 21 and 22.
    ★M-417 and DB-3333/37 and LCT-1042

Symphony No. 1
    Recorded October 25.
    ★M-507 and ★DB-3537/39 (single face) and LCT-1023

The British Broadcasting Corporation [B.B.C.] Symphony Orchestra
Recorded in Queen's Hall, London.

In 1935 and from 1937 to 1939 Toscanini appeared in London with the B.B.C. Symphony, which was increased to about ninety players for these concerts. The Maestro found it a sensitive and sympathetic ensemble. On these disks we hear performances that are clean, well balanced, and entirely suave and agreeable in sound; in other words, highly civilized and very British. These are nearly perfect examples of the best pre-war recording. The range is limited and the presence is not too good, but as shellac technique goes, the HMV Company here gave Toscanini much better recording than he received from Victor in the six years following.

The *Pastoral* has been a specialty of the Maestro, and for many years this was the definitive recording. The LCT version was made largely as a stop-gap measure until the 1952 edition could be put on the market, and since the later version is, if anything, a better performance and certainly is better recorded, this set can be put aside, although the transfer is satisfactory.

The *First* was recorded again in 1951, and the new performance is tighter, more classical, and faster paced. One may well prefer the broader treatment given the score here, and the recording and transfer to longplay reproduce it well.

BRAHMS

Tragic Overture
    The B.B.C. Symphony Orchestra
    Recorded October 25 in Queen's Hall, London.
    ★15383/85 (in ★M-507) and ★DB-3349/50 (inc. Beethoven No. 1, *Minuet*)

We have here another spectacular Toscanini recording that has died an undeserved death. The work was on his first concert program in 1896, so he had been playing it forty-one years when he made this recording, which reveals a practiced hand thoroughly familiar with the score. The work is full of stumbling-blocks, as Tovey points out so well, and Toscanini is equal to them. All the points at which lesser musicians go bad (to begin with an obvious one, the tympani roll in the opening bars, which must be quiet, as marked, and on no account *f* or *ff*) are navigated with the greatest skill, and the final climactic passage for the brass is a magnificent example of how Toscanini can get an entire section to play as if it were a single musician of exceptional skill.

The work tends to be pretentious (under some conductors quite intolerably so) but for me Toscanini refines this away. One can hope for a new recording, say from the 1953 broadcast performance, but lacking that the restoration of this one would be welcome. There is plenty of good sound on the shellac records for an acceptable transfer.

1938

BEETHOVEN

Quartet No. 16 (Op. 135): Lento and Vivace
★M-590 and ★DB-3904 and ★DB-3858 and LCT-1041

HAYDN

Symphony No. 88
★M-454 and ★DB-3515/7 and ★LCT-7

The National Broadcasting Company [N.B.C.] Symphony Orchestra
Recorded March 8 in Studio 8-H, Radio City, Rockefeller Center, New York.

On Christmas night, 1937, Toscanini returned to New York and at the age of seventy became conductor of the N.B.C. Symphony, a new orchestra that had been engaged and trained for him by Artur Rodzinski. Rodzinski's greatest ability, which exceeded his impressive accomplishments as a conductor, was as a builder of orchestras. The N.B.C. Symphony and the Cleveland Orchestra of the late 'thirties, the Philharmonic-Symphony of New York in the mid-'forties, and the Chicago Symphony Orchestra of 1947-48 (his last American appointment) provided unambiguous evidence of his skill in turning a hundred or more musicians into a well-integrated and fine-sounding ensemble, often within a matter of a few weeks.

The early recordings with the N.B.C. Symphony are classic examples of the dreadful things that can happen when an orchestra plays in an acoustically treated studio. The sound is completely dead and unnatural, and the introduction of artificial resonance in some transfers only makes this the more apparent. The highs and lows are greatly limited, the monitoring makes the range of volume shallow; and, with the high overtones of the instruments missing, one often hears only the grumbly, distorted sound of the fundamentals. This is especially true of the brass, which always has an unpleasant quality.

These works, being lightly scored, are somewhat more agreeable, although the Haydn is still not very pleasant in sound and, after being released in the LCT series, was withdrawn. It is a symphony of considerably lesser stature than those of the London period and has never been an important item in Toscanini's repertory. It is well played, but the orchestra does not have the beauty of sound revealed (say) in the 1953 recording of the *Surprise Symphony*. The Beethoven is beautifully played and preserves the feeling of a string quartet very well. It is unfortunate that this was never recorded again, and perhaps more unfortunate that Toscanini rarely ventured into the music of the late Beethoven quartets, although he regarded them as the greatest of the composer's works and was able to play them with a small string orchestra without destroying the texture, as commonly occurs when chamber music is played by larger groups than that for which it was intended. In the quartet the two movements come in the reverse of the order given here, and Toscanini has played them that way, but he feels that in concert it is better to close with the *Scherzo* and thus provide some resolution for the slow movement.

MOZART

Symphony No. 40
  The N.B.C. Symphony Orchestra
  Recording begun March 8, completed February 27, 1939, in Studio 8-H.
  ★M-631 and ★DB-3790/92

In spite of his reputation as a performer of Mozart, Toscanini has recorded only seven works of that composer, and only four of his Mozart recordings are satisfactory. This is one of the bad sets. The sound is poor (coarse, distorted, and generally disagreeable) and the performance is too intense. Toscanini wants vital, powerful Mozart, with blood in it, but often the more delicate parts of the works are scorched by such an impassioned approach. Happily, in this case we have a 1950 performance that is powerful without excess and beautifully recorded, and there is no point in giving further attention to this version.

The Magic Flute: Overture
   The B.B.C. Symphony Orchestra
   Recorded June 2 in Queen's Hall, London.
   ★15190 and DB-3550 and 49-0903

Having made three poor recordings in Studio 8-H, the Maestro took himself to an acoustically perfect hall (which was, unfortunately, to fall to Hitler's bombers within a short time) and made three fine recordings for the HMV Company. Of the group, this is the only one to have been transferred from shellac. In contrast to the set above, it is one of his finest Mozart recordings, and the nobility of the music is deeply felt.

ROSSINI

The Silken Ladder: Overture
   The B.B.C. Symphony Orchestra
   Recorded June 13 in Queen's Hall, London.

One of Toscanini's finest Rossini performances, with very pleasant recording and unusually good woodwind sound. An enjoyable disk which ought not to have been allowed to disappear from the American catalog. One would be well advised to obtain a copy.

WEBER (*Orch.* BERLIOZ)

Invitation to the Dance
   The B.B.C. Symphony Orchestra
   Recorded June 14 in Queen's Hall, London.
   ★15192 and DB-3542

Another fine recording, although in this case there is a 1951 version in which virtually the same performance is heard in the splendid sound of the new orthophonic technique. The music is highly enjoyable, and Toscanini plays it with exactly the right *élan.*

1939

BEETHOVEN

Symphony No. 5
  The N.B.C. Symphony Orchestra
  Recorded February 27, March 1 and 29 in Studio 8-H.
  ★M-640 and ★DB-3822/25 and LCT-1041

Technically this is rather dreadful, although the original performances must have been excellent. Old M-640, a notorious set
in its shellac form, has actually been improved in the process of
transfer to longplay, although much of the sound is still coarse
and wooden. Toscanini worked unusually hard to get this the
way he wanted it. An earlier attempt to do the symphony with
the Philharmonic had failed to produce anything he would approve, and his broadcast performance in October, 1938, earlier
in the same season, was quite different from the recording. The
LCT disk actually does not duplicate the shellac album, since
some of the transfer was made from second masters which had
not been used in the eight sides of the original issue. The fact
that three recording sessions are involved indicates there was
probably a great deal of alternative material.

This performance is fundamentally the same one heard on the
1920 records. The 1951 set is faster by over two minutes (one of
which reflects a quicker pace in the "slow" movement) and
represents the symphony as Toscanini has speeded it up in his
old age. If both approaches to the score could be heard with
the advantages of good recording it would be quite clear that the
slower tempi are the right ones. Among the things clearly heard
at this speed are the strings playing their parts with proper
accent and rhythm, rather than the somnambulistic yiddle-diddle-
diddle that slipshod conductors often allow to pass in place of
the surging voices that Beethoven demands. The broader singing
line of the 1939 recording is well suited to the music.

ROSSINI

William Tell: Overture
  The N.B.C. Symphony Orchestra
  Recorded March 1 and 29 in Studio 8-H.
  ★M-605 and DA-1695/96 and LM-14 (all are 10″)

An old clinker which can be given short shrift. The performance is wonderful, but the recording is cramped and wheezy

without being in any way venerable. The same marvelous statement of the score is available in the excellent 1953 version.

PAGANINI

Moto Perpetuo
   The N.B.C. Symphony Orchestra
   Recorded April 17 in Studio 8-H.
   ★15547 (in ★M-590) and ★DB-3858

An attractive piece of no particular weight, expertly played,
and given a mediocre recording typical of the period.

BEETHOVEN

Leonore Overture No. 1
   The B.B.C. Symphony Orchestra
   Recorded June 1 in Queen's Hall, London.
   ★15945 and ★DB-3846 and LCT-1041

Whether this is the first or last of the four overtures to *Fidelio*,
it certainly contains many passages of great force and beauty,
and were it not for the overpowering *Leonore No. 3* this piece
would certainly attract more attention than it usually receives.
Toscanini gives it a direct, striking performance with a firm,
singing line, and the recording reproduces this with adequate
fidelity by even contemporary standards.

Symphony No. 4
   The B.B.C. Symphony Orchestra
   Recorded June 1 in Queen's Hall, London.
   ★M-676 and ★DB-8733/36

The performance of the *Fourth* in this set is wonderfully relaxed, and the romantic and lyric qualities of the score are
realized in a much better manner than one finds in the overly
tense 1951 version. Apparently continuous recording was used;
the seventh side ends with a spectacular cliff-hanging effect. The
recorded sound is completely acceptable, which makes the lack
of an LCT transfer all the more saddening. This is the last set
Toscanini made in Britain, unfortunately.

Symphony No. 3 [Eroica]
   Recorded during a broadcast, October 28.
   ★M-765 and ★DB-6058/645
Leonore Overture No. 3
   Recorded during a broadcast, November 4.
   ★DB-5703/04

Egmont Overture
  Recorded during a broadcast, November 18.
    ★DB-5705
Leonore Overture No. 2
  Recorded during a broadcast, November 25.
    ★DA-1753/54 (10″)

  The N.B.C. Symphony Orchestra
  Recorded in Studio 8-H.

Victor drew this series from Toscanini's first Beethoven cycle with the N.B.C. Symphony. Technically it is butchery. Quite apart from the qualities of the studio, mentioned previously, and the introduction of a great many unpleasant audience noises (such as coughs between the opening chords of the *Eroica*), the sound has a rough and limited upper range, a coarse and poorly defined middle, and below that a grumbly and emaciated bass. It is the absolute low point of Victor's work with Toscanini, and one wonders how he could approve an *Eroica*, for example, in which the first note of the famous horn passage announcing the recapitulation (bar 394) is detached from the rest of the phrase in the infamous break between sides two and three, so that the effect of the E opposed to the B flat of the violins is totally destroyed. This type of technical failure, in which vital parts of the music are mangled or simply lost, is typical of the series.

  In spite of the poor sound and discontinuities of the recording, these are clearly performances of great power which ought to be preserved. *Aficionados* will, therefore, want to listen to these disks, bad as they are. There is a 1949 *Eroica*, a 1945 *Leonore No. 3*, and, best of all, a 1953 *Egmont*. It is to be hoped that the 1954 broadcast performance of the *Leonore No. 2* can be released, since even this poor one is unobtainable.

  It will be noted that only one of the four items in this series was ever released in the United States. All of them were approved by Toscanini for this purpose, and only the management of the Victor Company at the time knows why the disks were not put on the market.

Recordings with the N.B.C. Symphony Orchestra 1940-54

Since a large number of the recordings listed in this section are available on longplay and 45 rpm disks, a few special notes about these media, and high fidelity recording in general, might well be inserted at this point.

It is the best modern practice when cutting a disk to reduce the bass in volume below a predetermined point (500 cps for RCA Victor) and increase the treble to a predetermined level at 10,000 cps. This is done because bass, if highly amplified, makes a big, rolling cut which would require one to space the grooves quite widely apart, with a resultant loss of playing time, while the best way to eliminate the *sissss* noise of the surface is to make the higher frequencies much louder than the noise level, so that the music overpowers the surface, so to speak.

When a record is played back it must have the bass increased and the treble decreased by the identical amount of boost and cut introduced by the engineer who cut the disk. This restoration of the original levels is called "equalization," and it is of the greatest importance for the quality of the music that it be done accurately. I insist upon this because many record players, including some that belong to critics, appear to lack the degree of control needed to do this in every case, even if they profess to be of high fidelity standards. If one has not heard a recording played with proper equalization, he actually hasn't heard it at all. My notes refer to playbacks when equalization has been adjusted to the manufacturer's standards, and when I depart from that equalization or add other components to the playback circuit (such as an electronic filter) in order to secure pleasing sound, I indicate this.

Many of the Toscanini long-playing records have appeared in more than one edition, even though the number of the record has not been changed. The usual state of affairs is that the later editions are either new transfers of disks or tapes to longplay masters or are laboratory re-recordings of older disks or tapes in which major changes have been made to eliminate, as much as possible, flaws in the originals. Therefore, in those cases in which I know of several editions of a given disk, I shall review only the *latest* edition, which I shall indicate when necessary by its master number (which should be distinguished from the catalog number of the record, which appears on the label in large type). At the end of the master number is an "S number" (for example, E2RP-4373-1S). These indicate the place the master holds in a series of cuttings of the identical material, the first of which is designated 0S.

The RCA Victor Company has graciously supplied me with a set of the latest revised editions of its Toscanini longplay records which have appeared in alternate forms, and if my remarks seem a bit flattering to disks that the reader has and finds faulty, he might discover, by checking with a later edition, that earlier we were actually listening to two different things. Since the records I discuss are the ones actually on the market when this book appears, there seem to be no grounds for difficulties, but in doubt, check the "S number" against the one I give. If it's the same, *or higher*, the record ought to sound as described here.

I am, however, sometimes at a disadvantage, since I have not heard all the old editions in which some of these recordings have been issued. For example, I have only limited familiarity with the two limited editions which contained the Beethoven and Brahms symphonies. My impression is that, with the exception of the *Eroica* and the *Pastoral*, all the Beethoven symphonies were better in the later editions for general circulation than they were in the limited edition in which they were first offered at a premium price, while the Brahms symphonies were just about the same in both versions. My comments refer in all these cases to the editions for general circulation.

In April, 1956, Victor released as LM-*6901,* a new edition "pressed from the same masters as the limited edition" cited above, but selling for the same price as other records in the series. I have not had an opportunity to hear these records, but my inclination would be to recommend that one take the transfers available for general circulation in the past year. Before buying the reprint of the limited edition, the reader would be well advised to check the S-numbers against those given here.

1940

BEETHOVEN

Violin Concerto (Op. 61)
    Jascha Heifetz, violin
    Recorded March 11 in Studio 8-H.
    ★M-705 and ★DB-5724/285 and LCT-1010

Those who remember the cover of the Victor album may well think of this as the old diamond in the rough. Time has not made it any better. Since Heifetz is still active, one wonders why no attempt was made to do it over, rather than transfer the old records to long play. Again we hear the harsh, dry sound of the studio, and unless volume is boosted one loses *pp* and hears *ff* as wooden grunts. On the whole the recording is so dead and artificial that at times the thin line of violin sound reminds one of something from the golden age of Thomas Edison's tinfoil cylinder rather than 1940. Heifetz's performance is not my cup of tea, although there is some vitality and musical pleasure in Toscanini's fine handling of the orchestral part of the work.

BRAHMS

Piano Concerto No. 2
    Vladimir Horowitz, piano
    Recorded May 9 in Carnegie Hall.
    ★M-740 and ★DB-5861/66 and LCT-1025

Although some works of Brahms are clearly the product of a great composer's use of materials he can command with ease and utilize in the construction of large, solidly built compositions, others disclose faulty construction and the kind of pretension that invariably follows when one tries to make fairly ordinary things appear to be terribly significant and profound. Weingartner was aware of this, and in his book *The Symphony Since Beethoven* (Boston, 1904) went after Brahms quite soundly for his "mannerisms" and the fact that "entire sections of his works" are "built up."

I mention this because the *Second Piano Concerto* mixes fine pages with inferior ones, and the performer is therefore obliged, I feel, to present the work in a way which emphasizes its good points and does not underline the bad. Horowitz certainly does not play the ham actor, rather he appears to hold his feelings in check and content himself with making bright, percussive sounds, as if each note had been turned out of brass and chromium plated. Trills are rattled off with the brisk mechanical efficiency of a turbine. I confess this diminishes what pleasure there is for me in this work, which in the hands of an artist such as the late Artur Schnabel I could even come to enjoy. (Schnabel could even make me like parts of the *First Piano Concerto.*) Since the recording puts the piano in the foreground, whether or not this disk is likely to satisfy one depends, then, in large part, about his feelings on the subject of Mr. Horowitz. I find him unsympathetic.

In spite of a trip to Carnegie Hall, the recorded sound—especially that of the orchestra—is by modern standards lacking in definition and detail, and, of course, limited in range. Although in its day many persons found this a thrilling performance, well recorded by going standards, it now must be considered antique, and those who are interested in Toscanini's Brahms would do well to turn to his more recent recordings of that composer.

GLINKA

Kamarinskaya

Recorded during a broadcast, December 21, in Studio 8-H.
In LM-6026

The most interesting thing about this is the recording, which has been reprocessed from sixteen-year-old broadcast acetates and thus shows us what can be expected from this type of laboratory work. Judging by my ear alone (it is, however, a rather sensitive device), the frequency response is about 100-6,000 cps, which makes this recording superior in quality to a disk of the same year. What Victor has done is to up-date the sound to the "medium-fidelity" period of the late 'forties. The over-all effect is good: one simply lacks deep base, brilliant highs, and the definition and presence that a wider range provides.

The performance itself is splendid, satisfactory both in "Russian" feeling and delicacy. The rhythmic and lyric charm are undeniable, and the laboratory work has here gone toward a musically justifiable objective.

1941/48—V-DISKS BY TOSCANINI

The V-Disk project was carried on by the American armed forces from 1944-49. The records were twelve-inch 78 rpm disks pressed on vinylite for distribution in service installations in this country and abroad. The Toscanini series was taken from acetates of N.B.C. Symphony broadcasts. The recorded sound is generally equal or superior to his commercial recordings of the period. Because of union regulations, contractual obligations of the artists, etc., these records were never available commercially, and when the project ended the masters were destroyed. None the less, there are thirteen Toscanini items in the series that cannot be had in another form, though the remaining twenty-four Toscanini V-Disks duplicate other records. I offer the list so that collectors may take a morose interest in its contents. The date of the broadcast which supplied the source recording is given in each instance; also the numbers of the V-Disks.

Wagner: *Die Götterdämmerung: Orchestral Finale* [incorrectly labeled *Immolation Scene*], February 22, 1941–361

Rossini: *La Gazza Ladra: Overture*, April 12, 1941–461

Strauss: *On the Beautiful Blue Danube*, December 6, 1941–151

Smetana: *The Moldau*, December 13, 1941–121 [an exceptionally fast performance]

Brahms (*Orch.* Dvořák): *Hungarian Dance No. 1*, January 10, 1943–593

Grofé: *Grand Canyon Suite: On the Trail* and *Cloudburst*, February 7, 1943–561

Boccherini: *Quintet, Op. 13, No. 5: Minuet*, April 4, 1943–226

Hérold: *Zampa Overture*, April 4, 1943–95

Ponchielli: *La Gioconda: Dance of the Hours*, April 4, 1943–63

Sousa: *The Stars and Stripes Forever*, April 4, 1943–31

Rossini: *William Tell: Passo a sei* [incorrectly labeled *Dance of the Soldiers*], April 4, 1943–226

Tchaikovsky: *The Nutcracker Ballet: Suite No. 1*, April 25, 1943–261/62 also as 501/02

Verdi: *Don Carlos: O Don Fatale* [with Nan Merriman] and *Rigoletto: Quartet* [with Ribla, Merriman, Peerce and Valentino], July 25, 1943–75

Garibaldi's War Hymn, September 9, 1943–31

Bizet: *Carillon* from *L'Arlésienne Suite No. 1*, and *Carmen: Act IV, March of the Toreadors*, September 19, 1943–53

Glinka: *Jota Aragonesa*, November 7, 1943–593

Wagner: *Tristan und Isolde: Liebestod*, November 28, 1943–361

Prokofiev: *Symphony No. 1 (Classical)*, June 25, 1944–481 [a very rapid performance]

Beethoven: *Leonore Overture No. 1*, October 29, 1944–392

Sibelius: *The Swan of Tuonela*, January 13, 1945–333

Kabalevsky: *Colas Breugnon: Overture*, January 21, 1945–675

Debussy: *Prelude to the Afternoon of a Faun*, February 11, 1945–708

Rossini: *Il Signor Bruschino: Overture,* November 11, 1945—637

Vaughan Williams: *Fantasia for Double String Orchestra on a Theme of Thomas Tallis,* November 11, 1945—606/07

Elgar: *Enigma Variations: No. 7 "Troyte,"* November 18, 1945—606

Castelnuovo-Tedesco: *Overture to a Fairy Tale,* November 25, 1945—607

Mozart: *Symphony No. 40: First Movement,* January 27, 1946—638

Verdi: *La Forza del Destino: Overture,* January 27, 1946—638

Puccini: *La Bohème: O soave fanciulla* (Finale, Act I) [with Albanese and Peerce] and *Quando m'en vo* (Musetta's Waltz Song and Finale, Act II) [with Anne McKnight, other principals, chorus, etc.], February 3, 1946—654

Dukas: Excerpts from *Ariane et Barbe-Blue,* March 2, 1947—836/37 [Toscanini conducted the first American performance of this opera at the Metropolitan in 1911]

Gillis: *Symphony 5½,* September 21, 1947—826

Verdi: *Otello: Willow Song* and *Ave Maria* [with Herva Nelli], December 13, 1947—847

Martucci: *Noveletta,* March 13, 1948—848

1941

BEETHOVEN

Symphony No. 8
  Recorded February 24 in Carnegie Hall.
  ★M-908 and ★DB-6160/62

The best thing about this set when it was released was that it offered the first movement with the repeat marked by Beethoven and necessary for the form of the work to be properly revealed. Otherwise one could complain that the sound was inclined toward shrillness without bass or solidity in the middle registers and that Toscanini's performance was taut, hard driving, and often seemed to force the line into unnatural motion, although there were also moments of relaxation and great delicacy. Apparently recording was continuous with engineer-made breaks between the 78 rpm surfaces. There is now a 1952 version of this symphony that is better in every respect, and this can be forgotten.

WAGNER

Die Götterdämmerung: Immolation Scene
Helen Traubel, soprano
Recorded February 24 in Carnegie Hall.
★M-978 and LCT-1116

This is the first recording Toscanini made with the N.B.C. Symphony (after directing it during five seasons and recording with it for nearly three years) which deserves to be regarded as a classic. Its predecessors are (to treat them kindly) merely historical documents. This set, on the other hand, still yields musical satisfaction. Pale and tired as the sound appears to be, there is enough of it to make the final pages of the score powerful and impressive and convince us that in 1941 the N.B.C. Symphony was a great orchestra, fully capable of giving Toscanini anything he wanted.

During this period the musical director of Victor was Charles O'Connell, and there was tension between him and the Toscanini family much of the time. For one thing, O'Connell was himself a conductor, although apparently the Maestro could not take him seriously in this role. Something of a crisis followed Toscanini's rejection of this set on the grounds that trumpet passages were not well balanced with the voice. In his book, *The Other Side of the Record,* O'Connell says that it was Toscanini's own fault, but the Maestro stuck to his contractual rights, and the set could not be released. By this time the American Federation of Musicians' recording ban of 1942-44 was in force, and Victor went to James C. Petrillo, the chief of the union, who granted the dispensation necessary for Harry Glantz, first trumpet of the orchestra, to come before the microphone and record the passages again so that they could be dubbed into the original at the higher volume level Toscanini demanded. This re-recorded version was eventually released, and O'Connell claims that some of the freshness and impact of the sound was thus lost.

For all that, the performance is an exceptionally fine one and the sound adequate as a replica.

WAGNER

Lohengrin: Prelude to Act I
Recorded February 24 and May 6.
★11-8807

VERDI

La Traviata: Preludes to Acts I and III
    Recorded March 10.
    ★18080 and ★DB-5956

STRAUSS

Tritsch-Tratsch Polka
    Recorded May 6.
    ★11-9188 and 49-1082

Recorded in Carnegie Hall.

Two of these were duplications of popular recordings from the two series with the Philharmonic. They are lacking in bass and limited and thin on top, so there is nothing to recommend them over the newer versions: the 1946 set of the whole of *Traviata,* and the 1951 *Lohengrin.* The Strauss I suggest for the children and beer-busts.

BRAHMS

Symphony No. 1
    Recorded March 10 in Carnegie Hall.
    ★M-875 and ★DB-6124/28

Released to commemorate Toscanini's seventy-fifth birthday in 1942, this was a welcome set at the time, and I recall the pleasure I then secured from what seemed to be unusually good sound. The work is not one of my favorites, since it embodies the faults of the composer cited in connection with the *Second Piano Concerto,* but Toscanini's performance is a masterful one. Happily there is a 1951 version that duplicates and eliminates this set.

TCHAIKOVSKY

Piano Concerto No. 1
    Vladimir Horowitz, piano
    Recorded May 6 and 14 in Carnegie Hall.
    ★M-800 and ★DB-5988/91 and LCT-1012

In 1941 a song called "Tonight We Love" transformed the opening episode of this work into the adolescent's dream of tonal ecstasy; overnight everyone from hillbilly virtuosi on the washboard and harmonica to Toscanini and Horowitz was taking this old war horse for a ride. Nobody who lived through those days will ever want to hear this concerto again, but there is always a new generation, so it should be noted that the performance is a fine one, perhaps too intense but tremendously exciting, and that the recorded sound—coarse, clangy, and lacking in body—is ideal for juke boxes.

WAGNER

Die Götterdämmerung: Dawn and *Siegfried's Rhine Journey* and *Siegfried's Death and Funeral Music* [concert versions by Toscanini]
    Recorded May 14 and 17 in Carnegie Hall.
    ★M-853 and ★DB-5994/6

The second of the three recorded versions of the *Rhine Journey,* given here, is nearly a minute faster than the 1936 recording, which is better paced and has a solidity and weight which compensate for the slightly brighter, but thinner sound of this version. This set can be forgotten. The definitive performance of the first work is 1936; there are new versions of both, 1949 and 1952 respectively, with excellent recording.

1942

BARBER

Quartet (Op. 11): Adagio for Strings
    Recorded March 19 in Carnegie Hall.
    ★11-8287 and ★DB-6180

Toscanini gave the world première of this excellent score, which is the only really serious American work he ever recorded. The performance is a fine one, the sound adequate. Victor killed the disk off as soon as sales fell, although it remained in the HMV catalog as late as 1955. An LCT transfer is in order, I feel.

STRAUSS

On the Beautiful Blue Danube
    ★11-8580 and ★DB-6171

THOMAS

Mignon: Overture
    ★11-8545 and ★DB-6177

WAGNER

Tristan und Isolde: Liebestod
    ★11-8666 (in ★M-978) and 7ER5003

Recorded March 19 in Carnegie Hall.

The opening pages of the *Mignon* are of great beauty, but lovely as they are, this is not enough to compensate for the light weight of the music. In any case, the 1952 version is even finer. The Strauss and Wagner both document Toscanini's tendency toward fast, metronomic, inexpressive performances in 1941-42. The waltz is completely out of style, and ruined by the bloodless, mechanical execution of the figures. (Note especially the ludicrous effect produced by the rigid, expressionless playing of the passage that concludes the first side.) Some of the fine, clean attacks are admirable, but this is small compensation. The *Liebestod* was cut as a filler, and perhaps that accounts for the speed, since it had to come out as a single surface, but it, too, is ruthlessly inexpressive.

Some history is required at this point. During the summer of 1941 Toscanini had a falling out with N.B.C., and when he recorded in February, 1942, it was with the Philadelphia Orchestra. This Philadelphia series was the final showdown between Toscanini and O'Connell, who left Victor shortly afterward, and the Maestro eventually rejected the entire lot.

Victor thus took a heavy loss, since the orchestra and engineers had to be paid their fees exactly as if acceptable recordings had been made. Toscanini's time cost them nothing, but in return for his efforts he obtained no royalties and had thus exerted himself mightily for nothing. Meanwhile a union ban on recording loomed ahead, and with a pile of damaged Philadelphia masters confronting them, Victor persuaded Toscanini to make a few records with the N.B.C. Symphony, which he had consented to lead for War Bond Concerts. Seven twelve-inch sides were cut and approved from the March nineteenth session and these, with the sets listed above, constituted all the Toscanini material Victor had to release during the two years following, when, in the midst of war, tragedy, and crisis, music of adequate proportions was required.

With this Toscanini's commercial recording ended for thirty-one months, and the Great Petrillo Interdiction began.

1943

von Suppé

Poet and Peasant Overture
  Recorded during a broadcast July 18 in Studio 8-H.
  In LM-6026

Eventually, I suppose, there *had* to be a Toscanini *Poet and Peasant* to document the one Toscanini performance (at least of his American career), but of all the things lost in the period of the A.F.M. ban, why was this work the first to be resurrected, presumably with A.F.M. approval? It is rather like a ship going down and only the most depraved and unrepentant member of the engine-room gang escaping with his life; it causes one to doubt the existence of a moral order. The work is a stock item of village band concerts, secondary school orchestras, the most unimaginative "Pop" nights, and, for all I know, ensembles of dervishes or Tibetan lamas. There is some point in having this Toscanini recording, since the performance is undeniably a fine one, although it is certainly not a disk that I shall play very often. The recorded sound is limited but pleasant and quite adequate to convey the contents of the score.

1944

BEETHOVEN

Piano Concerto No. 3
    Artur Rubinstein, pianist
    Recorded during a broadcast October 29 in Studio 8-H.
    ★M-1016 and ★DB-9483/86 and LCT-1009

Technically this is among the poorest of the conductor's recordings; its faults include serious instability in pitch. The performance is ruined for me by the conflict in style between Rubinstein's romanticism and Toscanini's reserved, classical approach. None the less, Toscanini suggested this collaboration and showed unusual interest in having a recording made. The sound is thin, distorted and unpleasant. Many details of the orchestra part are obscured or lost entirely.

Fidelio
    Principals: Rose Bampton, soprano, Eleanor Steber, soprano, Jan Peerce, tenor, Nicola Moscona, bass, Herbert Janssen, bass, with chorus under Peter Wilhousky
    Recorded during broadcasts December 10 and 17 in Studio 8-H and incorporating a recording of *Abscheulicher!* (recitative) and *Komm, O Hoffnung* (aria) made December 19, in Carnegie Hall and the *Leonore Overture No. 3* made June 1, 1945, in Studio 8-H.
    LM-6025. The recitative and aria were released as ★11-9110;

for the other versions of the *Leonore No. 3* recording, see its separate listing.

Released in the United States exactly ten years after it was made, this recording must be regarded as a *tour de force,* a musical souvenir of a great performance which represented Toscanini's first presentation of opera in New York since 1915 and, for all but a few of his audience, served as the first experience of his art as an operatic conductor. For all that, although not comparable to a modern tape, the sound is not at all bad, and despite limitations, is agreeable. Therefore, since one must accept this set on the basis that an imperfect transcription is better than none, the imperfections are not such as to destroy the musical pleasure which the splendid playing of the orchestral parts and the excellent to routine singing of the cast provides. It has the usual faults of recordings made under concert conditions, but it also has the dramatic impact of Toscanini working with an audience, and the music is of self-evident greatness. The insertions are both well advised. Bampton's singing of the recitative and aria was much better controlled on the nineteenth than it had been on the tenth, and the 1945 disks of the overture were superior to the concert acetates.

The Creatures of Promethus: Overture
Recorded December 18 in Studio 8-H.
★11-9459 (in ★M-1098), also ★11-9006 (in ★SP-2) and ★DB-6425. LCT-1041 may have been taken from a "second master" cut in the same session. My remarks apply to it.

Opus 43 is one of the early masterpieces of the composer and is filled with the sort of things that Toscanini does superlatively well. For example, the way in which the opening chords establish a feeling of tension and a sense of continuity and rhythm, so that in the course of six chords and a fanfare the tempo has been established. We do not lose that sense of tempo in the quiet introduction that follows, and we have the feeling that we are still in time during the fast section, where the Maestro's sweeping motor energy carries us along with authority and strength. Beethoven used a similar introduction in his *Consecration of the House Overture,* which Toscanini recorded two years later.
As if to show us that a new day had arrived, Victor here made a very decent recording in Studio 8-H, proving to all doubters that it *was* possible (just as it was equally possible to make poor records in Carnegie Hall).

1945

GERSHWIN

An American in Paris
    Recorded May 18 in Studio 8-H.
    LM-9020 and ALP-1107

At the time it was made, this was technically the finest Toscanini recording in existence, and I nominate the engineer in charge
for the Star and Sash of the Grand Prix de Nipper, First Class.
The fact that this was done in Studio 8-H only adds to his glory:
a victory on a field where many battles had been lost. The sound
is spacious and well balanced—a faithful replica of the playing
of a great orchestra. I have been told that the new technique
used for some of the later (and better) 8-H recordings was to
take the orchestra off the stage and put it on the floor, thus
making use of the full resonance of what was, in fact, a fairly
ample concert room.

The performance has the fine plastic qualities one expects from
the Maestro; its only questionable aspect is that of style. This is
Gershwin's finest work for symphony orchestra and a first-class
piece of picture music. In its idiom it employs devices of both
French and American popular music, and the question is whether
symphonic jazz should be played as jazz or symphonic music.
Specifically, should the blues sections in this work be given the
traditional expressive inflections of blues style or not? Toscanini's
performance implies not, for either he has no feeling for the blues
style (I wonder, in fact, if he has any feeling for American popular music) or he rejects it. This performance gives a "straight"
reading of the French episodes, the blues section, the Charleston
theme and the rest. Those who want to hear the work on purely
musical terms will probably enjoy the freshness of Toscanini's
approach. But is that what Gershwin intended?

In spite of the date, this recording never appeared on shellac.
One had to wait until the 'fifties to find what could be done in
1945.

SOUSA

The Stars and Stripes Forever
    Recorded May 18 in Studio 8-H.
    ★11-9188 and 49-1082

The 1943 performance on V-Disk—31 was more relaxed, somewhat broader and more spontaneously expressive, particularly

in the final section. The recording ban prevented a commercial disk being made at that time; when this one was cut, a little more than two years later, Toscanini's performance had tightended up, with metronomic rigidity substituted for spontaneity in feeling. Even so, it is an exceptional reading of a score that is rarely given such careful attention to balance and detail. In the loud passages the sound is somewhat cramped; otherwise it is quite acceptable.

HAYDN

Symphony No. 98
    Recorded May 25 in Studio 8-H.
    ★M-1025

Why this recording was never issued in Britain and allowed to perish when the 78 rpm set was dropped, I do not know. The work is an exceptionally fine example of the composer's best, late writing for orchestra, and the test copies of the 78 disks that I heard on a Victor home-type machine in their New York studio gave me bright, agreeable sound, well placed in resonant space, and flawed only by a slightly cramped feeling in the climactic passages, which could no doubt be improved with a little laboratory work.

The majestic opening of the symphony is powerfully stated, and the slow movement, with its theme that suggests "God Save the King," is played with a growing intensity that other conductors rarely give Haydn. The minuet is a good *allegro*, unlike the excessively fast "real" *allegro* which Toscanini introduced into his later performances of Haydn (such as the 1953 version of the *Symphony No. 94*), and the finale goes with the greatest gusto. An amusing note is provided by a few stray tuning-up noises at the start of the surface with the minuet.

Coupled with the Mozart *Divertimento K. 287* of 1947, this would be a distinguished and welcome item in the catalog.

WEBER

Der Freischütz: Overture
    Recorded May 25.
    ★11-9172 and ★DB-6331 and 49-1228

BEETHOVEN

Coriolan Overture
    Recorded June 1.
    ★11-9023 and ★DB-6423 and ERA-91

MENDELSSOHN

Octet (Op. 20): Scherzo
  Recorded June 1.
  ★11-8966 (in ★M-1025) and ★DB-21105

  Recorded in Studio 8-H.

The 1952 version of the Weber is identical or possibly superior in performance to this and technically superb, so the sick and obscured horn tones at the opening of this disk are painful to hear in contrast. The *Scherzo* is all quicksilver and froth, and superior to that in the 1947 recording of the entire work recently issued. As for the *Coriolan*, the sound is not distinguished and the Maestro's intensity is a disadvantage, since there is insufficient contrast between the two main themes—both are agitated. The 1953 broadcast performance was the finest reading of this score I have ever heard, and it is to be hoped that it will appear on a record in time.

BEETHOVEN

Leonore Overture No. 3
  Recorded June 1 in Studio 8-H.
  ★M-1098 and ★DB-6424/25 and LM-1043 and LRM-7023 and in LM-6025 *(Fidelio)*

Just how many editions of this recording have been issued I can't even guess, but the three available at the moment reflect the confusion that multiplicity of this sort can introduce. No two editions have the identical sound one would expect from (supposedly) alternate copies of the same recording.

Best of the copies I have heard is the LRM version with the master number E3RL-4735-1S. It has a firmness and power that the others don't match, and it eliminates all the faults except a few bad horn notes that defy electronic correction. In this form I can recommend the disk as conveying the force of a great performance, limited only slightly in range, and, if a little dry, still robust enough for its purposes.

Few disks would be more appropriate for showing what can be done with fancy cutting. The LRM is a ten-inch surface, the LM a twelve-inch, and in LM-6025 the overture occupies *half* a twelve-inch side! My second place goes to the LM edition (15S), which has a bit more treble boost than I like, and the transfer for the *Fidelio* had to be reduced in volume to permit variable cut techniques. Of the older editions on 78 and longplay, some of which were pretty wooden and drab, I'll say nothing, since RCA has made up for its earlier failures with superlative laboratory work. Since a new recording is unlikely and the 1939 version is agreeable only in the soft passages, this will have to stand as the documentation of one of the basic works in Toscanini's repertory. Happily, it is equal to that role.

ROSSINI

The Barber of Seville: Overture
La Cenerentola: Overture
La Gazza Ladra: Overture
Il Signor Bruschino: Overture
William Tell: Passo a sei

Recorded June 8 and 28 in Carnegie Hall.
★M-1037 and *(Barber)* ★DB-6344, *(Cenerentola)* ★DB-6368, *(Gazza)* DB-6342 *(Bruschino* and *Passo)* ★DB-6345. The four overtures are now LM-1044 and ALP-1007; the *Passo* is on LRM-7005, *Bruschino* on 7ER5017

Of all the lighter music Toscanini has played, his unique performances of Rossini have been the most enjoyable, and although these overtures deal with matters of less weight than the symphonies of Beethoven, there is no ground for being patronizing about them. These versions are not likely to be matched by new performances within the next decade or so. The recorded sound is good, agreeably bright on top and full below, and well balanced except for a tendency for the strings to dominate the loud passages.

MOZART

Symphony No. 41 [Jupiter]
Recorded June 22 and March 11, 1946, in Carnegie Hall.
★M-1080 and LM-1030

Although Toscanini worked on this in two recording sessions, it is not a success and reveals what dismal results could be produced even in a Carnegie Hall recording. In my improved transfer the quality still is distorted and unpleasant, especially in passages for full orchestra, and with weak bass, coarse highs, and related evils, some passages of the final movement become a hopeless scramble of poorly defined sounds. Dubbed on to tape and reproduced at the proper pitch, but twenty-five per cent slower in tempo, by use of A. M. Springer's ingenious playback machine, the final movement shows up the frantic, insensitive quality of the performance. The men are obviously hard pressed just to get in all their notes, let alone shape their phrases with polish or beauty, and at the reduced tempo the faults in the ensemble are easily spotted. However, a twenty-five per cent reduction just about gives one the proper tempo for the fugue, which is far too tight, far too intense, and far too fast as played here. It loses power as a result, just as the rushed and graceless slow movement loses both dignity and beauty. The style simply is not appropriate to Mozart. This is a set to forget.

VERDI

La Forza del Destino: Overture
    ★11-9010 and ★DB-6314 and 49-1175

WALDTEUFEL

The Skaters Waltz [Les Patineurs]
    ★11-8949 and DB-21352 and LM-14 and LRY-9000 and
    7ER5017

Recorded June 28 in Carnegie Hall.

It is instructive to regard the fate of these disks. The Verdi is now just an uninteresting old recording, replaced by the 1952 version which offers the identical performance with better sound. The Waldteufel can be heard in the original LM transfer with the limitations of 1945 recording, or in a very spectacular "updated" transfer on the LRY disk which one would imagine to be a recent tape. In either case one hears a pleasant, old-fashioned waltz turned into a stunning concert piece by the apparently simple device of giving it an incisive performance, in contrast to the slack and rhythmically inexact run-throughs one is accustomed to hearing on Pop nights. The simplicity and beauty of the opening pages, especially as reproduced in the LRY edition, are quite striking.

BEETHOVEN

Piano Concerto No. 1
    Ania Dorfmann, piano
    Recorded August 9 in Carnegie Hall.
    ★M-1036 and ★DB-6460/63 and LM-1039
    In the opening bars the orchestra creates a lively, flowing musical line made expressive by changes in coloring and accent; into this framework the piano enters, blandly moving along with-

out the qualities of color, accent and continuity which Toscanini is exhibiting and which one would expect a perceptive soloist to duplicate. What is exciting about this performance, then, is the manner in which the orchestral part is played. But if one rightfully expects a concerto to reveal a unity of feeling on the part of soloist and conductor, this will not do. Miss Dorfmann has to scramble in the final movement, since the relentlessly pursuing Maestro hardly gives her time to get in all her notes. (This is a typical feature of a Toscanini "accompaniment" and one reason why so few artists would play with him.) He is clearly too much for her, although she is stylistically closer to him than was Rubinstein.

The recording is of middling fidelity, pleasant, and unexceptional.

BERLIOZ

The Damnation of Faust: Scene 3, Rákóczy March
Recorded during a broadcast September 2 in Studio 8-H.
LM-6026

There is no point in thinking that this is anywhere nearly as effective as a 1955 recording would have been. Ten years are too long a time to erase in a laboratory. For all that, I recommend this as a polished and expertly prepared version of a work that is all too frequently given a heavy, slipshod performance. In spite of the coarse and limited quality of some of the sound, the musical values are of the highest level.

GROFÉ

The Grand Canyon Suite
Recorded September 11 in Carnegie Hall.
★M-1038 and ★DB-6327/30 and LM-1004 and ALP-1232 and
On the Trail only 7ER5012

Although this is the *Grand Canyon Suite* it is the Comstock Lode recording. Fortunately, although not entirely immune to commercial temptation, Toscanini's morals were usually equal to the seductive lures of really gawdawful popular works. Had he and RCA Victor been interested in giving us a first-rate example of contemporary American music in a distinguished performance, this would not have been chosen. That such were not their motives can be seen in the short, happy life of the one such item that was recorded, Barber's *Adagio for Strings*. The *Grand Canyon Suite* was, in fact, available on 78 rpm as late as 1953 and proudly holds its place with the "101 All Time Best Sellers on RCA Victor Records." I am happy to say that the Toscanini Beethoven *Ninth* is on the same list; he did not have to play trash to make money.

Toscanini first prepared this work in 1943 during the recording ban—parts of that performance are on a V-Disk—and repeated it in 1945. The set was made after his second, and presumably last, public performance of the score. It receives a dazzling reading that it certainly never deserved and is not likely to receive again, and the recording preserves that experience for anyone who can't think of anything else he would rather hear.

1946

PUCCINI

La Bohème
> Principals: Licia Albanese, soprano, Ann McKnight, soprano, Jan Peerce, tenor, Francesco Valentino, baritone, with chorus under Peter Wilhousky
> Recorded during broadcasts February 3 and 10 in Studio 8-H. LM-6006 and ALP-1081/82

Seldom have the musical and dramatic qualities of this work been realized as well as they were in these broadcasts, and the integration of the fine singing and splendid orchestral playing makes this as enjoyable a performance of the score as one is likely to hear. However simple and direct its appeal to the ears and the tear ducts, *Bohème* is at its best in its gayest and least pretentious moments. As soon as Puccini attempts to be tragic or enlarge the scale of the drama, the weakness of his musical powers is betrayed, a fact that Toscanini has himself noted on occasion.*

The recordings from the broadcast line are good and have been well processed. The effect of *Che gelida manina* as a duet between Peerce and the Maestro is quite beyond description.

WAGNER

A Faust Overture
> ★11-9642/43 (in ★M-1135) and ★DB-6545/46 and LRM-7023
Die Meistersinger: Prelude
> ★11-9385 and 49-0297 [Pressed by HMV as ED-662 but apparently distributed only in Australia]

*For example, in Howard Taubman's account of a conversation, *The Maestro,* p. 288.

Siegfried Idyll
   ★11-9640/41 (in ★M-1135) and ★DB-6668/69 and LCT-1116
Die Walküre: Prelude to Act III [The Ride of Valkyries]
   ★11-9643 (in ★M-1135) and ★DB-6546 and ★WDM-1564 and
   7ER5003

Recorded March 11 in Carnegie Hall.

Three of these works appeared in the United States as an album set.

The *Faust Overture* is early Wagner and one of his few works which was written for the concert hall rather than the theatre. It was to have been part of a Faust symphony, a project which also appealed to Liszt, who managed to carry it to completion. Wagner never got any farther than this, but in comparing his version of the solitary Faust to Liszt's, Wagner's superior taste and musicianship become apparent. The performance is splendid and the recording satisfactory.

The *Meistersinger Prelude,* the *Eroica,* and *La Mer* are the three most frequently performed works of Toscanini's American career as a symphonic conductor. Of the two versions of the *Meistersinger,* both are superb, but I prefer the earlier and slower of the pair, given here, and apparently his "boys" in the orchestra feel the same way, since the version they recorded in 1954, without a conductor, is closer to this than the 1951 performance. This conductorless record was privately distributed in the United States to those who contributed to the orchestra's endowment fund. It was not issued by RCA Victor or commercially available.

There are three versions of the *Siegfried Idyll.* Between that of 1936 and this successor of a decade later the choice is primarily based upon sound. The performance here is warm, beautifully paced, and deeply felt, and the recording, although lacking the lustre of the upper string tones, is thoroughly acceptable. Since the 1950 version offers brighter sound at the cost of substituting an over-refined, cool, and slick reading of the score, this is the recording to take as the best statement of this distinguished performance.

Those who enjoy the dreadful concert setting of the Valkyries in flight can look forward to the superlative fidelity of the 1952 recording. This one was not a complete success and can be put down as obsolete and withdrawn.

BERLIOZ

Romeo and Juliet, Dramatic Symphony: Part II, Romeo Alone and *Great Festivities at the House of Capulet; Love Scene*
 Recorded April 8 in Carnegie Hall.
 ★M-1160 and ★DB-6665/67 and LM-1019

Toscanini prepared this work *in toto* with the Philharmonic in 1942 and with the N.B.C. in 1947. The 1942 performances were not recorded or broadcast because by that time the Philharmonic had become the exclusive property of the Columbia Broadcasting System and Columbia Records, but there are acetates of the 1947 performance, and if Toscanini loves us at all he will allow it to be released in the same manner as the operas.

Meanwhile, all we have of this brilliant and wonderful score are the two excerpts here and a 1951 broadcast recording of the *Queen Mab Scherzo*. Happily these give us three of the finest sections and a fair sample of one of the great triumphs of orchestral playing in our time, although I cannot hear them without recalling that the *Love Scene* opens with a delicious little choral nocturne which is omitted here, and that there are many other fine things in the missing portions of the work. Why Toscanini did not prepare and record this score in a later season is a mystery. If we have lost it, we have lost a great deal.

TCHAIKOVSKY

Romeo and Juliet: Overture-Fantasia
 Recorded April 8 in Carnegie Hall.
 ★M-1178 and LM-1019

Two composers' treatment of the same theme must have made for an interesting recording session. This is not a traditional Tchaikovsky performance, for Toscanini eschews the excesses and distortions often heard in this composer's music. This is surely the most powerful reading of the *Romeo and Juliet Overture* that I have ever heard, and yet the lyric passages sing freely. For me, one of the most interesting things about this disk is the fine statement of the little quasi-fugato episode that comes just after the exposition of the love music and builds up to the climax on the "conflict" theme. This interplay of brass and strings has continuity and meaning in Toscanini's hands that no other conductor gives it—at least none that I am aware of—and before hearing what he did with it I often thought that the section should be cut.

The recording needs proper equalization, but when the knobs have been set correctly (don't over-emphasize the top) it yields very good sound.

BACH

Suite No. 3: Air [Air on the G String]
  ★11-9344 (in ★M-1080) and 49-3301

KABALEVSKY

Colas Breugnon: Overture
  ★11-9978 (in ★M-1178) and 49-3156

Recorded April 8 in Carnegie Hall.

These were two fillers. The only Toscanini recording of anything by Bach has admirable clarity but is taken too fast. The Kabalevsky is an ugly piece of synthetic music in which clichés of romanticism are distorted to produce "modern" effects. Toscanini has feeling for the rhythmic vitality of the work and shapes it accordingly. The recording of both pieces is satisfactory.

GLUCK

Orfeo: Dance of the Spirits
  ★11-9903 (in ★M-1172) and ★DB-6993 or ★DB-21046 and 49-3301

MOZART

Symphony No. 35 [Haffner]
  ★M-1172 and LM-1038

Recorded November 4 in Studio 3-A, Radio City, New York.

A re-recording of a set (M-65) made with the Philharmonic seventeen years before. The 1929 performance is more relaxed, and the intensity of this one, though not excessive, may be more than some feel is appropriate. (I prefer the older version myself.) The studio sound has been reinforced by a number of echo chambers, and the artificial resonance is very pronounced and, for me, unpleasant. The Gluck lacks clean definition, the sound of the solo flute being particularly undistinguished. The Mozart is hard and cold, with the sound never quite in focus, as if one were hearing a concert played in a subway tube. The Gluck is newly available in the beautiful 1952 recording of the whole of Act II.

MENDELSSOHN

Incidental Music to "A Midsummer Night's Dream": No 1 Scherzo
  Recorded November 6 in Studio 3-A, Radio City, New York.
  ★11-9860 (in ★M-1167) and ★12-1130 (in ★M-1368) and
  ★DB-21105 or ★DB-21046 and 49-3156

The fourth of the five Toscanini versions of this celebrated *Scherzo* is of interest primarily for the contrast it provides with the brilliant 1947 version to follow. Essentially it is the 1921 and 1929 performance, and while the 1947 recording is lightness itself, swiftly flowing, yet wonderfully delicate and expressive, this one is, in contrast, much slower and rather heavily inflected, although when played by itself it seems more magical. The sound of the disk is not particularly clean or brilliant, but acceptable.

BEETHOVEN

Overture for the Consecration of the House
  Recorded November 11 in Carnegie Hall.
  ★M-1287 and ★LM-6 and LM-9022

One of Beethoven's finest works, this deserves to be played much more frequently. One reason for its neglect is a degree of uncertainty about the proper style for the piece. The traditional German approach is shown in the fine old Weingartner recording, based upon the premise that even though the writing is not "Beethoven style" it must be given a properly solid, four-square performance. Toscanini appears to recognize that the acknowledged influence on the work is Handel (who is not too dull and solid an individual, once we rescue him from the nineteenth century school of oratorio conductors) and that "Rossini fever" had reached epidemic proportions in Vienna at the time Beethoven was putting this work on paper. The Maestro's performance is not in the German tradition at all, and both Handel and Rossini have their say without having to don false, solemn faces. Although, in general, I don't always find Toscanini's fast tempi in fugues congenial, in this instance, I am convinced and find his reading stunning—although there are also beauties in a slower and more rhetorical approach to some of these passages.

As originally issued the recording was monitored too much. I am pleased to say that a new transfer in the twelve-inch series removes this fault—to the extent that it can be removed—and gives us much improved quality and a wide dynamic range. Recommended.

VERDI

La Traviata
> Principals: Licia Albanese, soprano, Jan Peerce, tenor, Robert Merrill, baritone, with chorus under Peter Wilhousky
> Recorded during broadcasts December 1 and 8 in Studio 8-H.
> LM-6003 and ★DB-9683/95 and ALP-1072/73

Toscanini's *Traviata* is to be taken on a basis similar to his *Fidelio*, that an imperfect recording of a great performance is better than none at all. It *is* a great performance, even though Toscanini is too tense during the portion that represents the first broadcast (fearful, perhaps, that he would not finish on time). No one could possibly do *Traviata* at this pace in an opera house with stage action taking place, but listening to a record is not going to the opera, and the fault is not too serious.

In a recent copy of this set in which the master numbers of the four sides terminate in 17S, 17S, 12S, and 18S respectively, some coughs have been expertly removed (when possible)—although Toscanini is as noisy as ever—and the sound is very much better than in early editions, bright and clear, seriously flawed only by being rather hard and cold on top and short of overtones. The singing still is not always of the best, and Merrill is quite unpleasant in quality at times when his own shortcomings are increased by those of the recording.

Great performances of opera being as scarce as they are, the thing to do with this set is forget the defects and listen to the beautiful things which are preserved here. I find that it repays such consideration, since its merits outweigh its flaws.

1947

SCHUBERT

Symphony No. 9 [sometimes called *No. 7*]
> Recorded February 25 in Carnegie Hall.
> ★M-1167 and LM-1040 and ALP-1120

Although this is one of the great Toscanini performances, adequately recorded, the 1953 version is superior on all counts, thus making the above disk obsolete. It will probably be withdrawn shortly.

MENDELSSOHN

Octet for Strings (Op. 20)
Recorded during a broadcast March 30 in Studio 8-H.
LM-1869

Although this set was released only recently, there have been two editions to date, 2S, which I presume to be the original, and a recutting designated by 3S after the master number. The difference is considerable. The 2S version is coarse, disturbingly limited on top and dry below, and not very nice to hear. In the 3S edition the sounds are more pleasant, although the frequencies present are no more extended than in the previous issue. On the whole, the fidelity is adequate, and although the expectation of further recordings of this quality from broadcast sources is not likely to excite some people, I shall welcome them for what they are.

It is hard to tell just how big an orchestra Toscanini used for this. It is studio sound, cramped and artificially condensed at its best, but I would gather that the eight players Mendelssohn called for have been roughly tripled. In some places this is good, in others this factor—plus the recording—makes for heavy textures lacking the effect of chamber music. The 1945 version of the *Scherzo* alone was, I think, a lighter and more polished performance. It is the most enjoyable movement, the work as a whole being a pleasant but rather small-scaled example of youthful romanticism.

HAYDN

Symphony No. 101 [Clock]
Recorded June 12 in Studio 3-A, Radio City, New York.
★M-1368 and LM-1038

Like the Mozart *Haffner*, this constituted a re-recording of a 1929 set, complete to the original filler. After playing the old records (Victor M-57) one may debate whether the spacious, relaxed quality of the 1929 performance is more or less effective than the faster and more intense reading of 1947. I am inclined to prefer the slow movement in the 1929 version and the fast movements as they are given here.

The recording is better than the *Haffner*, though still cold, hard, and shrill on top. A filter takes the shrillness out, fortunately, but leaves sound that lacks bass and warmth and is artificially resonant.

MENDELSSOHN

Incidental Music to "A Midsummer Night's Dream" "Complete"
Overture, No. 5 Intermezzo, No. 7 Nocturne, No. 1 Scherzo,
No. 10 Wedding March, No. 12 Finale [with Edna Phillips,
soprano, and female chorus]
Recorded November 4 in Carnegie Hall.
★M-1280 and LM-1221

During his American career, Toscanini played the *Nocturne*
and *Scherzo* from this set of pieces in twenty-four cities, making
it his perennial choice for touring. Indeed, so magical a performance could hardly fail to please any audience that was even
slightly fond of music, regardless of sophistication—or the lack
of it. He has never prepared the entire work, but in the literal
sense it almost never *is* prepared, except when the music is
actually used in connection with a production of the play, and
the "complete" score indicated here comprises all of the numbers
which are appropriate to the concert room and enjoyable as pure
music.

It is fortunate that when Toscanini remade this set—an earlier
version was among the items of the Philadelphia series—he was
given the benefit of good recording and was prepared to relax
and sing. What one hears, then, is incandescent tonal brilliance,
and playing in which the beauty, the delicacy of inflection, and
the plastic distinction of the moving line cause one to gasp as
wonder follows wonder. The volume level is low; with adequate
gain the recorded sound is excellent. Now that *La Mer* has been
issued in a new edition, this should be recoupled with *Don Juan*,
thus eliminating two duplicates and retaining the sales appeal
of two fine Toscanini performances.

MOZART

Divertimento for Strings and Two Horns (K. 287)
Recorded November 18 in Studio 8-H.
★DM-1355 and ★DB-9563/66 and ★LM-13

Both Toscanini and Koussevitzky were particularly fond of this
work. Toscanini's grasp of its form gave him the means to overcome what B. H. Haggin has identified as "the difficulty of
knowing what to do between the mere *p* here and the *f* eight
bars later." For Koussevitzky, as Haggin has pointed out, the
thing to do with this or any doubtful situation was to submerge
the music in a flowing gorgeousness of sound that dazzled the

ear, hoping thereby to conceal the essential lack of intensity in the music. That the sound was gorgeous, no one will deny, but if one asked for more than this Koussevitzky was often unable to provide it.

In his book, *The Maestro,* Howard Taubman tells us that Toscanini made this recording for other conductors as a demonstration of how Mozart should be played. Among other things it demonstrated that in the slow movement Mozart had clearly indicated a cadenza for the first violin by writing a six-four chord, a rest, and a trill leading back into the melodic line. Haggin reports that when Toscanini heard the Koussevitzky performance, in which the chord, the rest, and the trill were played through exactly as marked, he exclaimed, "This man is no musician. He is *ignorante!*"

What we have here is a simple, clear line of sound, moving at a speed appropriate to its melodic flow and expanding to *f* and *ff* and contracting to *p* and *pp* without changing the tempo of that flow or its plastic continuity. Whatever reservations one may have about Toscanini's other Mozart recordings, this one is very beautiful and technically satisfactory. It is, indeed, one of the great disks of all time, and it would be very good of Victor to let us have it again.

MOZART

Bassoon Concerto No. 1 (K. 191)
    Leonard Sharrow, bassoon
    Recorded November 18 in Studio 8-H.
    ★M-1304 and ★DB-20182/83 and LM-1030

Mozart's only bassoon concerto (*No. 2* being considered spurious) is a pleasant work of no great weight with a number of fine passages that are capably realized in this performance. The recording is good.

TCHAIKOVSKY

Symphony No. 6 [Pathétique]
    Recorded November 24 in Carnegie Hall.
    ★M-1281 and LM-1036

Two reactions are engendered by this performance. The first, which I share, is that it is a definitive version of a much-abused score. The second is that Toscanini's approach to the music is unsympathetic to an extreme, that he forces upon it a style quite unsuited to it.

Toscanini gave the first Italian performance of this work over
fifty years ago, and though it is true that he has never played
another Tchaikovsky symphony in either Britain or the United
States (indeed, that he never even played the *Pathétique* while
with the Philharmonic), I do not subscribe to the suggestion
that Toscanini really dislikes the music and has played it in recent
seasons only in deference to popular taste. A part of his great
honesty as a musician, reflected again and again in his programs,
is that when he has no real feeing for a work he does not play it
at all.

What one hears on this record is an effort to play the score
with the same respect for the composer's markings that one normally gives, say, to a symphony by Beethoven. The traditional
banalities, the excesses, the exaggerations, the departures from
the spirit of the printed music heard in the performances of other
conductors are not reproduced here. In their place is the disciplined intensity of Toscanini. If one is so accustomed to hearing
this music "interpreted" that he cannot appreciate it in an honest,
musician-like performance, then this is not for him.

The first movement is played with great power and beauty,
the second (always an irresistible temptation to any flaw in a
conductor's morals) is played with muted restraint, perhaps too
much. The march is dazzling and the final movement reveals its
stature and tragic grandeur without falling to the level of tub-
thumping bathos and glycerine tears. The recorded sound is good
except for some unpleasantness in the strings in a few loud passages. The bass should be boosted.

VERDI

Otello

Principals: Herva Nelli, soprano, Nan Merriman, mezzo-
soprano, Ramon Vinay, tenor, Giuseppe Valdengo, baritone,
with choruses under Peter Wilhousky and Eduardo Petri
Recorded during broadcasts December 6 and 13 in Studio 8-H.
LM-6107 and ALP-1090/92

Bernard Shaw remarks that *Otello* is Shakespeare writing an
opera libretto, a tragedy based upon a farce plot in which the
coincidences all work out and the structure holds up until the
eventual denouement. The Boito adaptation of the play is a
masterpiece among opera libretti, but it increases the strain on
the dramatic structure. Therefore, it is for Verdi's magnificent
score—a work of enchanting beauty which reveals his powers at

their highest level (and a very high level it is)—that I wish to hear *Otello*. In this recording, the brilliance of the performances compensates for the weaknesses in the logic of the drama.

Toscanini plays the music with clarity, force, and a lovely singing quality that is always compelling, for example in his wonderful statement of the opening scenes. The singers are equal to the Maestro's demands and obviously give the performances of their lives in these roles, although Nelli seems, at times, to be lacking in tragic force. The recording is marred with a coarse, hard quality at times, but once more the musical values are more important than radiant high frequencies and undistorted tutti passages. On the whole the sound is good. The Victor booklet is unusually fine, with Henry W. Simon's parallel Boito-Shakespeare text deserving particular study.

SCHUMANN

Manfred Overture
Recorded December 16 in Carnegie Hall.
★M-1287 and ★DB-6992/93 and ★LM-6 and LM-9022

Schumann has appeared regularly in Toscanini's programs, yet this is the only Toscanini recording to date of any of his music. The Maestro shows a special sympathy for the early romantics, and he plays this fine work so that its power and beauty are fully realized without sentimentality and distortion. The original form of the recording was over-monitored; however, in the twelve-inch edition the sound is rich and the dynamics excellent.

Although it is unlikely that anyone knew it at the time, Toscanini was not to lead another recording session for nearly two years. When he resumed, he would be recording on a new medium for a revolutionized industry.

1949

VERDI

Aïda
Principals: Herva Nelli, soprano, Eva Gustafson, mezzosoprano, Richard Tucker, tenor, Giuseppe Valdengo, baritone, Norman Scott, bass, with the Robert Shaw Chorale
Recorded during broadcasts March 26 and April 2 in Studio 8-H and corrected with recordings made in Carnegie Hall, June 3 and 5, 1954.

Although approved for release, this set has not yet been scheduled for production. Its appearance, whatever the date, will be musically noteworthy, for the performance was without parallel in recent seasons, and the recording should be distinguished.

BEETHOVEN

Symphony No. 2
Recorded November 7 in Carnegie Hall.
LM-1723 and in ★LM-6900 and ALP-1145

No other conductor reveals the stature of this score in the manner Toscanini does. He makes it a work of great force, a logical phase in the development from the young genius who wrote the *First Symphony* to the mature one who composed the *Eroica*. The recording is disappointing, and those who have a generous margin of control on their playback equipment will be able to make more out of it than those who lack this flexibility. The thing to do is lighten the bass by giving it less than the normal boost in the equalization and accentuate the top slightly. This takes out both the unpleasant, cramped highs and the boom, but it doesn't, alas, take out the muddy horn sounds near the end of the slow movement. The master number should be 5S or higher.

RAVEL

Daphnis and Chloe: Suite No. 2
Recorded November 21 in Carnegie Hall.
★DM-1374 and LM-1043 and ALP-1070

Toscanini's approach to this music is that everything should be heard; thus, in balance and general effect, he offers a performance that is frequently quite different from the great Koussevitzky-Boston Symphony reading which many of us will hear in our minds as long as we live. (Toscanini insisted that Koussevitzky's version was not "correct.") In a new transfer of this recording, master number EO-LRC-3816 31S, I heard far more detail than I imagined possible to extract from the originals, deftly re-recorded, and presented with satisfactory gradations in volume. (The HMV edition is similar in quality.) Although the age of the recording is still, unfortunately, easily detected, it now has a degree of impact which it did not possess before and is roughly equal to the task of preserving a satisfactory replica of the marvel of balance and virtuosity which the original must have been.

BEETHOVEN

Symphony No. 3 [Eroica]
Recorded November 28 and December 5 in Carnegie Hall.
★DM-1375 and in ★LM-6900 and LM-1042 and ALP-1008

The 1939 edition of this symphony was a horror, and the original release of this 1949 recording was something to weep about, since it was shrill, cramped, and nasty in sound. This is what one found in the 78 rpm set and in the first LP editions, including the HMV. With the LM-6900 set one heard a new transfer of the tape with added resonance and a good deal of repair work. On first impression this seemed greatly superior to the first master. This, or a closely related, transfer was then made generally available in the United States as EO-LRC-3814-29S/15-32S. On further hearing one could well form doubts and misgivings about the improvements, and there is no use pretending that the disk approximates the minimum contemporary standards of high fidelity recording.

The choice was, thus, between a transfer with a high degree of distortion and some downright unpleasant sounds, but a certain degree of clarity and force, and a transfer with pleasanter sounds and far less distortion, but with the clarity sacrificed to excessive resonance and a "soft focus" effect, over-all, which made much of the musical detail indistinct or, worst of all, indistinguishable.

Since this is the symphony Toscanini has played more than any other during his American career, the lack of a satisfactory recording is a really black mark against Victor. The 29/30S transfer is the only one now available in America: one must accept its faults or do without the Toscanini reading of the score.

The *Eroica* belongs to the nineteenth century—although just barely—but it is scored for the eighteenth century orchestra that Beethoven used until he added trombones in the *Fifth Symphony*. In the *Eroica*, although we are hearing a work of double the length and five times the harmonic and intellectual complexity of *Symphony No. 104 [London]* of Haydn, we are hearing an orchestra that differs from the one Haydn used in that work only by the addition of a horn, giving the ensemble not four (as in the *Ninth*) or eight, as Bruckner and Mahler demand on occasion, but a total of *three* horns! The textures in the *Eroica* are, therefore, not heavy, and although we expect the *Eroica* to sound rich and full and "Beethovenish," to achieve this it must be played with great force, just as a powerful and exceptional performance of the Haydn *No. 104* (such as that of Munch and the Boston Symphony on Victor LM-49 or HMV ALP-1061) can make it sound like a "little *Eroica*."

There is a full analysis of the performance in Chapter II. Suffice it to say here that the inflections of the 1939 version have given way to a singing line that is pulse-stirring in its intensity and cumulative power. Let us hope there is a release of the 1953 broadcast performance with higher fidelity.

TCHAIKOVSKY

Manfred Symphony [generally called a "symphonic poem"]
    Recorded December 5 in Carnegie Hall.
    ★DM-1372 and LM-1037 and FLP and QLP-150 [i.e., HMV French and Italian series]

The only real example of a neglected score of great power and beauty which Toscanini has revived and sponsored with frequent performances. To him it is an opera without human voices, Taubman tells us. The recording gives us another masterful demonstration of how fine Tchaikovsky's music can be when played with honesty and force. Without sacrificing any of its lyricism, Toscanini holds this somewhat loosely structured score together with a firm hand and makes a judicious cut in the final movement. The sound of the current edition is exceptionally fine. Recommended.

RESPIGHI

Roman Festivals
    Recorded December 12 in Carnegie Hall.
    LM-55 and BLP-1011

High fidelity is really with us here; the bell notes in the last half inch of side 1 are as good as those on any disk. When told that the final section of the work might overload the recording equipment, Toscanini shouted: "I don't care! Break everything, but get it on!" What we have, then, is a thrilling performance of a score that is good picture music but not much else, recorded as a decibel champion of its day. The two sides should be 10S and 5S for the best sound.

WAGNER

Die Götterdämmerung: Dawn and *Siegfried's Rhine Journey*
    [concert version by Toscanini]

Recorded December 22 in Carnegie Hall.
LM-1157 and in LM-6020 and ALP-1173

This recording, as the *Eroica* above, is analyzed in Chapter II. Of the three versions of the score, this is second best in performance, first in sound, and since the difference in this respect is very great, no doubt this is the recording that one will want to play. Certainly it is still a fine performance, and the sound is excellent, although the LM-6020 transfer is the better of the two, apart from being a better value.

Parsifal: Prelude and Good Friday Spell
Recorded December 22 in Carnegie Hall.
★DM-1376 and LM-15 and in LM-6020 and ★DB-21270/72 and BLP-1033

The very low bass one hears toward the close of the first statement of the theme on the LM-6020 transfer (which offers superior sound to the alternate editions) is a Seventh Avenue, New York, subway train, from which one can conclude (a) that Carnegie Hall is not the ideal concert room—especially for making high fidelity recordings, and (b) this recording is pretty good. Both counts are correct, which is one reason why Victor used 8-H as long as they did. (Columbia records in a mellow old room named Liederkranz Hall beneath whose wooden rafters many a seidel of beer has, in years past, made its contribution to the general happiness of mankind.)

The qualities of this playing, the tensile strength of the sound, the unity of the ensemble, the incisiveness of the attack, the expressive force of the inflection and accent make for a statement of the music with an impact that others almost never achieve. I find what appears to be an equal performance in the ancient recording by Karl Muck, who inherited the score from Hermann Levi, the conductor whom Wagner selected for the first production. Muck gave *Parsifal* at Bayreuth until 1931, when Toscanini succeeded him for one season. I feel it is proper to regard this dedicated performance as being within the apostolic tradition of the Festspielhaus. The brilliant playing of Harry Glantz, the first trumpet, is especially noteworthy, and the recording reproduces his unique tone very well.

1950

MOZART

Symphony No. 40
_Recorded March 12 in Carnegie Hall.
LM-1789

Of the eight Toscanini recordings of Mozart by the electrical process which have been commercially distributed this is the second best. I recommend it, the 1947 *Divertimento*, and the 1938 *Magic Flute: Overture* without reservations, and the 1947 *Bassoon Concerto* is satisfactory. The remaining four items are either inferior performances or sonically obsolete. Thus, this single item is all we have of Toscanini playing Mozart on high fidelity.

Taubman quotes Toscanini as saying of Mozart, "He was too perfect. . . . Some of his music I find cold. . . . But he was a unique genius." And going on to recall how his first experiences of this symphony (in Italian performances) sounded as if it went "tweet, tweet," so only after Puccini reported to him how von Bülow played it in Berlin, with "bite in the strings" and "the first theme . . . strong and passionate" did he realize, "that was the way for me."

None the less, as the chapter following documents, Toscanini never explored the Mozart symphonies adequately in concert, and although he studied them in score and read Mozart's life and letters, he still did not always grasp his musical language with a sense of security which would have permitted him to prepare the more distinctive of his great works with a proper approach to their unique expressive content.

Similarly, it must be noted that this is not German Mozart (for that listen to Furtwängler's fine recording on Victor LHMV-1010 or DB-6997/99) or the unique Mozart of Sir Thomas Beecham, but Toscanini Mozart, played with a passion, intensity, and sense of "blood" that is appropriate to Italian music, but is not required for music as delicate and subtle, and yet as seemingly unlimited in its expressive range, as that of the Salzburg master. What is offered here is a deeply felt and impelling performance that avoids the excess of tension and the demoniac qualities of the older recording, but still must be regarded as a personal interpretation of the score. It is artistically honest, even convincing, but I am not prepared to say that it is in every way what Mozart intended.

SCHUBERT

Symphony No. 8 [Unfinished]
Recorded March 13 and June 2 in Studio 8-H.
★DM-1456 and ★LM-54 and LM-9022 and BLP-1038

This was the last Toscanini recording to be issued on 78 rpm disks in the United States. It preserves a reading of the score that is unusually impassioned (some moments could actually be described as fierce) even for the Maestro, who had, on other occasions, given it a more relaxed and lyric statement. Those who think of the work in terms of *Blossom Time* will find this completely uncongenial, and others, who do not find this quite so unsympathetic, may prefer a more romantic approach. Since this is a work I have studied with some care, I confess that I find Toscanini's heroic portrayal of the young artist more in keeping with my own feeling for the music than the more relaxed, romanticism of other conductors. The recording is much better in the twelve-inch edition, which offers considerably more agreeable sound over-all, greater clarity, and improved dynamics.

DUKAS

The Sorcerer's Apprentice
Recorded March 19 in Studio 8-H.
LM-1118 and FALP and QALP-130 [i.e., released by HMV in France and Italy only]

One of the most enjoyable of the lighter works in the supposedly serious repertory, given a delicious performance that is far more lyric, relaxed, and enjoyable than the 1929 version. However, the use of a full, twelve-inch, longplay surface for a single piece of ten minutes' playing time is a needless inflation of the cost of the music.

SMETANA

The Moldau
Recorded March 19 in Studio 8-H.
LM-1118 and ★DB-21496/97 and FALP and QALP-130 [i.e., French and Italian series]

Does this river flow into the Elbe or the Adriatic? The performance has a clarity and drive that one rarely hears, and the inner voices are beautifully revealed, but the spirit could not be less Bohemian and the scanning of the excerpt of folk music is completely Italian in manner.

VERDI

Falstaff

Principals: Herva Nelli, soprano, Teresa Stitch-Randall, soprano, Nan Merriman, mezzo-soprano, Cloe Elmo, mezzo-soprano, Giuseppe Valdengo, baritone, Frank Guarrera, baritone, Norman Scott, bass, and the Robert Shaw Chorale Recorded during broadcasts April 1 and 8 in Studio 8-H. LM-6111

Falstaff is frequently cited as Verdi's masterpiece. It might well be regarded as Boito's finest work and Toscanini's most distinguished operatic interpretation. For many years connoisseurs of Italian opera have insisted that *Falstaff*, more than any other score, has drawn forth Toscanini's most remarkable achievements in the opera house and, although other conductors could challenge him in other works (Furtwängler in Wagner and *Fidelio*, de Sabata in the Italian repertory, etc.), that the Toscanini reading of *Falstaff* remained a unique musical experience. It was natural that one would hope for a recording, and eventually it appeared—just as the announcement of a 1955 performance at the opening of La Piccola Scala suggested a second opportunity to record the work and the possibility of an even finer cast. Unfortunately, after thus whetting the sense of anticipation, the 1955 performance failed to materialize, and the 1950 recording remains as the *Falstaff* performance that must stand the inspection of coming generations of operatic historians.

The performance is a personal triumph for Toscanini. Under a lesser conductor it would be merely routine. Valdengo seems to have been coached within an inch of his life, but for all that one need only follow with the libretto to see how many lines are simply thrown away, how many others receive far less than one would imagine they deserve. Valdengo is simply attempting to do a role that has been imposed on him from without, and lacking any spontaneous feeling for the right thing to do, he continually does what he feels to be the *safe* thing. The result is we have a *Falstaff* with a Falstaff who is not fat, or lecherous, or amusing, but *dull*, and that is what is hardest to resign oneself to, for it is as violent a disruption of the order of things as someone playing *Otello* for laughs.

Of the female singers, Cloe Elmo is outstanding and walks away with the opening scene of Act II without even a struggle. Mesdames Nelli, Merriman, and Stitch-Randall have been attentive pupils at the Maestro's school and deserve high marks (they often are quite charming), but the diligent student and the accomplished actress are two different things. Bardolph and Pistol emerge as distinctly subdued ruffians, and although Ford has moments of personal force, one feels his impact could be greater. The chorus is excellent.

I find the recording bright, clear, and agreeable, with the balance usually fine and never disturbingly faulty. The sound is clearly that of a studio (our venerable friend 8-H), happily without phony resonance, so one must be prepared for the compression of sound that it provides. The natural resonance of a good hall, with the resultant separation of the lines of sound, would be preferable, of course.

For all the faults mentioned above, I feel that this is a set to acquire and play. The work is a marvel; the performance of the orchestral part is astonishing; and the singing, if not awe-inspiring, is at least quite pleasant to hear.

DEBUSSY

La Mer
  Recorded June 1 in Studio 8-H.
  LM-1221 and LM-1833 and ★DB-21453/55 and ALP-1070

If the American tour of the N.B.C. Symphony was Toscanini's greatest triumph of the 1949-50 season, this recording surely comes second. *La Mer* is the work he played fifty-three times in his twenty-nine seasons as a symphonic conductor in the United States, and although there had been several efforts to record it, the best known of which was (once more) during the 1942 Philadelphia sessions, none had yielded a version with the clarity and perfection of detail which he demanded. Even the Philadelphia recording, the first movement of which was so fine he said it was "just like reading the score," failed to please him because of errors in the later pages, and it is possible that, had the electroplating accident not taken place, it still would not have been approved.

Made in the final recording sessions held in 8-H, this was a performance prepared for the tour and polished by a series of six concerts before the recording was made. Some say that the final concert performance, in Philadelphia, was even finer than this. I didn't hear it, so I can't comment, but if it was better, I can't imagine how. This is one of the miracles of orchestral virtuosity, and I think it can be said with safety that there are only three other orchestras in the world, the Boston, the Philharmonic, and the Philadelphia, which, under a Toscanini, might duplicate it. The two things which are the most striking are the phenomenal clarity (*everything* sounds) and the cohesion of the parts, each of which is perfectly executed—but always in proper relation to the whole and the other strands of sound. I think that is really the chief point on which this reading of the score is superior to the great Koussevitzky performance; with Koussevitzky it added up to ninety-six per cent, with Toscanini it is unquestionably one hundred per cent.

Toscanini edited this score with great care, doubling lines in the subtlest fashion when necessary to make them sound, and his text should be printed for general use, now that he no longer requires it. These changes were made with Debussy's permission, and had the composer been wise he would have had his publisher incorporate them into the printed score he had issued.

Of the two transfers of the tape available in the United States, the newer with "enhanced sound" is clearly the better of the two, although it should not be thought from this that the first had anything seriously wrong with it. The new edition is improved chiefly in giving the effect of a hall recording and offering more brilliance, solidity, and a wider dynamic range, so that one really gets a Toscanini *ff* in unmonitored contrast to a Toscanini *pp*.

Saint-Saëns

Danse Macabre
Recorded June 1 in Studio 8-H.
LM-1118 and 7ER5012

That Toscanini could in the same recording sessions perform three transcendent masterpieces and this work poses a baffling question on the mentality of genius, quite as if Cezanne had paused between his two greatest canvases to turn out a crudely voluptuous pin-up. What can one say? It is a fine performance, well recorded. Who cares?

Debussy

Images, Third Set [for orchestra—sets 1 and 2 are for piano solo]:
No. 2 Iberia
Recorded June 2 in Studio 8-H, and incorporating corrections from the broadcast performance of November 2, 1938.
LM-1833

The three *Images* for orchestra are (1) *Gigues,* (2) *Iberia*—in three movements, the final two played without pause, (3) *Rondes de printemps.* Heard as a work of three contrasting parts they have an effect which cannot be duplicated if they are played singly, but, in fact, in all his American career, Toscanini never played either the first or third of these three works, although *Iberia* became one of the core items in his repertory. I can offer no explanation for this, save that the expressive medium of the first and third of the *Images* is more deeply felt than that of *Iberia,* and perhaps he did not understand it.

The 1950 recording issued here was not approved until corrections were made in the second movement by means of splicing in material from a broadcast. This was expertly done, and cannot be heard. The whole set was then "updated" by electronic manipulations which are difficult to explain but easily understood in terms of the fine sound they yield.

Toscanini's *Iberia* is *sec* rather than sensuous. So far as balance, unity, precision, and rhythmic accuracy go, there is no touching it. Let there be no doubt about it being a great performance, but I sense that it is a somewhat over-refined one. In the past it probably had redder blood in its arteries.

The Saint-Saëns, these two Debussy recordings, and parts of the Schubert *Unfinished* were the last things Toscanini made in Studio 8-H (R.I.P.) which was converted into a television studio in the summer of 1950.

1951

STRAUSS

Don Juan
    Recorded January 10 in Carnegie Hall.
    LM-1157 and ALP-1173

An impassioned statement of one of Strauss's most effective pieces of portraiture, quite sufficient to rebut the charge that Toscanini's performances of his music are over-refined and lack vigor. The recorded sound is excellent.

VERDI

Requiem [in Memory of Alessandro Manzoni]
    Herva Nelli, soprano, Fedora Barbieri, mezzo-soprano, Giuseppe Di Stefano, tenor, Cesare Siepi, bass, and the Robert Shaw Chorale, Robert Shaw, conducting
    Recorded during a public performance and broadcast January

27 in Carnegie Hall.
LM-6018

The most impressive quality of this recording is the sense of presence that it gives. Heard over equipment that can handle the large masses of sound without distortion, one can shut one's eyes and actually feel that in some magical way one has been transported to Carnegie Hall on that memorable evening. The fidelity, then, is spectacular, with the sound vivid, natural, and agreeable, and if one must contend with a few realistic coughs, one is compensated by hearing a performance that is actually *better than* the original, since the flaws have been expertly corrected in tape editing. Toscanini prepared this fine work regularly from his first New York season in 1908-09 and was here captured in a period of sustained intensity which was held in check by the urge to sing; thus even such hair- (and roof-) raising moments as the opening of the *Dies Irae* are perfectly under control and avoid any excess. As one hears Verdi's description of the Last Judgment, one is impressed by the manner in which, with a few powerful strokes, he paints the scene and achieves a greater effect than Mahler ever secures after pages of preparation in the *Resurrection Symphony*. The Toscanini performance is dramatic rather than liturgical in feeling, but it is not operatic, and the work is held together in a firm grip that does not allow the movements to appear to break up into episodes. Unfortunately, although the orchestra plays with amazing virtuosity and precision, the force of that master hand sometimes makes the soloists appear trapped in the unyielding framework of Toscanini's concept of the score. It is the splendor of that concept that makes this set the marvel that it is.

BEETHOVEN

Symphony No. 4
Recorded during a broadcast February 3 in Carnegie Hall.
LM-1723 and in ★LM-6900 and ALP-1145

I have listened to a copy of the original tape and can report that the disk reproduces the sound of the source recording well, though it is not less cramped and dry for that. Toscanini was driving the orchestra very hard and obviously wanted clarity and dramatic force, which are here preserved at the cost of tonal splendor. The more relaxed 1939 performance is the one to have.

Of the editions which RCA Victor have issued, the limited one was the worst, and the refurbished master, numbered E2RP 4361

10S (or higher), is still faulty with excessive treble and phony-sounding resonance and insufficient bass. With a good pre-amplifier one can fix some, but not all, of this, but in any case the performance is unsatisfactory, and it is better to apply oneself to making the 1939 set sound a little brighter.

ROSSINI

Semiramide: Overture
Recorded September 28 in Carnegie Hall.
LRM-7054

Before writing this, I played the 1936 recording for the tenth or eleventh time, and this in succession and tried to answer the question: "Why is the earlier one better?" in terms that would exclude sentimental bias for a set that was once, by the going standards, exceptionally beautiful, that thrilled me again and again, and that still preserves with remarkable force the wonderful sound of the Philharmonic of nearly two decades ago. The answer at which I arrived is that, although the 1951 version is superior in sound and presence, the 1936 recording is played more lightly and delicately, with subtler inflections and greater verve, and that, in contrast, the 1951 version seems mechanical, less expressive, and well drilled rather than deeply felt. As I write this I feel I must add that hearing the 1951 recording *without* the 1936 set as a preface, it appears to be convincing and quite satisfactory, so that those who acquire it won't be disappointed.

WEBER (*Orch.* BERLIOZ)

Invitation to the Dance
Recorded September 28.
ERA-125 and 7ER5021

DONIZETTI

Don Pasquale: Overture
Recorded October 10.
LRM-7028 and LM-6026
Recorded in Carnegie Hall.

Both of these are modern duplications of older recordings which offer polished and propulsive versions of scores Toscanini plays extremely well. The Donizetti is almost the identical performance as that of thirty years before, and the Weber, with the prelude and postlude stated in the beautiful tone of Frank

Miller's 'cello, is a charming synthesis of precision and grace. Since the postlude is usually lost under premature applause (as happened to Toscanini in the broadcast concert of December 13, 1953), a record is about the only chance one has to hear it.

PROKOFIEV

Symphony No. 1 [Classical]
    Recorded October 15 in Carnegie Hall.
    LM-9020 and ALP-1107

Has this symphony a slow movement? Toscanini has decided in recent years that it does, and his tempo for the *Larghetto* is quite a bit slower than that of other conductors. It is convincing, but the great Koussevitzky performance (which never got on to modern records) was convincing too, though quite different. An unusual and effective reading of a fine score, then, well worth some thought.

WAGNER

Lohengrin: Preludes to Acts I and III
    Recorded October 22 in Carnegie Hall.
    LM-6020 and LRM-7029 and (Act I) DB-21574

Two more modern duplications of older recordings which have the life and strength of the originals. There is a noticeable (but inoffensive) tape splice near the beginning of the *Prelude to Act I;* both preludes could use a little more solidity and bass.

Siegfried: Forest Murmurs
    Recorded October 29 in Carnegie Hall.
    LM-6020 and LRM-7029 and DB-21599

Of all the raw and bleeding fragments of Wagner which reach the concert room, this one reaches the level of "groveling imbecility" according to Tovey, whose judgment I second with a lusty *aye!*

The American 45 rpm set matches the level of the music: after twenty-four seconds of *Forest Murmurs* there is a break to the side following! Those who can stand the piece with its lack of form and silly climax (how can Toscanini tolerate it?) will find it beautifully played here.

WEBER

Euryanthe Overture
    Recorded October 29 in Carnegie Hall.
    LM-6026

This recording completes the famous trio in Toscanini performances of unique clarity and vigor. Why *Freischütz* and *Oberon* were not coupled with it for release some time ago is a question only RCA can answer. In any case, the three are now together, and this performance in particular—with its freedom from the rhetorical excesses that often pass as "German style"— is particularly welcome. The sound is not quite so full as I would like, but otherwise very good.

BRAHMS

Symphony No. 1
Recorded November 6 in Carnegie Hall.
LM-1702 and in ★LM-6108 and ★DB-9768/72 and ALP-1012

I confess that I do not like the Brahms *First Symphony*, even though I am aware that millions of people do and that performances which stress the very pretentious qualities which repel me, such as those of Stokowski and Furtwängler, arouse many admirers of the work to rapturous enthusiasm. The portions of the score which I am able to hear with pleasure, most of them in the final movement, Toscanini states with dignity and exemplary good taste, and the crude, crosscut-saw effect in the exposition of the first movement is, with similar good taste, minimized. The score, thus, is beautifully played and beautifully recorded here, and for those who enjoy the rest of the work, it is expertly done.

BEETHOVEN

Symphony No. 7
Recorded November 9 in Carnegie Hall.
LM-1756 and in ★LM-6900 and ALP-1119

There are fifteen years of time between this and the 1936 version, but there aren't fifteen years of improvement in the recording, and if Victor made a better than usual set in 1936, in 1951 they fell below the standard of the day. In limited edition this symphony was especially bad and the commercial version, although improved in resonance and brightness, was still cramped, inclined to stridency, and needlessly drab and harsh, particularly in view of the natural and agreeable sound RCA Victor engineers had given the same work when they recorded it with Munch and the Boston Symphony the season before. Technically this is better than 1936, then, but not by a great deal. E2RP-4290/91-5S (or higher) is a "rehabilitated" master.
When we consider the two performances it becomes clear that

at eighty-four the Old Man was not up to duplicating what may have been the Beethoven performance of his life in the 1936 sessions. Even with its dated sound the slower tempo in the introductory pages is more impressive, and point by point the earlier version scores over the later one. One difference, which may partly be due to the recording, is in the final pages, bars 358-405 where the wind are playing sustained harmonies over the moving figures in the strings. In 1936 this was beautifully balanced and very thrilling, and in the Munch recording it can be heard with striking effect. In the 1951 Toscanini the balance is faulty in these bars and the woodwinds are obscured. I fear, in terms of really adequate sound, that this great performance has been lost, but the disk is worth having for its undeniable merits.

BERLIOZ

Romeo and Juliet, Dramatic Symphony: Part II, Queen Mab Scherzo
Recorded during a broadcast November 10 in Carnegie Hall.
LM-6026 and LM-1951

Sheer orchestral sorcery from beginning to end, this music has finally been recorded and approved by the Maestro. For those who have been waiting ever since word leaked out that it had been done with the Philadelphia Orchestra in 1942, its release is a long-anticipated pleasure, and the wait justified, since modern engineering captures literally everything, including the distinctive tone of the antique cymbals in the final pages, an effect that is frequently lost even in the concert room.

TCHAIKOVSKY

The Nutcracker, Ballet: Suite No. 1
Recorded November 10 in Carnegie Hall.
LRY-9000

Certainly the most remarkable of the two "Toscanini" versions of this score is the one made without him, in October, 1954, to be used as a gift to those who contributed to his former orchestra under its new incorporation as the "Symphony of the Air," which I mentioned in connection with the 1946 Wagner recordings. Although they had not played the work under Toscanini since the day they made the 1951 recording, nearly three years previously, they duplicated the performance as well as any musician can duplicate a performance, showing to anyone who was interested that once a Toscanini taught them a piece they could play it forever if necessary. However, by slowing down the tempo twenty-five per cent with the Springer device one finds that they played with much heavier inflections under the Maestro, and their performance without a conductor is lighter and more sensitive both melodically and rhythmically. The Philharmonic had given the world a similar demonstration of their ability to re-create Toscanini in 1942 and 1945, but it had not been documented by recording, and in that case Toscanini was present and in charge.

This work was on the program of Toscanini's first symphony concert in 1896; fifty-five years later he was playing it with a freshness, zest, and degree of attention to balance, and coloring such as it rarely has been given. A thoroughly delicious performance that transforms a score that one is probably tired of into a delightful musical experience once more.

BEETHOVEN

Septet (Op. 20)
Recorded November 26 in Carnegie Hall.
LM-1745 and ALP-1106

This is chamber music played with orchestra forces, but the sound is still delicately scaled and the textures are those of an ensemble of—if not seven—few players. The work is a sort of divertimento in a relaxed, youthful style reminiscent of the *Second Symphony* at times. Extremely popular when it was written, it was soon overshadowed by the mature Beethoven, and although one finds it fresh, melodic, and romantic, none of the matters of which it treats are particularly weighty. It is pretty Zerlina rather than Donna Anna.

WAGNER

Die Meistersinger: Preludes to Acts I and III
Recorded November 26 in Carnegie Hall.
Both in LM-6020; Act III only LRM-7029 and DB-21564

In terms of performance alone the slower and more relaxed 1946 version of the *Act I Prelude* is better than this. None the less, both performances are longer than a "standard" German one, such as Muck's. The 1951 version, with its brilliant sound (but boost the bass a little), is highly effective and enjoyable. The *Act III Prelude* is magnificently achieved and gives us some of the best pages Wagner wrote. Increase bass here, too.

BRAHMS

Symphony No. 4
  Recorded December 3 in Carnegie Hall.
  LM-1713 and in ★LM-6108 and ALP-1029

The most perfectly conceived work of Brahms and one of the supreme masterpieces of the nineteenth century, this work has been audible in many Toscanini performances which ranked as the finest reading of the score to be heard. From the siren song of the opening bars to the towering heights of the concluding passacaglia the work is filled with traps for the unwary conductor of dubious musicianship or taste, and Toscanini invariably navigated the course without slipping into them. Particularly, he gave us a reading of the final movement in which, by holding the tempo steady, *as it must be* (and as it almost always is *not*), he achieved the great climactic passage at the close of the variations in a manner which could serve as the paradigm for all who play the score.

That being said, let us consider this recording. The sound is not Victor's absolute best, but its deficiencies are not serious. With a folded horn enclosure my Tannoy speaker produced some splendid full tones from this disk. Smaller units, I found, did not do it justice. The performance is still an extremely fine one, but, as happened in these later years, it is now slightly over-refined, with absolute smoothness and uncanny precision taking the place of the subtle variations of expressive playing. This is most noticeable in the slow movement, which Toscanini fails to probe to the depths of its feeling or content, indeed, which he does not even reveal fully in terms of tonal beauty. (The old set of the Koussevitzky, Boston Symphony performance contains a more probing statement of the score in terms of sonorities alone.) In fact, Toscanini's final performance of the symphony, in London the October following, was more expressive, since the Philharmonia is a mellower instrument than the N.B.C. and had not played the work with the Maestro before.

I sum it up this way: there is no finer recording of the final movement to be heard, and although cool and highly polished where they should be warmer and more robust, the first three movements are still wonderfully achieved. It *is* a great recording, but there have been greater performances from the Maestro, and one might well desire to have a second, warmer, more "German" version of the work in his record collection.

ELGAR

Variations on an Original Theme [Enigma]
  Recorded December 10 in Carnegie Hall.
  LM-1725 and ALP-1204

To the British, Elgar is a great composer, although I doubt if he holds this reputation in any other country, certainly not in the United States where his *Pomp and Circumstance No. 1* is the invariable processional at secondary school graduations, but his larger works are unheard except for occasional performances of the violin concerto and these variations. This is the only work of Elgar which Toscanini performed with any regularity, and his recording commands our attention, for it is a lovely score, played here with obvious affection, and containing a wealth of fine moments. The recording is excellent.

RESPIGHI

The Fountains of Rome
  Recorded December 17 in Carnegie Hall.
  LM-1768 and ALP-1101

More Roman pictures with the colors splashing wet out of the tubes, brilliantly recorded. The final pages are an unusually fine picture in sound.

BEETHOVEN

Symphony No. 1
  Recorded December 21 in Carnegie Hall.
  LM-6009 and ★LM-6900 and ALP-1040

Within the style imposed (a severe, unyielding classicism) this is a consistent and cogent reading of the score. Some may prefer a warmer and broader performance, such as that of 1937. The 21S master is considerably better than its predecessors, although any one over 1S counts as refurbished, and its quality eliminates any misgivings I might have had about this disk.

1952

WAGNER

Die Götterdämmerung: Siegfried's Death and Funeral Music
  [concert version by Toscanini]
  Recorded January 3 in Carnegie Hall.
  LM-6020

This powerful statement of the hero's death is slower and more dramatically paced than the *echt* German version by Muck. It is one of the basic Toscanini repertory items, most welcome in its return to the catalog. Increase the bass a little and this becomes a real thriller!

Die Walküre: Prelude to Act III [The Ride of the Valkyries]
Recorded January 3 in Carnegie Hall.
ERA-249

I dream, at times, of a non-existent Spike Jones recording of this work with a background of high wind, thunder, pelting hail, and rain, a chorus of Valkyries fair overflowing from their cups, and a great many horsy effects. (In the same reveries I think of sensational interpretations of the *1812 Overture* and a few other "concert favorites.") Unfortunately, this is a straight performance, and "thems as likes it can have it."

WEBER

Der Freischütz: Overture
Recorded January 3 in Carnegie Hall.
LRM-7028 and LM-6026

One of the great works of German romanticism given a performance and recording which fully reveal its lyric and dramatic qualities.

FRANCK

Psyché No. 4: Psyché and Eros
Recorded January 7 in Carnegie Hall.
LM-1838 and ALP-1218

This would make a better effect if it did not tail the sensational *Pictures at an Exhibition* and reveal the big difference in Victor recording between early 1952 and a year later. The only Toscanini recording of Franck's music, it offers an agreeably melodic excerpt from a longer score. Bass requires an extra boost.

WAGNER

Tristan und Isolde: Prelude and *Love-Death*
Recorded January 7 in Carnegie Hall.
LM-6020

In Alma Mahler's biography of her husband, we learn of Mahler's misgivings about Toscanini's performances of *Tristan* in the 1909-10 season at the Metropolitan Opera, when they both conducted there. I share Mahler's reservations. The performance (there is no reason to believe it has changed greatly in the intervening years) is over-refined, the antiseptic souvenir of passion rather than its full-blooded actuality. In *Tristan* this will not do, although it is easily understood when we see that these two works rank fourth and fifth in frequency in Toscanini's repertory: they have had all the life played out of them. There is a noticeable break in continuity in bar 55 of the *Love-Death*, right after the strings have played a wonderful phrase in a cool, polished and unfeeling manner, more appropriate to Verdi than to this period of Wagner's music.

BEETHOVEN

Symphony No. 6 [Pastoral]
    Recorded January 14 in Carnegie Hall.
    LM-1755 and in ★LM-6900 and ALP-1129

There are two *Pastoral* symphonies. One is a warm, German work, relaxed and reflecting the mood of rustic poetry; the other is this, a dazzling classical landscape, brilliantly illuminated by the Mediterranean sun. Those who want the former work need only secure the recording of any one of the great German conductors, and for the second there are the two Toscanini recordings (and close to them a very similar version by De Sabata). The greatest marvels are in the second movement, in which the delicacy of coloring and the plastic quality of the unfolding line of sound are a unique musical experience, but the other movements are equally fine in their respective ways, and if the village band Beethoven suggests in the trio of the *Scherzo* never appears (the refined sounds one hears are no rural musicians) the storm that follows is forceful enough, and the thanksgiving sincerely conveyed.

The recording is excellent, although the high tones of the strings are sweeter if the top is turned down just a bit. Apparently the first side of this was better in the limited edition than in the commercial version, although I find the latter satisfactory. The master numbers should be 10S or higher.

BRAHMS

Variations on a Theme of Haydn [St. Antoni Variations]
    Recorded February 4 in Carnegie Hall.
    LM-1725 and ALP-1204

The sixth ranking item in frequency in Toscanini's repertory with forty performances in twenty-nine seasons. For all that, the duplication of the 1936 set is very successful (there are one or two minor differences of an expressive character), giving one a well-remembered performance in the excellence of modern sound.

Symphony No. 2

Recorded February 11 in Carnegie Hall.
LM-1731 and in ★LM-6108 and ★DB-9773/76 and ALP-1013

The sound of this 1952 Toscanini series is good, but it is not so fine as that of the 1953 series, and one of the differences is that the later recordings capture the full brilliance of the brass, while these occasionally slice just enough off the top to take away its full lustre and make it seem a bit hard and coarse. To correct this the top must be depressed just a bit below normal equalization, and those with multiple speaker systems should take care that their high frequency driver is not out of balance, since if it starts free-wheeling on a record such as this, it could make it sound much less pleasant than it actually is.

With that warning out of the way, one can remark that this is a fine performance of the symphony, well reproduced by the disk. It is of interest to me to contrast this reading of the score with that Toscanini gave with the Philharmonia Orchestra in London the autumn following. This is a disciplined performance: intensity is the predominant feeling in the work, and the propulsive force of the dramatic line carries all before it. In London the symphony had "loosened" somewhat, it was warmer and more expressive, there were variations in tempo (not all of them completely to my liking), and a more relaxed, singing quality was dominant in the performance. There is a tape of this September concert in Walter Toscanini's collection of broadcast material, and I wish we had it on disks as well as this version, for nowhere else have I heard the two main approaches to this score from a single conductor within a short span of a few months.

CHERUBINI

Symphony in D

Recorded March 10 in Carnegie Hall.
LM-1745 and ALP-1106

Cherubini once ranked with the great and now is forgotten and all but unperformed, a process of deflation that may well affect some of the more celebrated composers of today. (I wonder, for example, what Bartók's reputation will be in fifty years.) Toscanini's occasional revivals have, therefore, been welcome, and it is interesting to have this symphony, since it is a fine score, full of enjoyable things, but not bearing the marks of genius one finds in the music of Beethoven. Beethoven was ahead of his times; Cherubini, unfortunately, was just abreast of them.

STRAUSS

Death and Transfiguration
   Recorded March 10 in Carnegie Hall.
   LM-1891

Although there is no denying the popularity of this score, I find it the weakest of the six "big" Strauss tone poems of the decade 1888-98. *Don Juan* and *Till Eulenspiegel,* which flank it on either side, are both more vital not merely in thematic invention, but also in the symphonic development. The material in *Death and Transfiguration* is dangerously close to banality in its simplest form, and its treatment is frequently obvious and pretentious. The transfiguration theme is as good an instance of this as any.

The person who is fond of this score presumably admires some of its defects and, if record sales are any guide, enjoys a broad, rhetorical performance in which the melodrama is played for all it's worth. Toscanini, as one would expect, does not comply. His approach is cooler, more sublime, and also more detached. Never have I heard the opening phrase achieved with such clarity and polish, and throughout the playing is equally distinguished. I have heard part of the rejected Philadelphia recording of 1942 and can assure the reader that this performance is as fine in every way and sonically beyond comparison. If one wants *Death and Transfiguration* played for all the dignity it possesses, and if one will accept the brilliant (and rather chilly) sound of Toscanini's strings, this is the performance without peers.

BEETHOVEN

Symphony No. 5
   Recorded during a broadcast March 22 in Carnegie Hall.
   LM-1757 and in ★LM-6900 and ALP-1108

The 1939 recording of this work was faster than I thought necessary, and this one preserves a further increase in tempo, which is thrilling, if the sheer sensation of speed thrills one, but is increasingly dubious as an interpretation of Beethoven's intentions. I feel that the work is rushed, that the slow movement is not slow enough, that the decrease in tempo required for the "second subject" of the first movement is a bad effect, causing a lessening of force, and that an excess of intensity has robbed the music of much of its communicative power. The recording does not compensate for this. The quality is inferior to that of the Verdi *Requiem* of the previous year and well below what one had a right to expect in 1952, with the bass weak, the top limited, and the voices run together into a wooden, lustreless mass of sound at *ff*. The deterioration in Toscanini's performance is an unfortunate thing in itself, coupled with this recording it gives the present disk more of a documentary than a musical function. Master numbers of 15S or higher are refurbished transfers.

Symphony No. 9 [Choral]

Eileen Farrell, soprano, Nan Merriman, mezzo-soprano, Jan Peerce, tenor, Norman Scott, bass, the Robert Shaw Chorale, Robert Shaw, directing
Recorded (final movement) March 31, (first three movements) April 1, in Carnegie Hall.
LM-6009 and in ★LM-6900 and ALP-1039/40

"I'm almost satisfied" was Toscanini's comment on this recorded performance. Undoubtedly he knows how he could do it better, with angelic choirs that never sing off key or need to breathe, for instance, but in terms of human resources this is as personal and fine a *Ninth* as one is likely to hear. The two middle movements are as close to perfection as anyone is likely to get, although I feel that in earlier years Toscanini set a slower pace for the *Adagio molto e cantabile*, and playing a tape of the recording at a twenty per cent reduction in tempo (by means of the Springer invention mentioned earlier) I found no loss of continuity, so firm and clean are the phrases as Toscanini's men play them.

If one wants to register objections, it is possible to debate the tempo of the first movement, although this classical approach, lean and completely without rhetoric, appears to me wholly legitimate and undeniably effective. In the final movement, where most conductors go astray, Toscanini gives himself considerable interpretive freedom in the *recitatif* for the lower strings and adopts some fast tempi that run against German tradition. Peerce lacks the weight of tone required to do justice to the *Alla Marcia,* and the double fugue that follows—a section that in the hands of German conductors often seems to break the movement in two—is here a bit rushed, but does not assume a disproportionate place in the scheme of the whole. Make up your own mind about the tempo best suited to the choral passage beginning in bar 542. The soloists are the weakest part of the proceedings, and Farrell does not seem to be able to sing a long phrase on a single breath, which makes for a choppy quality at times. In the final *Prestissimo* there is too much triangle, cymbals and gong for my idea of the dignity of the passage, and I have an idea that Beethoven intended a gong of lower pitch than Toscanini's and not quite so much tone from the cymbals.

Don't let any of this scare you, though. It's a wonderful recording.

WAGNER

Siegfried Idyll
Recorded July 29 in Carnegie Hall.
LM-6020

Students of concert life in New York should note that this ends with a fanfare of automobile horns; in fact, the constant penetration of noise into the hall caused the engineers to use a "close-in" technique which lost much of the natural resonance of the auditorium. The performance is not my favorite of the three, a little chilly and lacking intimacy. The 1946 version is best. Note the midsummer recording date of this and the following; unusual for Toscanini.

LIADOV

Kikimora
LRM-7014

PONCHIELLI

La Gioconda: Dance of the Hours
LRM-7005 and LM-1834 and DB-21587 and ALP-1235

THOMAS

Mignon: Overture
LRM-7013 and LM-6026

Recorded July 29 in Carnegie Hall.

All these are "Pops" (or, if you prefer, "Prom") items, pleasant, but of no great musical weight. The recordings were made close-in and then given artificial resonance, the effect of which was to coarsen the sound. The playing is very lovely indeed. It is also an interesting contrast to note that the Ponchielli was issued in Britain as a 78 rpm disk, the newer speeds then still considered secondary rather than "standard."

BIZET

Carmen: Orchestral Suite No. 1
  LRM-7013 and LM-6026

CATALANI

Lorelei: Dance of the Water Nymphs and *La Wally: Prelude to Act IV*
  ERA-101 and LM-6026

HÉROLD

Zampa Overture
  LRM-7014 and LM-1834 and ALP-1235

HUMPERDINCK

Hansel and Gretel: Prelude
  LRM-7014 and LM-6026

  . Recorded August 5 in Carnegie Hall.

Further spectacular performances of light music with the recorded sound coarsened by the needless addition of resonance. The *Carmen* is sensational. The Humperdinck has many lovely moments, but particularly the first entrance of the strings. Hearing it I unconsciously wait for the announcer to break in with "This is the Ford Sunday Evening Hour."

SIBELIUS

Finlandia
  Recorded August 5 in Carnegie Hall.
  LRM-7005 and LM-1834 and ALP-1235

Toscanini's only commercial recording of music by a composer he has played sparingly. The performance is simple, forceful, and direct. Recording is satisfactory.

WEBER

Oberon: Overture
  Recorded August 5 in Carnegie Hall.

LRM-7028 and LM-6026

The 45 set has this tagging *Don Pasquale* without a separating band. Toscanini does things with the early romantics that others just can't manage; this is no exception. Recording is excellent.

BRAHMS

Symphony No. 3
    Recorded November 4 in Carnegie Hall.
    LM-1936 and in ★LM-6108 and ALP-1166

Toscanini put off recording this symphony until the end of the Brahms series because he was uncertain how he wanted it to go. After several days of listening to tapes of his broadcasts, he put together an ideal performance (first and fourth movements of October 15, 1938, second movement of March 31, 1946, third movement of November 20, 1948). He listened to this until he thought he had it well in mind and then attempted to duplicate it in the recording session. He was unsuccessful. The "ideal version" is consistently taut, hard driving, and intense. This performance is slower and suffers, of all things, from both a lack of continuity and changes in the rhythmic pulse and scanning of phrases. The conclusion to be drawn is that the Old Man is still unable to get this to go as he would like. The recording, however, is the best of the Brahms series, and the important repeat in the first movement is observed. Incidentally, speeded up ten per cent by the Springer device it is much improved.

STRAUSS

Till Eulenspiegel's Merry Pranks
    Recorded November 4 in Carnegie Hall.
    LM-1891

The word "definitive" has not appeared very often in these pages, although Toscanini is one of the few conductors to whose performances it might frequently be applied. Here I break down. This is the definitive *Till*. Why? First because no other performance I have ever heard—and I have heard some good ones—had the impact of this. The Old Man's power here is unbelievable until one has heard it for himself. Then it becomes inexplicable. The "trial scene" in particular is played as I had no idea it could be played with human resources. Second, for all the success with which the individual sections of the score are achieved, the work has a higher degree of unity and cumulative force here than in any other performance I have ever known. A bad conductor makes this work a string of episodes; Toscanini makes it a tightly integrated whole. Third, the clarity is astonishing, and the details of the scoring, down to the striking reproduction of some very unusual instrumental timbres, are faultlessly reproduced. The violins, unfortunately, sound as if they had steel strings throughout. Perhaps they did, although I would sacrifice some of the brilliance of their tone to greater warmth. None the less, from every standpoint, this is one of the great Toscanini disks.

BEETHOVEN

Symphony No. 8
  Recorded November 10 in Carnegie Hall.
  LM-1757 and in ★LM-6900 and ALP-1108

It would be nice to report that the last of the Beethoven nine to be recorded was given a brilliant taping, but, plagued by some unknown disability, again Victor failed to produce a recording up to the highest standards of the day. The limited edition was raucous and strident, and the improved commercial version is frequently harsh and without sufficient warmth and lustre. E2RP-4363-15S (or higher) is a new master. None the less, it is the only recording I know that does justice to the score, which is usually treated as a merry quadrille, full of jolly little tunes, and by no means a serious business. So reduced in scale it provides material for commentators to develop, starting with their astonishment that he should write such a work during a period of crisis in his life. In the Toscanini performance it is restored to its proper stature, as a score equal in power and intensity to the *Seventh* which precedes it. I am, therefore, obliged to call this a definitive performance, in spite of the deficiencies of the sound. Note the big difference made by repeating the exposition of the first movement. In seeing the necessity for this Toscanini reveals his superb sense of form.

VERDI

La Forza del Destino: Overture
  Recorded November 10 in Carnegie Hall.
  LM-6026 and 7ER5021

A successful re-make of the 1945 disk. This is Toscanini playing his beloved Verdi with affection and sympathy. For those who enjoy the piece it is a brilliant version.

SAINT-SAËNS

Symphony No. 3 [with organ]
Recorded during a broadcast November 15 in Carnegie Hall.
LM-1874

The *Third Symphony* of Saint-Saëns is the only one of his three works in this form to remain in the present-day repertory, a rather melancholy fate for one who was once known as "the French Beethoven." Indeed, even this *Third Symphony* belongs to that second division of scores that, although containing many fine pages, cannot truthfully be ranked as masterpieces. Under a sympathetic interpreter they reveal their merits, and under a less understanding artist their weaknesses predominate.

What, then, of this Toscanini performance? The rhetoric which is inherent in much of the music, and which many performers underline with varying degrees of skill and taste, is, as one would imagine, underdone rather than stressed. On first hearing, this approach may seem disappointing, unsympathetic, a typical conflict of style between Toscanini's ideas and a romantic composer's intentions. Further hearings, however, convinced me that Toscanini's approach to the score is valid and in excellent taste, and that if there are some passages where a little less intensity and a touch of rhetoric might be a good thing, there are others, often played with great rhetorical excess, that Toscanini reveals strong and firm in their inherent musical force—which needs no rhetorical underpinning.

The audience is a little noisy and coughs off the beat. (If they were in time it would not be so bad!) Otherwise the recording is excellent. There are, even in this short time since the release of the disk, two editions: the original (both master numbers terminate in 1S) and the later version, both master numbers of which end in 3S. The 3S set has firmer bass, better balance, and more accurate registration of the dynamic range of the score. Apparently the engineer who cut 1S got frightened of the loud passages and tried to monitor them, and one disagreeable effect of this type was present on the second side of the original edition.

GLUCK

Orfeo: Act II
Barbara Gibson, soprano, Nan Merriman, mezzo-soprano, the Robert Shaw Chorale under Shaw

Recorded during a broadcast November 22 in Carnegie Hall.
LM-1850

Although in the period after 1926 Toscanini prepared only two scores of Gluck, he plays his music with a sense of mastery and stylistic elegance that causes one to wonder why more works of this composer were not included in his programs. We should thank him for this set. *Orfeo* is just about the oldest opera in the repertory (when older ones are produced it is usually a special revival, steeped in the spirit of antiquarianism) and the second act contains its finest music, much of which is unfamiliar and very beautiful indeed. Toscanini and the singers are perfectly in harmony, and lyricism touched with the wonderful *melos* that Toscanini can (on occasion) provide is the predominant mood. Except for a tendency to harshness in some of the louder passages, the recorded sound is extremely good. No libretto is provided: an unusual omission for Victor.

1953

BEETHOVEN

Egmont Overture
   LM-1834 and ALP-1235

BERLIOZ

Roman Carnival Overture
   LM-1834 and ALP-1235

ROSSINI

William Tell: Overture
   LRY-9000 and LRM-7054
   Recorded January 19 in Carnegie Hall.

Two of these are duplications of old and unsatisfactory recordings in terms of modern sound. The third item, the Berlioz, is itself duplicated on the 1954 "Symphony of the Air" disk, *sans* Toscanini. Of the Beethoven and Rossini, one can only say that the performances are spectacularly fine and the recording equal to them, so one feels he really is hearing what the original sounded like. The Berlioz is much more expressive here than in the conductorless version, since Toscanini plays it with subtle changes in pace and slight deviations from strict tempo which are impossible for a conductorless orchestra to duplicate (they have to be metronomic to stay together). Heard by itself, however, the Toscanini-less version is thrilling. (There isn't an orchestra in Europe that could duplicate it *with* a conductor!)

HAYDN

Symphony No. 94 [Surprise]
  Recorded January 26 in Carnegie Hall.
  LM-1789

A warm and radiant performance of a symphony in which the most celebrated of the various surprises is not the most amusing. (The best of Haydn's surprises is in fact the Great Bassoon Joke in the final movement of *No. 102.*) The theme of the minuet is unhappy at the pace Toscanini takes it; otherwise all is relaxed and beautiful.

MOUSSORGSKY (*Orch.* RAVEL)

Pictures at an Exhibition
  Recorded January 26 in Carnegie Hall.
  LM-1838 and ALP-1218

Ravel's orchestration was commissioned by Koussevitzky, but Toscanini plays it with a dramatic flair and growing excitement that I have not heard from any other conductor. The quality of the sound makes this a real showpiece.

DVOŘÁK

Symphony No. 5 [From the New World]
  Recorded February 2 in Carnegie Hall.
  LM-1778 and ALP-1222

The traditional performance of this work contains a good deal of unrefined corn which Toscanini removes. If you like the corn, if you think it is inherent in the thematic material and the way it is developed, then you won't find this a sympathetic reading of the score. Not being a corn lover, I call it definitive.

SCHUBERT

Symphony No. 9 [sometimes called *No. 7*]
  Recorded February 9 in Carnegie Hall.
  LM-1835

One of the greatest Toscanini performances, his reading of the last of the Schubert symphonies is also one of his most controversial, since his departure from German, Viennese (name it what you will) tradition is absolute and uncompromising. Critics invariably are obliged to comment on the clarity and virtuosity of the playing, only to raise their hands in horror at the tempi (particularly that for the *Andante con moto*) and suggest that the record collector buy an "orthodox" version by Herr Bratwurst and the Wiener Philharmoniker. Let us, therefore, look at the score and clear up this matter, if possible. Schubert writes *Andante con moto* at bar one, and nowhere else does he indicate a change of tempo. Now Schubert was no fool, and when he indicates all one tempo for the movement, he means all one tempo. What does Herr Bratwurst do? He begins slowly, *mit* Sentiment, and so dawdles along until roughly bar 160. Here the music begins to build up to an impressive climax that is the point of the whole movement. Now this must be taken at a faster tempo in order to be at all effective and remotely like Schubert's clear intentions, so Herr Bratwurst increases the tempo, gradually, suddenly, or otherwise, until bar 250, when, after the pause, the orchestra returns in the same, flabby rhythm as before. Why does Herr Bratwurst need to read Schubert's score? He has tradition to guide him! In the Toscanini performance the single tempo for the movement is set by the tempo necessary for its climax, and here (and throughout this recording) we hear, as we almost never hear otherwise, a correct statement of the composer's expressed desires. The orchestration is not good, and Toscanini's corrections are splendid. Take this, then, for a magnificent performance, magnificently recorded.

BRAHMS (*Orch.* DVOŘÁK)

Hungarian Dances Nos. 1, 17, 20 and 21
    Recorded February 17 in Carnegie Hall.
    LM-1834 and ALP-1235

Brahms, of course, did not write these wonderful melodies; he collected them and arranged them for piano—a form in which they are almost never heard. Dvořák orchestrated part of them, and his versions are scored with the same mastery he gave his own collection of *Slavonic Dances*. Toscanini plays these with great bravura, but the way he places the accents in *No. 1* ought to have every last gypsy fiddler up in arms. It is wonderful. It is thrilling. But it is completely Latin!

RESPIGHI

The Pines of Rome
    Recorded March 17 in Carnegie Hall.
    LM-1768 and ALP-1101

"It sounds better here than the orchestra in the hall," was the Maestro's comment on this disk, and that is sufficient, I think.

SCHUBERT

Symphony No. 5
Recorded March 30 in Carnegie Hall.
LM-1869

Toscanini's only performance of this score in either the United States or Britain after 1925 was recorded in one of his final N.B.C. broadcasts. For the many persons who learned to admire this work through the medium of the 1938 Beecham recording, this Toscanini reading may well seem another example of the Maestro's rushed, graceless, and over-intense performances of works that call for lightness, delicacy, and, above all, lyricism and warmth. I confess, as young romantic Schubert it seems wanting, revealing more of Toscanini's tendency in a "quick study" to impose upon a work his familiar style rather than attempt to probe its own intrinsic qualities too deeply. This may be doing Toscanini an injustice. However, it seems fair to note that the opening movement is too fast. The melody is obviously in distress, requiring a more relaxed and gentle hand before it can unfold itself or reveal its full beauty. The last movement is probably that most successfully stated in this version. The slow movement is affected by the chill, and the minuet is too high powered. All in all it's fine Toscanini; unsympathetic Schubert.

BEETHOVEN

Missa Solemnis
Lois Marshall, soprano, Nan Merriman, mezzo-soprano, Eugene Conley, tenor, Jerome Hines, bass, with the Robert Shaw Chorale, Robert Shaw conducting
Recorded March 30, 31, and April 2 in Carnegie Hall.
LM-6013 and ALP-1182/83

I have heard an air check recording of Toscanini's first performance of this work during his 1933-34 New York Philharmonic season, with Rethberg, Onegin, Althouse, and Pinza in the solo parts. The pace is slower, the inflection of the melodic line more pronounced, and the power even greater, and it is tragic that we have no recording of that period. (Victor made the work in Boston with Koussevitzky.)

This is a faster performance, as lean and ascetic as an El Greco saint, with lighter-weight soloists and a single-microphone technique which puts them at a disadvantage. It is full of remarkable things, for example the perfect handling of the solo violin (which in less than expert hands can sound disturbingly like a concerto); without doubt, we have here as great a statement of the score as one is likely to hear. But its lack of rhetoric may be a little severe, particularly at the close of the *Agnus Dei* where the final chords seem an inadequate resolution of the crisis that has gone before.

With the exception of those given to the correction of the operas in June of 1954, these three recording sessions were the last Toscanini led with the N.B.C. Symphony.

BRAHMS

Tragic Overture

STRAUSS

Don Quixote
    Frank Miller, 'cello, and Carleton Cooley, viola
    Broadcast November 22 from Carnegie Hall.

These two works began Toscanini's final season of eleven broadcast concerts. Recordings were made, and if approved will appear.

WAGNER

Tannhäuser: Prelude to Act III [original version]
    This work was also recorded, and if approved will be issued.

BERLIOZ

Harold in Italy
    Carleton Cooley, viola
    Broadcast November 29 from Carnegie Hall.
    LM 1951

Scheduled for release in April, 1956, this should provide a welcome addition to the pathetically small group of Toscanini recordings of Berlioz. I heard the actual performance in Carnegie Hall and found it excellent, so I have no doubt but that the disk will be a brilliant achievement.

BEETHOVEN

Coriolan Overture
Symphony No. 3 [Eroica]
    Broadcast December 6 from Carnegie Hall.

Both of these were performances of unbelievable brilliance and power, the *Coriolan* in particular exceeding all my previous experience of the score. New versions of both works are needed, and it is therefore to be hoped that Toscanini will approve these broadcast recordings.

MOUSSORGSKY

Kovanchina: Prelude

FRANCK

Les Éolides

Broadcast December 13 from Carnegie Hall.

Two lovely performances which would be welcome on disks. The Weber-Berlioz *Invitation to the Dance,* which was also played, duplicates the 1951 version and is not likely to be released.

MENDELSSOHN

Symphony No. 5 [On the Protestant Reformation]
Recorded during a broadcast December 13 in Carnegie Hall. LM-1851 and ALP-1267

The first of these 1953-54 recordings to appear, this disk is exceptionally fine and raises hopes that the other items in the series will be equally distinguished. Mendelssohn is here revealed in his best Victorian parlor manner, and I confess I find the stately thumping-out of chorales and bits of chorales and the less than flamingly inspired material that connects them rather pompous and dull. The entrance of the clarinet with the fragment of *"Ein' feste Burg"* at the start of the *Allegro vivace* (right at the close of the chorale itself) reminds me of the appearance of the *Dies Irae* in the final movement of the Berlioz *Fantastic Symphony,* an association that is hard on Mendelssohn's effect. What we have here, then, is a superlative recording of a second-rate work which Toscanini evidently prefers to the finer *Scotch Symphony* (which he played only once in his final twenty-nine seasons). The distance from the Mediterranean to the Highlands and foggy Hebrides must be too far for Toscanini to bridge, but it is unfortunate that such excellent sound and such an inspired performance should be expended upon an inferior work when some of Toscanini's finest readings are available only in defective recordings.

1954

VERDI

A Masked Ball
   Principals: Herva Nelli, soprano. Virginia Haskins, soprano,
   Claramae Turner, mezzo-soprano, Jan Peerce, tenor, Robert
   Merrill, baritone, Nicola Moscona, bass, with the Robert
   Shaw Chorale, Robert Shaw conducting
   Recorded in Carnegie Hall during broadcasts January 17 and
   24 and corrected with additional material recorded June 3
   and 5.
   LM-6112 and ALP-1252/54

All other values apart, this recording would be of considerable
historical importance, since it documents what in all probability
will prove to be the last operatic production under Toscanini's
direction (the Scala *Falstaff* of 1955 having failed to be realized)
and (together with the still unreleased *Aïda* recording of 1949
and 1954) probably the final time Toscanini led his N.B.C.
Symphony or any other orchestra. (The longest portion of the
score which can be identified as coming from the final session is
the duet in the second act, where the emotional effect of both
the actual and the operatic situation carries Peerce and Nelli to
what is possibly their highest dramatic point in the performance.)
   I am at an advantage in evaluating these records, since I
heard the Carnegie Hall broadcasts from which the greater part
of the set was derived and am competent to assure the person
who listens to the recording that what he hears is superior in a
number of ways—particularly balance—to what one heard in the
actual performance. Merrill sounds better on the records than he
did in person, and everywhere the recording reveals detail that
has never been so clearly set forth before. In only one place do
I sense a loss. The effect of the distant, mocking laughter of the
conspirators at the close of the second act, which Toscanini produced so strikingly in the hall (by having them move toward the
back of the stage), is diminished. They are too close to the
microphone.
   Toscanini lined the singers up in front of him with the orchestral ensemble around them and the chorus to the rear of the
stage. The sonic perspective of the microphone unerringly reveals
the arrangement. It is not an effect one would ever encounter in
an opera house, but I am not disturbed by it. The audience is
quiet, and the quality of the sound, if a bit *sec* and direct, is

splendid—far and away the best of the Toscanini operatic recordings, and high fidelity without any refurbishing, compromises, or reservations.

The booklet with the Victor edition is typical of their fine productions of this type and contains an excellent discussion by Henry W. Simon of the problems of the libretto. A rather strange tragedy in which chance plays into the hands of blackest villany and only the nobility of the music provides any basis for catharsis, the opera survives only through the beauty of the score. Included in the booklet is an article by the late Olin Downes in which Toscanini is reported to have said in 1939 that the strain of producing an opera of the dimensions of *Tristan* had become beyond his powers. (He was then a youth of seventy-two.) The fact that five years later he began a series of operatic presentations that eventually comprised seven major works (one of them as long and demanding as *Aïda*) is, I think, ample proof of his continuing energy. *A Masked Ball* is not one of the operas I admire above all others, but I accept this production with the deepest gratitude, for it is a miraculous thing, worthy of a conductor in the prime of life, and without the remotest suggestion that Toscanini was on the verge of complete retirement. All of his powers, including his lyric gifts, are as fully represented as ever before, and I am sure it will be many years before I hear the score played this way again.

Peerce took over his role at short notice, slipping out of another engagement to assist the Maestro when Bjoerling, who had been engaged for the part, was prevented from singing by illness. Peerce was on familiar ground, since the part has been his at the Metropolitan many times, although his voice is now somewhat dry and not so pleasant as Bjoerling's might have been. Peerce sings well, however, and with force and dramatic impact. The remaining members of the cast are about as one would have expected from previous Toscanini operatic productions. No one is bad or musically inaccurate, but several tend to be dull and dramatically ineffective. Nelli, Turner, Haskins, and Merrill all sing in a good musical and dramatic manner, although only momentarily do they suggest commanding presence. The Old Man and Verdi have the field pretty much to themselves.

MENDELSSOHN

Symphony No. 4 [Italian]
  Recorded during a broadcast February 28 in Carnegie Hall.
  LM-1851 and ALP-1267

Here the beautiful sound and controlled intensity of a Toscanini performance is lavished upon a score worthy of it, and this is the version of the *Italian Symphony* that one is likely to regard as standard for many years. It is unfortunate, therefore, to have to add that it is marred in a way that one might expect from lesser conductors, but that is shocking from an intelligent student of form such as Toscanini has shown himself to be. As I have mentioned before, Toscanini invariably plays repeats, even when other conductors fail to do so, when they are necessary for the proper exposition of the work. It is therefore with sorrow that I report that in this symphony, which more than any other needs the execution of the marked repeat for the proper statement of the first movement, Toscanini has followed the practice of his inferiors and disregarded Mendelssohn's instructions.

Mendelssohn writes an exposition of 186 bars which is followed by a quiet and lovely transitional passage of 23 bars' length. Even in this quick tempo, 23 bars is a not inconsiderable amount of music. At the close of the transition one is to repeat 183 bars of the exposition, which then leads into the development section (the fugato). The Toscanini recording, by omitting the repeat, eliminates 206 bars of material which Mendelssohn intended one to hear, 23 of which were "new" and remain unplayed in this recording. The whole first movement is thus foreshortened.

In spite of the violence done to it, the first movement is miraculously well played, and the three that follow are polished and radiant. One cannot possibly do anything other than recommend the set; but Toscanini should be ashamed of himself for that first movement cut.

The Strauss *Don Juan* and Weber *Oberon: Overture*, played on this broadcast, are not likely to appear on records.

BEETHOVEN

Leonore Overture No. 2
Broadcast March 7 from Carnegie Hall.

It is to be hoped that this fine performance will be available on a record. The *Pastoral Symphony*, played on the broadcast, is not likely to be released, since it duplicates an excellent disk.

BOITO

Mefistofele: Prologue
Nicola Moscona, bass, Robert Shaw Chorale, Robert Shaw conducting, and Columbus Boys' Choir, Herbert Huffman, conductor

Recorded during a broadcast March 14 in Carnegie Hall.
LM-1849

I heard this concert from one of the best seats (acoustically) in the hall, and can report that the presence of this recording is one hundred per cent—you *are* there. The musical experience I recall vividly, from that afternoon, was repeated when I played the recording for the first time and was just as strong on later hearings. For those who don't know the music, I can say that it is an important, if less familiar work, full of beautiful and powerful things, and in this inspired performance shaped with the greatest sensitivity. Toscanini's brass, after all the times it has been recorded with a coarsened and distorted sound, is here exactly right, and the off-stage instruments, always a problem in records, are superbly placed in sonic perspective.

VERDI

Te Deum
   The Robert Shaw Chorale, Robert Shaw conducting
   Recorded during a broadcast March 14 in Carnegie Hall.
   LM-1849

It is fitting that this fine work, virtually the last of his beloved Maestro Verdi, should have been played at the last (save two) of Toscanini's New York concerts. The performance is filled with the perfection of dedication and faith in his art, and the recording gives it to us unblemished.

VIVALDI

Concerto in D Minor [presumably *No. 11*]
   Broadcast March 14 from Carnegie Hall.

This opened the program from which the two recordings cited above were drawn. (It was followed by the Verdi.) I hope it, too, can be released in time.

On March 21 Toscanini played the *Barber of Seville: Overture* and the *Pathétique*. The Rossini might be released, if Victor want to replace a tolerable recording, and the *Pathétique,* if it was taped in the dress rehearsal (which I heard) as well as the concert, might be managed, but the public performance showed signs of fatigue, and I doubt if Toscanini would approve it.

His final concert on April 4 is not likely to yield any tapes. An all-Wagner program, four of the five items *(Lohengrin Prelude, Forest Murmurs, Dawn* and *Rhine Journey, Meistersinger*

Prelude) exist in high fidelity recordings. The *Tannhäuser Overture* and *Bacchanale,* which came fourth in the series, were tragically flawed.

To the obvious question, will there be more new Toscanini recordings?, the answer now seems to have become clear. Apparently the Maestro will not conduct, even for the microphone. He has retired, his orchestra is no longer connected with N.B.C., and he no longer feels equal to the strain of creating a performance. This is understandable, and one cannot do more than accept the situation with regret and wish him happiness and good health.

However, the resources of earlier years—the tapes of the seventeen seasons of N.B.C. Symphony broadcasts housed in the basement of the Riverdale villa—are being explored with care for possible material. Some of these things already exist in adequate recordings, as the discussion in the chapter following documents. In these cases, the existing disks will, presumably, stand. Other scores, however, can be added to Toscanini's recorded repertory when the broadcast version, after editing and laboratory refurbishing, can be raised to his standards. It is an open question how much music can be made available as a result of this work. Toscanini and his son, Walter, are, apparently, giving their full time to the project, and now that he cannot expect to remake a faulted recording, the Maestro may allow a few slips to pass for the sake of the greater whole. Everything which might possibly be released as a result of this project is to be found in the first Appendix, where the repertory of the N.B.C. Symphony under the Maestro is indicated in full. Obvious candidates are the scores for which no recording is cited in the lists at the beginning of the chapter following. (See page 195.)

A sample of the type of sound possible in these broadcast recordings is to be found in the Berlioz, Glinka, and von Suppé items in the "pop" concert released as "A Toscanini Omnibus" (LM-6026). It is pleasant, bright, and reasonably well detailed, but offers no more. If a series of otherwise unavailable performances can be obtained from the Riverdale files, they will be welcome. Tragically, however, we cannot expect another *Pictures at an Exhibition.* The limits of Toscanini in high fidelity are set, apparently for all time, by the lisitings given above. Whatever further documentation of his art we may receive, it is certain to be on a lesser scale.

IV

Toscanini's Repertory

1

IF ONE were to study Toscanini's repertory in a thorough fashion from the beginning of his career it would be necessary to have data from his early years as well as a representative sample of his later programs. The materials for such an investigation do not exist. Toscanini himself has always been indifferent to keeping records of this type, and those which his family have assembled cover only his later period and, even then, are incomplete. In making the survey on which this chapter is based I restricted myself to Toscanini's concerts in the United States from the season 1925-26 through the season 1953-54, his concerts in Britain, and his tours with American orchestras in 1930, 1940, and 1950. This gives one the programs of the field of his major activity as a symphonic conductor during the final seasons of his career, and for that period it is unquestionably valid. During that time he may have played some works in his concerts on the Continent that he did not prepare in the United States or Britain, but I do not think the additional data from these programs, if it could be secured, would have a significant effect on my conclusions.

Excluded from this survey, then, is Toscanini as an operatic conductor (although his operatic repertory is suggested in Chapter I), and the early years of his career in the concert hall. I regret this omission, but since full, accurate data could not be secured, I felt such a survey could not be attempted. My sample represents Toscanini in the role in which he was best known during the years in which he was most conspicuous to a world audience, and what follows is, therefore, the account of the music played by this celebrated artist during the climactic period of his career.

During the seasons in question Toscanini prepared *471 works* by my count. (Another count might differ by ten or twenty items, depending on how one considers parts of longer compositions when played separately.) Of this impressive amount of music, *202 works were prepared for performance only once,* that is, they were rehearsed and given in one or more symphonic programs (usually within a single week), or they were heard in a single broadcast. *One hundred and fifty-five compositions were prepared on two to four occasions,* and *a final group of 114 scores were prepared five or more times.* Of these a nucleus of sixteen works received thirty or more performances in twenty-nine seasons, and this group I regard as the core of Toscanini's repertory.

The Toscanini repertory consisted, then, of (1) a small core of works which he played repeatedly, (2) a larger group of scores which he prepared with some regularity at one time or another, and (3) a final group of compositions which were heard infrequently. Beyond this there are the scores prepared only once, which (with a few exceptions) cannot be regarded as repertory in the usual sense of that word. It should be noted, as the list in Appendix I will reveal on examination, that sometimes a work would be played frequently for a short period and then dropped, never to be prepared again. On inquiry, one is forced to conclude that the process by which Toscanini selected the music he was to perform was essentially emotional, based, apparently, on whatever he was interested in, or had particular feeling for, at the moment. These repertory lists should not, therefore, be taken as a basis for deducing Toscanini's relative evaluation of scores. We know, for example, that he admired some of Mahler's music, but he never played any of it because he said he did not have a proper grasp of the style. The choices recorded here are those of an honest man who usually did not play music he did not like or thought he did not understand and who was guided primarily by his feelings at the time he was called upon to select programs. He reflects as well the common tendency for a conductor as he grows older to concentrate on a small group of scores which are thoroughly familiar to him rather than add significant amounts of new music to his repertory.

It will be seen that compositions which require soloists appear far less frequently than those for orchestra alone. Although his heart was always partly in the opera house, Toscanini produced opera in this period only when his conditions of perfection could be realized. Thus in these twenty-nine years he gave opera in Italy and at Salzburg and Bayreuth, but never in Britain, and in the United States only in concert form (and then on only seven occasions). New York had good choruses, however, and thus he performed the Beethoven *Ninth Symphony* eighteen times, led the *Missa Solemnis* nine times, and gave the Verdi *Requiem* on six occasions. All three of these works were heard in London under Toscanini, but on the whole he played them less frequently in Europe than America. The difficulty of finding instrumental soloists who would accept his domination of the work, including their execution of the solo part, or who were of sufficient stature in his eyes to permit them to play as they wished, resulted in infrequent performances of concerti even by composers whose works form the backbone of his repertory.

Toscanini's recordings are not a safe guide to his repertory in every instance. Strauss's *On the Beautiful Blue Danube,* which he performed in public exactly once, exists in two recorded versions, while the *Tannhäuser Overture,* a staple item, was never released on disks. Even some of his greatest recordings, for example the Mozart *Divertimento K. 287,* are based upon performances that were heard only once or (as in this instance) twice. His Debussy, which is not likely to be equaled again for many decades, is represented by only two commercial recordings, and considering the many tries that were required to get them, we probably should be grateful that we have anything at all of that composer from Toscanini's hand.

The three lists that follow give the contents of groups (1) and (2) indicated above. Here is group (1), the works Toscanini performed thirty times or more in the seasons 1925-26/1953-54, with the dates of the definitive recording(s) appended:

Composer	Work	Recording(s)
Beethoven	*Symphony No. 3 [Eroica]*	1949
Beethoven	*Symphony No. 6 [Pastoral]*	1952
Beethoven	*Symphony No. 7*	1936 & 1951
Brahms	*Symphony No. 2*	1952
Brahms	*Variations on a Theme of Haydn*	1936 & 1952
Debussy	*Iberia*	1950
Debussy	*La Mer*	1950
Mendelssohn	*Nocturne* and *Scherzo* from "A Midsummer Night's Dream"	1947

COMPOSER	WORK	RECORDING(S)
Strauss	*Death and Transfiguration*	1952
Wagner	*Die Götterdämmerung: Dawn and Siegfried's Rhine Journey*	1936 & 1949
Wagner	*Die Meistersinger: Prelude*	1946
Wagner	*Parsifal: Good Friday Spell*	1949
Wagner	*Tannhäuser: Overture and Bacchanal* [Paris Version]	No recording approved
Wagner	*Tristan und Isolde: Prelude and Liebestod*	1952

Of sixteen works we have fifteen recordings, all of which are adequate, although it is ironic that the *Eroica*, which Toscanini has played more than any other symphony, should never have been given as fine a recording as was lavished upon many lesser works. The frequency of Wagner in this list should be no surprise, since Toscanini has been an insatiable Wagnerian since he was seventeen, but Strauss's banal tone poem comes as a shock, as does the absence of eighteenth century music. The most recent work on the list is *Iberia* (1908).

Here is the second group which is made up of the works played twenty to twenty-nine times, that is on an average of once a season or slightly less for the period we are considering. Again I append the dates of definitive recordings.

COMPOSER	WORK	RECORDING(S)
Bach-Respighi	*Passacaglia and Fugue in C Minor*	No recording
Beethoven	*Egmont Overture*	1953
Beethoven	*Leonore Overture No. 3*	1945
Beethoven	*Symphony No. 1*	1937 & 1951
Beethoven	*Symphony No. 4*	1939
Beethoven	*Symphony No. 5*	1952
Beethoven	*Symphony No. 9*	1952
Berlioz	*Romeo and Juliet: Queen Mab Scherzo*	1951
Brahms	*Symphony No. 1*	1951
Brahms	*Symphony No. 3*	1952
Brahms	*Symphony No. 4*	1951
Debussy	*Prelude to the Afternoon of a Faun*	V-Disk recording
Haydn	*Symphony No. 101 [Clock]*	1929 & 1947
Moussorgsky-Ravel	*Pictures at an Exhibition*	1953
Ravel	*Daphnis and Chloe: Suite No. 2*	1949
Respighi	*The Pines of Rome*	1953
Respighi	*Roman Festivals*	1949
Rossini	*The Italian Woman in Algiers*	1936
Schubert	*Symphony No. 9*	1953
Smetana	*The Moldau*	1950

Composer	Work	Recording(s)
Wagner	*The Flying Dutchman: Overture*	No recording
Wagner	*Die Götterdämmerung: Siegfried's Death and Funeral Music*	1952
Wagner	*Parsifal: Prelude*	1949
Wagner	*Siegfried: Forest Murmurs*	1950
Wagner	*Siegfried Idyll*	1946
Wagner	*Tannhäuser: Overture* [Dresden]	No recording

Of twenty-six works in this group we have twenty-two recordings, a high standard of success considering the man with whom we have to deal. Only one work of a composer belonging wholly to the eighteenth century appears: the Bach is in a transcription that is modern in feeling and instrumentation. Once more the heart of the list is nineteenth century music. If one does not regard transcriptions as new composition, the most recent scores are those of Respighi, *Pines* (1924) and *Festivals* (1929).

The third list gives the seventy-two scores which Toscanini has prepared and played at least five times; in other words, those which received five to nineteen performances in the seasons under discussion. In some instances this is only one performance more or less than that given a work listed in the previous group or assigned to the lower division (works prepared and played two to four times). The three lists taken together give the contents of the group of 114 works cited earlier as the scores Toscanini could be said to have played at one time or another with some degree of regularity, and I think from these lists we get a reliable impression of the music Toscanini admired, understood and enjoyed. Full details of the remaining works which he performed appear in Appendix I.

Composer	Work	Recorded
Beethoven	*Coriolan Overture*	1945
Beethoven	*Leonore Overture No. 1*	1939
Beethoven	*Leonore Overture No. 2*	1939
Beethoven	*Missa Solemnis*	1953
Beethoven	*Prometheus Overture*	1944
Beethoven	*Prometheus: Adagio and Allegretto*	No recording
Beethoven	*Quartet No. 16, Opus 135: Lento and Vivace*	1938
Beethoven	*Symphony No. 2*	1949
Beethoven	*Symphony No. 8*	1952
Berlioz	*Damnation of Faust: Rákóczy March*	1945

Composer	Work	Recorded
Berlioz	*Harold in Italy*	1953
Berlioz	*Romeo and Juliet: Love Scene*	1946
Brahms	*Liebeslieder Waltzes*	No recording
Brahms	*Tragic Overture*	1937
Busoni	*Rondo Arlecchinesco*	No recording
Cherubini	*Anacreon Overture*	No recording
Debussy	*Nocturnes: Nuages and Fêtes*	No recording
Dukas	*The Sorcerer's Apprentice*	1950
Dvořák	*Symphony No. 5 [New World]*	1953
Elgar	*Enigma Variations*	1951
Franck	*Les Éolides*	No recording
Franck	*Symphony in D Minor*	No recording
Glinka	*Jota Argonesa*	V-Disk recording
Gluck	*Iphigenia in Aulis Overture*	No recording
Haydn	*Symphony No. 99*	No recording
Kabalevsky	*Colas Breugnon Overture*	1946
Martucci	*Notturno*	No recording
Martucci	*Noveletta*	Recorded on V-Disk
Mendelssohn	*Symphony No. 4 [Italian]*	1954
Mendelssohn	*Symphony No. 5 [Reformation]*	1953
Mozart	*The Magic Flute: Overture*	1938
Mozart	*Symphony No. 35 [Haffner]*	1929
Mozart	*Symphony No. 40*	1950
Mozart	*Symphony No. 41 [Jupiter]*	1945/46
Paganini	*Moto Perpetuo*	1939
Pizzetti	*Rondo Veneziano*	No recording
Prokofiev	*Symphony No. 1 [Classical]*	1951
Ravel	*Bolero*	No recording
Respighi	*The Fountains of Rome*	1951
Rossini	*Barber of Seville: Overture*	1945
Rossini	*La Cenerentola: Overture*	1945
Rossini	*La Scala di Setta: Overture*	1938
Rossini	*Semiramide: Overture*	1936
Rossini	*William Tell: Overture*	1953
Roussel	*The Spider's Feast*	No recording
Saint-Saëns	*Danse Macabre*	1950
Scarlatti-Tommasini	*The Good-humored Ladies*	No recording
Schubert	*Symphony No. 8 [Unfinished]*	1950
Schumann	*Manfred Overture*	1947
Schumann	*Symphony No. 2*	No recording
Schumann	*Symphony No. 3 [Rhenish]*	No recording
Sibelius	*En Saga*	No recording
Sibelius	*The Swan of Tuonella*	V-Disk recording
	"Star-Spangled Banner" [J. S. Smith, Toscanini orchestration]	No recording
Strauss	*Don Juan*	1950
Strauss	*Don Quixote*	No recording

Composer	Work	Recorded
Strauss	*Till Eulenspiegel*	1952
Tchaikovsky	*Manfred Symphony*	1949
Tchaikovsky	*Romeo and Juliet*	1946
Tchaikovsky	*Symphony No. 6* [Pathétique]	1947
Tommasini	*The Carnival of Venice*	No recording
Verdi	*Requiem*	1951
Verdi	*Te Deum*	1954
Wagner	*A Faust Overture*	1946
Wagner	*Lohengrin: Prelude to Acts I and III*	1951
Wagner	*Die Walküre: Act I, Scene 3*	No recording
Wagner	*Die Walküre: Act III, Ride of the Valkyries*	1952
Weber	*Euryanthe Overture*	1951
Weber	*Oberon Overture*	1952
Weber-Berlioz	*Invitation to the Dance*	1951

In this group of seventy-two works, forty-nine have been made available in commercial recordings, but since some of these disks are technically obsolete, or of poor quality, I would say only about forty really count as documentation. This leaves us with some great Toscanini performances lost, but considering the number of years in which he took no interest in making records, plus the fact that only about sixty per cent of the music he recorded was drawn from these lists of the most frequently played, the Victor company can be credited with having preserved a remarkably large amount of his repertory. Roughly seventy per cent of the works listed here have been recorded, and some of the scores which have not been put on disks are lightweight compositions which cannot be viewed as a serious loss.

Looking over this final list one is again impressed by the small amount of eighteenth century music, and the almost complete omission of contemporary scores. Toscanini drew his programs from a group of nineteenth century works augmented by a small number of eighteenth century compositions and a sprinkling of scores from the early decades of this century. On the whole, he played the music he knew as a youth and had programmed from the beginning of his career.

Writing of a celebrated virtuoso, B. H. Haggin remarked, ". . . he has gone on recombining into programs of one pattern the limited group of works that he learned fairly early—a group that has included a large quantity of trashy salon and display pieces . . ." and from this he goes on to speak of the way in which Koussevitzky, apart from the preparation of contemporary music, returned constantly to the same group of older scores rather than study different works by the well-known composers, and thus ". . . ends up going over the same limited ground year after year—much the same limited ground as all conductors go over year after year" (*Music in the Nation,* pp. 4-5). This was true of the virtuoso in question, and it was true of Koussevitzky (as a study of his repertory has further convinced me), but both points were also true of Toscanini. The pattern of his programs was unchanging, the core works, listed above, returned season after season. Usually scores which were not already fixed in this familiar sequence were heard only once or twice and then disappeared in favor of other novelties which survived for an equally short time. The last new work to find a place in his standard repertory was the *Colas Breugnon Overture* of Kabalevsky, a piece of rhythmically bouncy junk which evidently appealed to him. Indeed, many works reappeared every season or so almost on the anniversary of their previous hearing, as if the new programs had simply been copied, with slight modification, from the old. There are numerous examples of this in Appendix I.

Actually Toscanini was no innovator. His programs were conservative, meat and potatoes affairs, in which one not only failed to hear any representative selection of the notable orchestral music of the present century, but one did not even hear all the major scores by the composers for whom he had a special affinity. Even forgetting Mozart and Haydn, whom he neglected in a shocking fashion, there are important works of Beethoven, Berlioz, Brahms, Wagner, and Debussy which never were given Toscanini performances, or were played only on rare occasions. He did not look for new music of high quality, and in the established works he stuck to a limited stock of standard items. Finally, it must be noted that much of the unfamiliar music he introduced was trashy, and that some of the works he played repeatedly were of inferior quality and undeserving of the pains and skill which were wasted upon their realization. There were, and are, Toscanini addicts who would listen, with awe, to anything he chose to play. I am not among their number. The best performance of the *Dance of the Hours* that anyone can conceive is still nothing I want to hear more than once or twice, and then not when my mind desires the nourishment of a significant musical statement. Unfortunately, in addition to his masterful achievements in scores of the greatest worth, Toscanini always was inclined to offer a certain number of barrel organ tunes as well.

2

Let us consider Toscanini's repertory, alphabetically by composer, from a strict set of absolute criteria (which may, for that reason, be a little severe) resting upon the idea that a great conductor ought to be capable of offering representative and adequate statements of the music of all the great composers (although, as noted earlier) not necessarily presenting the music of different periods and styles "with equal skill and understanding." Similarly, let us note in anticipation of our discussion, that Toscanini seems to meet this absolute criterion a little less successfully than certain other conductors of our times. Scores which Toscanini played well, Koussevitzky, for example, could frequently play equally well (or nearly so) and he could give performances of Mozart, Haydn, and Bach masterpieces for which Toscanini evidently did not feel sufficient affinity to cause him to give them a single preparation. Therefore, without diminishing our respect for Toscanini's unique achievements, let us avoid the misguided statement that he had a comprehensive repertory of music of all periods. He did not.

One would think that the music of Bach, with its fine, robust themes, its harmonic solidity, and its splendid instrumental coloring would make a direct appeal to Toscanini, but it had no such effect. Of the six *Brandenburg* concerti, two appeared briefly in his programs (one for only two performances), and of the four suites, which one would consider perfectly suited to his gifts, he prepared only one, and that for merely three performances. Except for a program of excerpts in 1934, he ignored the *St. Matthew Passion* and the other great choral works, including the *B Minor Mass*. Indeed, the only music of Bach that he played at all frequently was the *Passacaglia and Fugue in C Minor* in the Respighi transcription. This was heard nine times during the season (1930-31) and was selected to display the excellence of the Philharmonic to his audiences in Milan, Turin, and Rome. Since Toscanini evidently viewed this wretched caricature of Bach as an honest representation of his music, and his performance (which a perceptive friend described as "sounding as if he *wanted* to show how badly Respighi had orchestrated it") was, in fact, his idea of how Bach ought to go, we may conclude that the reason for Toscanini's virtual exclusion of Bach from his programs was, clearly, that he had little feeling for his music and, therefore, no desire to play it. The same applies, in all probability, to J. C. Bach, two of whose sinfonias were heard in one season, and to the other major composers of the period, whom Toscanini ignored. In this he simply reflected Italian attitudes of the nineteenth century, for Bach has never had the fame south of the Alps which he eventually secured in Germany and the United States.

In the performance of the symphonies of Beethoven Toscanini had few rivals, and it is on this music, as much as any, that his reputation is founded. None the less, it is interesting to see the large-scale works of that composer that Toscanini played rarely, or, in some cases, not at all. Of the five concerti for piano and orchestra, the *Fourth* achieved the record of two preparations and four performances, while the *Third* was heard twice, the *First* and *Fifth [Emperor]* only once, and the *Second* not at all! The *Violin Concerto*, with eight performances, triumphs over its natural rivals, the violin concerti of Brahms and Mendelssohn, which scored five and six performances respectively. The reason for this has been suggested: Toscanini was notorious for his inability to get along with soloists because of his unremitting demand that they shape their performance to the pattern he cut, and when he allowed a virtuoso such as Rubinstein to play with the freedom he desired, the result often was a conflict of styles and a poor statement of the work. Thus, of the many celebrated instrumentalists who have appeared in concert regularly while Toscanini was directing the Philharmonic or the N.B.C. Symphony, only Vladimir Horowitz, his son-in-law, could be said to have played with him with any regularity. Even during the Toscanini Beethoven Festival in London in May, 1939, the concerts featuring concerti were, very wisely, assigned to the direction of Sir Adrian Boult.

Actually the staples of Toscanini's Beethoven repertory were seven symphonies and the *Leonore Overture No. 3*, to which the symphonies *No. 2* and *No. 8*, the *Egmont* and *Coriolan* overtures, and the *Missa Solemnis* were added from time to time. Beyond that there is a large group of scores, many of them of considerable interest and value (such as the *Overture for the Consecra-*

tion of the House) which Toscanini prepared infrequently or ignored, and, for all the brilliance of his Beethoven performances, he cannot be credited with having revived any neglected compositions of interest or even playing everything that other conductors were offering, such as the whole of *Prometheus* or the *Incidental Music to Egmont.* His beautiful performances with string orchestra of movements from the late quartets led to the hope that he would prepare an entire work in this manner, but he never did, although he gave the unimportant Verdi quartet in this fashion twice.

Berlioz poses another mystery. Toscanini anticipated the revival of interest in this master by over a decade and gave the complete *Romeo and Juliet* in 1942 when many people were only dimly conscious that the work existed. For all that, Toscanini played only a few works of the composer, and one might assume that he was satisfied to repeat the *Queen Mab Scherzo* again and again rather than prepare a different score. There is no doubt but that his performance of the *Mab* was a miracle, but one cannot help but wish that the *Fantastic Symphony* and the *Requiem* had been heard under his baton, as they never were. Here is a case in which Toscanini seems to have ignored works which were ideally suited to him and which, had he chosen to do so, he could have achieved with the most brilliant success. For example, when he played the *Roman Carnival Overture* (and in twenty-nine years he prepared it only three times!) it was a performance without equal. Happily, it was captured on a modern record.

Next to his reputation as a Beethoven specialist, Toscanini is famed, and justifiably so, as a performer of Brahms. Again he centered his attention on a few scores, the four symphonies and the *Haydn Variations,* and played other major works less frequently than they appear to deserve. Thus the fine *Academic Festival Overture* was prepared only four times, while even the inferior *Serenade No. 1* received more attention. Considering the relative size of Brahms's output of orchestral music compared with Beethoven's, Toscanini gave a hearing to a somewhat more representative sample of the whole. Of the concerti, that for violin and 'cello was prepared four times, always with first desk players from the orchestra and, presumably, entirely in agreement with Toscanini's desires. The *Second Piano Concerto* received four preparations, three of them with Horowitz, the *Violin Con-*

certo was prepared twice with Heifetz, and Horowitz shared in the single preparation of the *First Piano Concerto*. Three times Toscanini applied himself to the dreadful *German Requiem* which, as Bernard Shaw remarked, could be "patiently borne only by the corpse," and his performances of the pretentious *First Symphony* were more numerous than those of the finer *Third*, which he still seems to find baffling in places.

Toscanini has studied the symphonies of Bruckner, and two of them were prepared, each on two occasions. What his version of the *Romantic Symphony* was like I do not know, but the majestic slow movement of the *Seventh*, heard on an old recording from the air, combined the traditional slow, German tempi with the clarity and wonderful singing quality of a Toscanini performance and made me regret that he had not played the work again at a later date or recorded his unique achievement with it. Actually, Bruckner did not figure in Toscanini's repertory after 1935.

Cherubini is unjustly neglected, and the Toscanini revivals of his music were welcome. Unfortunately only the *Anacreon Overture* became a steady repertory item, and only the *D Major Symphony* was recorded.

Toscanini's performances of Debussy include some of his greatest achievements, and here we have special grounds for concern over his tendency to play one or two scores again and again rather than prepare new works. Thus of the set of *Images for Orchestra*, *No. 2, Iberia*, was given thirty-one performances, while *No. 1* and *No. 3* were not played at all. Since they are compositions of equal merit, there seems to be no logic in such complete omission, not to mention the slight to Debussy in presenting only the central portion of a work conceived as three contrasting parts. In the twenty-nine seasons considered here there are fifty-three performances of *La Mer*, placing it second to the *Meistersinger Prelude* as the most frequently played score. In contrast, the *Prelude to the Afternoon of a Faun* was given only twenty-three times, the *Nuages* and *Fêtes* thirteen and fourteen times respectively, and apart from these there are only a few isolated performances of other works.

Toscanini prepared six compositions of Dvořák in the seasons we are examining, but the *New World Symphony* (with six performances) is the only one to be heard with any frequency, and one can fairly say that Toscanini has not offered a comprehensive selection of works by the Bohemian master.

Of the many scores of Elgar, Toscanini played two, but only the *Enigma Variations* can be considered a part of his repertory, and although he played them with obvious affection, they appear to represent the limit of his interest in the composer.

De Falla, a fellow Latin with an idiom one feels Toscanini would find congenial, is represented here by a single score, *El Amor Brujo*, which received four preparations.

César Franck appeared regularly in Toscanini's programs, and although he never played the *Symphonic Variations,* most of the other familiar works were heard, with *Les Éolides* and the *Symphony in D Minor* heading the list. His readings of Franck were unusually sympathetic and beautiful, and it is unfortunate that only a single work of the composer received a Toscanini recording.

The virtual omission of Grieg from Toscanini's repertory comes as no surprise, but the neglect of Handel is rather startling. None the less, except for a single concerto grosso *(No. 12 in B Minor),* which he played four times, and two shorter works which received one preparation each, the master simply was not represented in Toscanini's repertory. There has never been a Toscanini *Messiah* or a Toscanini performance of the *Water Music.*

Of 104 Haydn symphonies, Toscanini performed only eight: three of these were prepared only twice, and the greatest of them all, *No. 104 [London]* only once! Until 1938 he performed the inferior *No. 88* with some degree of regularity, and *No. 98* and *No. 99* were given from time to time, although *No. 101 [Clock],* is the only work of Haydn heard with much frequency. Since Toscanini played Haydn's music with brilliance and evident mastery, one is perplexed why more of his works have not figured in the Maestro's programs.

Certainly Honegger is not a composer one would imagine Toscanini promoting, but *Pacific 231* actually received a dozen performances from him in the period 1928-30.

Mendelssohn is obviously close to Toscanini's heart, and his performances combined affection and understanding with incandescent virtuosity. None the less, Toscanini played few Mendelssohn scores with regularity. The *Incidental Music to "A*

Midsummer Night's Dream" was given, in part, often enough, and the *Italian Symphony* was frequently heard, but the *Scotch Symphony* received but one performance, while fifteen performances were lavished upon the inferior *Reformation Symphony*. There was only a single playing of the *Hebrides Overture*! Again we find three or four works repeated season after season while the rest of the composer's music was ignored.

Much the same could be said of Moussorgsky, whose *Pictures at an Exhibition* was a staple item, and whose other works for orchestra (few as they are) were inadequately represented.

Most surprising is the extent of Toscanini's neglect of Mozart. Of forty-one symphonies Toscanini prepared eight, but of this group three received a single preparation, reducing the Maestro's actual repertory to *five* Mozart symphonies! Of the five, *No. 38 [Prague]* was never played after 1930, and *No. 29* was prepared only twice. In fact Toscanini played *three* Mozart symphonies regularly: *No. 35 [Haffner]*, *No. 40*, and *No. 41 [Jupiter]*, although none of the three was played nearly so regularly as the dreadful *Forest Murmurs* from *Siegfried*. Apart from these works his Mozart repertory consisted of the overture to *The Magic Flute*! A number of works, by no means representative and the longest way from being exhaustive, received one, or possibly two, preparations and one to four performances.

Toscanini has a reputation as a conductor of Mozart that is hardly consistent with the actual number of scores he played or the number of those performances which can be considered truly distinguished. Sir Thomas Beecham, a Mozartian of unique powers, has said that "something like two hundred" of the composer's works, "are of striking originality and beauty" and he has explored his scores and performed them with an enthusiasm Toscanini has never shared.

In the *Divertimento K. 287* Toscanini's fine plastic sense allows him to create an amazing structure of harmonic and rhythmic continuity within a changing dynamic pattern, and since it is a minor work, without strong feeling or the use of the most distinctive features of Mozart's style, we do not sense a lack of penetration into the composer's deeper thoughts. In the *Symphony No. 40* it is a different matter, and the old recording preserves a reading of the score that was too intense, and revealed, in its subjugation of the music to an inappropriate, hard-driving style, that Toscanini simply did not understand the work. In his new recording this has changed, but his recorded version of the *Symphony No. 41 [Jupiter]* is bad, and of his two versions of the *Symphony No. 35 [Haffner]* the earlier, which is relaxed, is good, while the later, overly intense version is unsatisfactory. In the *Symphony No. 39*, in which Mozart's style is revealed in the purest form, Toscanini is clearly at a loss, and the acetates of his single performance, in the years here considered, preserve a reading that is brutally unsympathetic and uncomprehending.

In the 1922-23 season at La Scala and at Salzburg in 1937 Toscanini prepared *The Magic Flute*, which he "always slept through" under German conductors, but which "had life" in his faster tempi. Judging from the recording of the overture, it must have been a fine performance, although able critics who heard it tell me it was disappointing, but I find no evidence of Toscanini ever preparing any other Mozart opera, nor do I believe that he ever gave the Mozart *Requiem*. The root of this neglect is not accidental but a conscious rejection of music which Toscanini finds uncongenial. Italian audiences have generally preferred other operas to *Figaro* or *Don Giovanni*, and Toscanini seems to share to a degree the blind spot of his compatriots. He is too simple, forceful, and direct to grasp the language of Mozart's *Figaro* or the emotional and intellectual content of the *Symphony No. 39*, and in these works conductors who were far from being his peer in Beethoven could put him to shame.

Of the many compositions of Prokofiev, Toscanini has prepared only the *Classical Symphony*, which is stylistically the least characteristic of his works, and his performance changed remarkably from one of the fastest to one of the slowest to be heard.

Ravel is represented in Toscanini's repertory by three works, one of which received only three preparations, while another was dropped, except for one revival, in 1934. The *Second Suite* from *Daphnis and Chloe*, which one heard reasonably often, is perhaps the best of the composer's scores, but it would have been interesting to hear what Toscanini could have done with certain of the other works.

Respighi appeared in Toscanini's concerts with the three Roman tone poems and as a transcriber of Bach. His other works,

among them the *Suite No. 1* of *Ancient Airs and Dances,* which
Toscanini played in his American tour with the La Scala Orchestra, had been set aside.

Rimsky-Korsakov was represented by one preparation of a
single minor work; Borodin had fared little better with two scores
played.

Rossini was a staple in Toscanini's programs, and invariably
the performances were brilliant and enjoyable. For some reason
the overture to *La Gazza Ladra* was played less than it deserved.
Every conductor plays a certain amount of light music, and
Toscanini played Rossini. We can be grateful to him for unique
performances of these scores.

Although Roussel's *Symphony No. 4* was prepared once with
the Philharmonic, his appearance in Toscanini's programs was
otherwise limited to *The Spider's Feast,* which, however, became
a reasonably frequent item.

Of the symphonies of Schubert, Toscanini played four, although of these only the *Unfinished* and the *Ninth* were heard
often enough to count as repertory items. (The *Fifth* actually
received only a single preparation and performance.) There was
a performance of the *Gastein Symphony* as reconstructed by
Joachim from the *Grand Duo,* and that is the lot. Even the
Rosamunde incidental music was ignored. What, then, can we
say? That the Maestro made his reading of the *Ninth* a miracle
of modern orchestra performance and revealed the powerful
structure of the *Unfinished* as no other conductor, but apart from
this he neglected Schubert.

Schumann fared little better. The *Spring Symphony,* the opening pages of which seem perfectly suited to Toscanini's unique
powers, never was given a Toscanini performance. The *Fourth,*
which one feels would suit him perfectly, he prepared once!
There were scattered preparations of the two middle symphonies
and the *Manfred Overture.* The *Concerto for 'Cello* received four
performances; the fine *Piano Concerto* he never played.

After this it comes as a shock to find that the Shostakovich
First was prepared and given in four concerts during 1931 and
repeated in three later seasons. The *Seventh* had its celebrated
American première under Toscanini in 1942, but was never
played again after that year, nor has any other music by Shostakovich figured in Toscanini's repertory, although he was not

unaware of contemporary Russian composers and even felt adventurous enough to give Mosoloff's *Iron Foundry* in 1933.

Normally one does not think of Toscanini as a conductor of Sibelius, and, indeed, only two of the seven symphonies (the *Second* and *Fourth*) ever were heard on his programs. Two of the tone poems evidently appeal to him, the lovely *Swan of Tuonella* and the inferior *En Saga*, and there have been occasional appearances of other works, although Toscanini seems to have had no interest in offering the composer's major compositions comprehensively, and left the two finest symphonies (*Five* and *Seven*) unplayed.

Smetana, another nationalist, was represented in Toscanini's programs by two scores only, neither of which was given in anything resembling a Bohemian style under his baton.

Stravinsky, one of the few composers of our day whose high place in the history of music seems assured, appears to have no appeal to Toscanini, who prepared *Fireworks* once and offered the opening and closing tableaux of *Petrouchka* (in other words, the folk-song material) in three seasons. Of the rest of Stravinsky's music Toscanini has given us nothing.

Of the better known works of Richard Strauss, Toscanini lavished the most performances on one of the worst, *Death and Transfiguration,* and gave the fewest preparations to one of the best, *Don Quixote. Don Juan* and *Till Eulenspiegel* were heard regularly, there were a few readings of *Ein Heldenleben* (all but one with the Philharmonic), and two preparations of the *Dance of the Seven Veils.* Once more a small group of works makes up the whole of his repertory, leaving major scores unperformed. *Der Rosenkavalier,* equal in its enchantment to *Figaro* and *Don Giovanni,* shared with them his frigid rejection.

Toscanini's offerings of Tchaikovsky amounted, essentially, to four works, all of which (for obvious reasons) he recorded, and one memorable but strictly occasional performance, which may be the most widely distributed of all his recordings. The latter item is the *B-flat Minor Piano Concerto (No. 1)* which he prepared with Horowitz in 1941, recorded shortly after the initial broadcast, and repeated, apparently out of sentiment, two seasons later. That his attitude was not wholly commercial is shown by the fact that he did not prepare the symphonies *No. 4* and *No. 5,* broadcast them once, make recordings, and drop them. In fact,

Toscanini has, to my knowledge, only played one Tchaikovsky symphony anywhere at any time, and that is the *Pathétique,* which he neglected with the Philharmonic but revived with the N.B.C. and played frequently and well during his seventeen seasons with that orchestra. The *Manfred Symphony,* a fine example of large-scale musical thought in the best Tchaikovsky manner, blessed with some excellent thematic material, and brilliantly scored, Toscanini revived from the general neglect into which it had fallen and played with both the Philharmonic and with the N.B.C. In this case he can be praised for giving us a splendid work which counts as unfamiliar. The *Romeo and Juliet Overture* and *Nutcracker Suite* were also staple items.

Toscanini prepared two scores of Ralph Vaughan Williams, giving a single broadcast performance of the *London Symphony* and playing the *Fantasia on a Theme of Thomas Tallis* in both New York and Britain.

Verdi, whom he admired, perhaps more than any other composer, actually played a small part in his symphonic programs. The *Requiem* and *Te Deum* were frequently heard in his magnificently impassioned readings, but there was little effort to find concert excerpts from the operas, and with the exception of the two scores cited, three preparations are the maximum attention given to any of the overtures, preludes, or scenes which he extracted for broadcast purposes. His countryman Vivaldi, although stylistically close to his heart, was perhaps a bit too refined, too reserved in his classicism to appeal to a fundamentally warm-blooded animal such as Toscanini. A single concerto grosso (*D Minor*) received four preparations, and the five other works which he played were heard only once or twice.

Wagner, with twenty-eight works performed, comes second to Beethoven in Toscanini's repertory. The magic of Klingsor of Bayreuth has always had the most potent effect upon him, and all but two or three of these works received, not scattered, but frequent performances. One would expect that a conductor with a sense of form as fine as Toscanini's would be sensitive to the problems involved in making cuttings from larger works, but surprisingly enough, Toscanini played a number of the worst Wagner extracts.

Taking the items in order, the *Faust Overture* is a concert work, and the overture to the *Flying Dutchman* stands well by itself. *Dawn* and *Siegfried's Rhine Journey* and *Siegfried's Death and Funeral Music* from *Die Götterdämmerung* Toscanini performed in his own fine concert versions (rather than the inferior, and more common, Humperdinck settings), and the *Immolation Scene* has an acceptable beginning and closes with the final pages of the opera itself. The preludes to *Lohengrin* and *Meistersinger* are frequently played by themselves, so one cannot really object, although the *Meistersinger Prelude* certainly ends more powerfully when it leads into the first act chorale, and I am unhappy about the flat taste one gets from the third act prelude when the theme is simply carried to a resolving chord that Wagner, wisely, does not sound in the opera. The *Parsifal Prelude* can stand alone. I am not so sure about the preludes to acts two and three of that opera, and the *Klingsor's Magic Garden* episode certainly lacks a good beginning and end. As for the *Good Friday Spell,* I am more or less resigned to being alone in my preference for it with vocal parts and within the context of the drama. The *Rienzi Overture* can stand alone; I want nothing to do with it, either.

It is here that difficulties commence. The *Forest Murmurs* starts nowhere, goes nowhere, and has the next thing to no form at all, since the whole piece is scrappy cuttings (there is no such interlude in the opera, where the raw materials of this "excerpt" are separated by other passages) which are brought to a climax by the most patently trivial means. None the less, Toscanini has played this patchwork twenty-eight times and carried it to twelve cities on tour. I am overcome. The *Siegfried Idyll,* in contrast, is a real piece of music, and so is the overture to *Tannhäuser.* The prelude to *Tristan* exists in a concert arrangement by Wagner which almost no one ever plays;* instead one hears the prelude with its operatic ending which trails off, *pp,* in the general direction of nowhere, but invariably is found to lead to the opening bars of the final scene of the opera, invariably played *p* or *mf* rather than *pp* as marked, and moving by way of a C minor splice to a system of key relations which makes no sense in terms of the A major/minor tonality of the prelude. Further, in most cases Isolde is silent, and we hear the piece without either a soprano or an instrumental double sounding the notes allotted

---

* Toscanini *may* have played it with the Philharmonic; the evidence is unclear.

to the lady. Toscanini has accepted this situation and done nothing about it, offering the *Prelude* and *Love-Death* (if we are going to keep *Liebestod* we might just as well make no bones about it) as the standardized concert item that it is. The fine prelude to the third act of the opera, invariably lacking the effect in the opera house that, in a "full" arrangement (with the English horn solo), it can produce in the concert hall, he never played. Toscanini prepared the love duet from the second act on one occasion, although I don't know how he ended it, and on five occasions he prepared the final scene of the first act of *Die Walküre*, which can stand alone. This is more than can be said for the *Ride of the Valkyries*, which is absolute hash in the concert version without vocal parts; but apparently this is not enough to overcome his liking for it.

Four of the overtures to Weber's works for the musical stage have been heard, although one of them was given in only a single season. Apart from these, there have been Toscanini performances of the *Invitation to the Dance* in the Berlioz orchestration.

I wish now to consider three topics: Toscanini's performances of Italian music, American music, and contemporary music.

It seems clear that if there is a school of living composers whom Toscanini has elected to champion, it is the modern Italian school. This is partly national pride and partly attributable to the fact that these composers use an idiom for which he has both feeling and understanding. Respighi is the most important member of the group, certainly his name comes to mind first as we think of Toscanini's repertory, but Busoni, Castelnuovo-Tedesco, Mancinelli, Martucci, Pizzetti, De Sabata, Sinigaglia, and Tommasini, along with others of the same school, have appeared in his programs from time to time. The question of who is a great composer, and who is worth playing, is, of course, a difficult one, particularly when feelings of national culture are involved. Sibelius is a great composer in parts of Northern Europe and the United States, but has slight reputation in Italy. Bernard Zweers is a great composer in his native Amsterdam, but not in New York. It must be said in all fairness that Toscanini was the only conductor to give the American audience a chance to hear the modern Italian school; but, at the same time, a great many

Americans did not especially wish to make their acquaintance. Moreover, some of these works which Toscanini offered regularly with the Philharmonic and N.B.C. were not popular, simply because they were felt to be of poor quality, making use of banal thematic material, and developing it along lines which only emphasized its conventionality and inherent vulgarity.

Thus when Lawrence Gilman wrote in 1931: "There is an impression hereabouts that Mr. Toscanini as conductor of the Philharmonic-Symphony Society has performed this season an excessive amount of inferior music," he may have been thinking of at least some of these scores. Certainly Deems Taylor, writing in September, 1930, not merely as a critic but as an American composer of some status, had one specific item in mind, and with it a complaint that raises the second issue. Commenting on the recently completed European tour of the Philharmonic, he notes ruefully, ". . . about the only kind of music that [the orchestra] did not play in Europe was American music. I think this was a mistake. In the first place, it would have been tactful toward us poor Americans, whose orchestra, after all, it is. In the second place, it would have been only just. If the programs had comprised nothing but undisputed masterpieces, the exclusion of Americans would have been all too understandable. But they did not. To say that MacDowell, Chadwick, Foote, and Carpenter, for instance, have written music as good as such gaudy rubbish as Tommasini's *Carnival of Venice* variations—which Mr. Toscanini conducted [in Milan and Rome] *con amore*—is to pay them no compliment." One can go on from this and note that Toscanini made a graceful gesture by playing Kodály in Hungary, offering Elgar in Britain, and so on, and that in this light the omission of even the briefest American work from the repertory of the tour seems an undeserved disparagement of American musical creativity.

Koussevitzky felt that he had an obligation to encourage the composers of his adopted country (even when they weren't writing masterpieces), by giving a hearing to their work, and in so doing he stimulated the creative powers of a number of able persons and enriched American music with a group of notable scores. Toscanini did nothing analogous. An American composer waiting for him to play his work would have abandoned his musical ambitions for steady employment early in Toscanini's

Philharmonic period when it became clear that no interest or support could be expected from the Maestro.

During his seasons with the Philharmonic, Toscanini played next to no American music, and the four composers named by Taylor, in fact, never appeared on any of his programs at any time. Ernest Schelling's *Impressions from an Artist's Life* was given, with the composer at the piano, during two seasons, the first of them as early as 1928-29. Chasin's *Flirtation in a Chinese Garden* and *Parade* were prepared in 1931. The *Symphony No. 2* of Bernard Wagenaar was played the following year, and the *Second Symphony* of Howard Hanson in 1933. Unless I am mistaken, these five works given a total of eighteen performances constitute Toscanini's cultivation of American music in eleven seasons with the Philharmonic. There is no doubt but that this is a blotted page in his copybook. Although in charge of one of the finest orchestras in the United States, he ignored the American composer as if he did not exist, in spite of the fact that he found time to prepare and play quantities of second-, third-, and fourth-rate European music, which I list in detail in Appendix I. One may read it and form his own judgment.

With the N.B.C. the situation changed somewhat, although no American piece ever became a staple of Toscanini's repertory, and the maximum number of performances which any American score got from Toscanini was *five*. The work so honored was nothing less than Barber's fine *Adagio for Strings*, of which Toscanini gave the world première in 1938. During his South American tour with the N.B.C. in 1940, Toscanini actually played this work in two cities, which was a refreshing change from the decade before. The *Essay for Orchestra*, which had its première in the same program as the *Adagio*, only got one further performance. Copeland has been represented in Toscanini's broadcasts by a single performance of *El Salon Mexico*, one of his weakest scores. The *Choric Dance No. 2* of Paul Creston struck Toscanini's fancy momentarily in the 1942-43 season and he prepared it with three orchestras! Unfortunately illness prevented him from giving it more than four times. Three seasons later he gave a performance to that composer's *Frontiers*. Gershwin's music draws upon a style and a manner that Toscanini cannot have found congenial. He played three Gershwin scores. The *Piano Concerto in F* and the *Rhapsody in Blue* he chose to drop after a single hearing; *An*

American in Paris was prepared a second time and recorded. Henry Gilbert's *Comedy-Overture on Negro Themes* was played twice, and the *Symphony 5½* of his producer Don Gillis once. One performance sufficed for Morton Gould's *Lincoln Legend,* Griffes' *The White Peacock,* the *Third Symphony* of Roy Harris, and G. T. Strong's *The Night,* all of them better works than Grofé's trashy *Grand Canyon Suite* which was played twice and recorded. Two performances were the lot of Kent Kennan's *Night Soliloquy,* and Loeffler's *Memories of My Childhood.* One performance was given to Elie Siegmeister's *Western Suite.* Apart from these, Toscanini played three Sousa marches and "The Star-Spangled Banner."

Twenty-six scores (not including the national anthem) is a rather poor record for twenty-nine seasons, especially if one realizes the total number of performances of all American music are fewer than those of the pedestrian *Tannhäuser Overture* in its two forms.

Most of the important works by American composers are modern in style as well as time and may well come under Toscanini's general lack of interest in contemporary music. His taste seems to have been formed early in his life, possibly in his years at the conservatory, and it has not developed as the times have changed. In his heart, he is devoted to Wagner, to Verdi, to the nineteenth century romantics and post-romantics, and to their impressionist successors. As we have seen above, in the core of his repertory, the newest score is by Debussy, and it was with an all-Wagner program such as few other conductors continue to give with regularity (they were common in the 'nineties) that he said farewell to his New York audience in 1954. Toscanini's understanding best encompassed what was, more or less, contemporary with his younger self, and the length of his career has made evident the changes in style since he began his musical life.

With his honesty and his consistent practice of not playing works which he felt he did not understand, he studied many scores which he never prepared, for example works by Mahler, as mentioned before. This seems wise. (I cannot imagine that a Toscanini performance of a Mahler symphony would have been good.) For much the same reasons he chose, apparently, to ignore Bartók and Hindemith, Stravinsky (except for two items), Prokofiev (apart from the *Classical Symphony*), Berg, and others.

Toscanini wanted a melodic line, relatively consonant harmony, and simple rhythmic vitality. Respighi suited him, and Stravinsky repelled him; but, unfortunately, Stravinsky remained, for all that, a great composer, and Respighi, however well played, remained commonplace.

Those who suggest that Toscanini's avoidance of modern scores was purely commercial, based upon his respect for the box office, do him an injustice. He never had any trouble filling a hall, even when he played modern Italian works that had less of a following than even the twelve-tone school. When he turned to broadcast concerts the tickets were not sold and he was free to play whatever he wished. As I have mentioned before, if Toscanini had wanted to exploit popular symphonic works, he could have performed a number of scores that he ignored.

There is a second group which suggests that we should not take exception to Toscanini's choice of scores, since his performances were of such unique quality that they were worth one's attention, whatever the music. I do not subscribe to that. Certainly it has been of interest to see what he could do with rather crude works such as the *Zampa Overture* but there is a limit to my interest in such music, however miraculously played.

Similarly, there is a limit to anyone's interest in a steady diet of the few works which Toscanini repeated, season after season. The truth is, the Toscanini repertory was superficially large and functionally small, restricted in time to about a century, in style to the varieties of romanticism, in harmony to the tonic-dominant tradition, and in the choice of programs to the familiar and well worn rather than the new or the unusual. Thus, although Toscanini gave us performances which none of his contemporaries could duplicate, he did not always play the music which the most critical and appreciative element of his public desired to hear, even when (as in the case of Berlioz) he could have played it with supreme mastery. Habit enslaved him.

APPENDIX ONE: *The Toscanini Repertory*

This list includes every work performed by Maestro Toscanini during his career as a symphonic conductor in the United States from the season 1925-26 through his final season, 1953-54. It includes all works performed in Britain, and all works performed outside the United States with American orchestras, that is on tour with the Philharmonic-Symphony Orchestra of New York in 1930 and with the N.B.C. Symphony in 1940.

The figure in brackets after the title of the work gives the total number of performances.

The names of assisting artists are given in brackets.

Unless another city is named, the concert took place in greater New York.

Unless another orchestra is named, if the date is set in Roman type, the concert was played by the Philharmonic-Symphony Orchestra of New York. If the date is set in *italic* type, the concert was played by the N.B.C. Symphony Orchestra of New York. On the whole, Sunday afternoon concerts of the Philharmonic-Symphony Orchestra of New York and all concerts of the N.B.C. Symphony were broadcast. The exceptions were usually special concerts, or concerts while on tour. All broadcast concerts of the N.B.C. Symphony were recorded by network engineers.

The sign § is used to indicate divisions between *seasons*. Thus an entry is to be read as follows: *Jn. 22–40,* reads June 22, 1940 [with the N.B.C. Symphony]; Jan. 30/31/Feb. 2/22–36, reads January 30, 31 and February 2 and 22, 1936 [with the Philharmonic-Symphony Orchestra of New York].

AQUIRRE
Two Dances [1]
  Jn. 22–40 [Buenos Aires]

ATTERKERG
Symphony No. 6 [1]
  Nov. 21–43

BACH
Brandenburg Concerto No. 2 [6]
  Jan. 30/31/Feb. 2/22–36 § May 23–38 [BBC Sym, London] § *Oct. 29–38*

Brandenburg Concerto No. 6 [2]
  Ap. 5/7–33
Cantata No. 209: "Non sa che sia dolore" [2]
  [Rethberg] Ap. 26/27–34
Christmas Oratorio: Pastoral Prelude to Part II [4]
  Mar. 29/30/31/Ap. 1–28
Concerto for Violin in A Minor [5]
  [Busch] Nov. 26/27/Dec. 14 [Philadelphia]/15 [Washington]/ 16 [Baltimore]–31

CONCERTO FOR TWO VIOLINS IN D
   MINOR [2]
[Piastro, Bolognini] Ap. 26/27–34
MASS IN B MINOR: KYRIE [2]
[Schola Cantorum] Ap. 26/27–34
THE PASSION ACCORDING TO ST.
   MATTHEW: FINAL CHORUS [3]
[Schola Cantorum] Ap. 26/27–34
§ [chorus under Wilhousky] *Ap.
1–45*
SUITE NO. 3 IN D [3]
Ap. 26/27–34 § *Nov. 22–47*
. . . 2ND MOVEMENT ["AIR ON THE
   G STRING"] only [1]
Ap. 4–42

BACH (orch. Albert)
PRELUDE, CHORALE, AND FUGUE [2]
Jan. 17/Feb. 1–26

BACH (orch. Respighi)
THREE CHORALE PRELUDES: [5]
1) NUN KOMM' DER HEIDEN
   HEILAND
2) MEINE SEELE ERHEBT DEN
   HERREN
3) WACHET AUF, RUFT UNS DIE
   STIMME
Nov. 13/14/16/Dec. 5 [Philadel-
phia Orch., Philadelphia]/6 [ibid.]
–30
PASSACAGLIA AND FUGUE IN C MINOR
   [27]
Ap. 16/17/May 6 [Zurich]/8
[Milan]/10 [Turin]/13 [Rome]/Jn.
4 [London]–30 § Dec. 11/12/14/
15 [Philadelphia]/16 [Washing-
ton]/17 [Baltimore]/27–30 and
Ap. 16/17–31 § Nov. 16/18/19–32
§ Feb. 3/4–34/Jn. 14–37 [BBC
Sym, London] § *Oct. 14–39* § Jan.
9 [Philadelphia Orch., Philadel-
phia]/10 [ibid.]/13 [Philadelphia
Orch., Washington]–42 § *Nov. 22–
47*
PRELUDE AND FUGUE IN D MAJOR [4]
Jan. 24/25/26/27–35

BACH (orch. Schoenberg)
PRELUDE AND FUGUE IN E-FLAT
   MAJOR [6]

Oct. 6/7/8/9/24 [Philadelphia]/
25 [Washington]–32

BACH (orch. WOOD)
TOCCATA AND FUGUE IN D MINOR [4]
Feb. 20/21/22/23–36

BACH, J. C.
SINFONIA IN E-FLAT MAJOR, OP. 18,
   No. 1 [4]
Dec. 3/4/5/6–31
SINFONIA IN D MAJOR, OP. 18, No.
   3 [3]
Ap. 16/17/19–31

BARBER
ADAGIO FOR STRINGS [from QUARTET,
   OP. 11] [5]
Nov. 5–38 § *May 14* [Washing-
ton]/*Jn. 27* [Buenos Aires]/*Jly. 3*
[Montevideo]–40 § *Dec. 13–41*
ESSAY FOR ORCHESTRA [2]
Nov. 5–38/Jan. 24–42

BAZZINI
OVERTURE TO ALFIERI'S "SAUL" [1]
Jan. 14–39

BEETHOVEN
CONCERTO FOR PIANO No. 1 [1]
[Dorfman] *Nov. 12–44*
CONCERTO FOR PIANO No. 3 [2]
[Rubinstein] *Oct. 29–44* § [Hess]
Nov. 24–46
CONCERTO FOR PIANO No. 4 [4]
[Serkin] Feb. 20/21/23–36 § [Ser-
kin] *Nov. 26–44*
CONCERTO FOR PIANO No. 5 [1]
[Horowitz] Ap. 23–33
CONCERTO FOR VIOLIN [8]
[Busch] Nov. 26/27/Dec. 14
[Philadelphia]/15 [Washington]/
16 [Baltimore]–31 § [Menuhin]
Jan. 18/19–34 § [Heifetz] Ap. 29–
36
TRIPLE CONCERTO FOR PIANO,
   VIOLIN, AND 'CELLO [2]
[Carreras, Piastro, Wallenstein]
Ap. 16–33 § [Dorfman, Piastro,
Schuster] May 1–42
CORIOLANUS OVERTURE [16]
Nov. 7/8/10–29 § Ap. 16–33 § Jan.
30/31/Feb. 1–36 § May 26–37

[BBC Sym, London] § *Nov. 12–38* and *May 8–39* [BBC Sym, London] § *Nov. 11–39* § *Ap. 26–42* § *Nov. 26–44* § *Nov. 24–46* § *Feb. 19–49* § *Dec. 6–53*
EGMONT OVERTURE [20]
Mar. 26/Ap. 15–33 § Jan. 11/12–34 § Mar. 24–35 [Broadcast, "General Motors Symphony Orchestra"] § May 3–39 [BBC Sym, London] § *Nov. 18–39* and *May 14* [Washington]/*Jly. 4* [Montevideo]/*8* [São Paulo]/*9* [Rio de Janeiro]*–40* § Ap. 24–42 § *Nov. 12–44* § *Sept. 25–45* § *Ap. 25* [New Orleans]/*May 3* [Pasadena]/*13* [Denver]/*21* [Cleveland]/*25* [Washington]*–50* § *Jan. 17–53*
FANTASIA FOR PIANO, CHORUS, AND ORCHESTRA IN C, OP. 80 [1]
[Dorfman, Westminster Choir—Williamson] *Dec. 2–39*
FIDELIO [1]
[Bampton, Steber, Peerce, Janssen, Moscona, etc., chorus under Wilhousky] *Dec. 10 and 17–44*
. . . OVERTURE [2]
Oct. 28–39 § May 1–42
. . . "KOMM HOFFNUNG" [aria] [1]
[Lehmann] Feb. 11–34 [Broadcast, "General Motors Symphony Orchestra"]
KING STEPHEN OVERTURE [1]
Ap 23–33
LEONORE OVERTURE No. 1 [7]
Jan. 25/26/Feb. 25–34 § Ap. 29–36 § May 7–39 [BBC Sym, London] § *Nov. 25–39* § *Oct. 29–44*
LEONORE OVERTURE No. 2 [7]
Feb. 25–34 § *Nov. 25–39* § *Feb. 21–40* § *Nov. 19–44* § *Sept. 25–45* § *Jan. 12–52* § *Mar. 7–54*
LEONORE OVERTURE No. 3 [23]
Jan. 24–26 § Mar. 27/28/31–29 § Nov. 20/22/23/24–29 and May 16 [Munich]/18 [Vienna]/27 [Berlin]/Jn. 1 [London]–30 § Nov. 24/25–32 § Ap. 23–33 § Feb. 25–34 § Ap. 26–36 § May 3–39 [BBC Sym, London] § *Nov. 4–39* and *Jn. 23* [Buenos Aires]*–40* § *Dec. 17–44* [in FIDELIO] § *Mar. 6–48* § *Feb. 3–51*

MISSA SOLEMNIS [11] [This is the total for Toscanini's entire career.]
[Rethberg, Onegin, Althouse, Pinza, Schola Cantorum] Mar. 8/9/11–34 § [Rethberg, Telva, Martinelli, Pinza, Schola Cantorum] Ap. 25/26/28–35 § [Milanov, Thorborg, von Pataky, Moscona, BBC Choral Society—Woodgate] May 26/28–39 [BBC Sym, London] § [Milanov, Castagna, Bjoerling, Kipnis, Westminster Choir—Williamson] *Dec. 28–40* § [Kirk, Castagna, Johnson, Kipnis, Westminster Choir—Williamson] Ap. 22–42 § [Marshall, Merriman, Conley, Hines, Robert Shaw Chorale—Shaw] *Mar. 28–53*
OVERTURE FOR THE CONSECRATION OF THE HOUSE [3]
Mar. 16–47 § *Oct. 25–47* § *Mar. 19–49*
PROMETHEUS OVERTURE [8]
Jan. 18/19/Feb. 11 [Broadcast, "General Motors Symphony Orchestra"]–34 § May 12–39 [BBC Sym, London] § Ap. 29–42 § *Mar. 5–44* § *Ap. 20–49* § *Feb. 3–51*
PROMETHEUS: ADAGIO [13]
Nov. 14/15/17–29 § Jan. 25/26/Feb. 3/4–34
. . . WITH THE ANDANTE [1]
May 22–39 [BBC Sym, London]
. . . WITH THE ALLEGRETTO [5]
Nov. 25–39 § *Mar. 5–44* § *Oct. 29–44* § *Mar. 16–47* § *Mar. 19–49*
QUARTET, OP. 59, No. 3: FUGUE [1]
Nov. 26–44
QUARTET, OP. 130: CAVATINA [1]
Nov. 26–44
QUARTET, OP. 135: LENTO AND VIVACE [7]
Jan. 11/12–34 § *Jan. 1–38* § May 22–39 (order reversed) [BBC Sym, London] § *Nov. 25–39* § *Nov. 12–44* § *Oct. 25–47*
SEPTET, OP. 20 [4]
Nov. 18–39 § *Dec. 6–41* § *Dec. 3–44* § *Nov. 24–51*
SYMPHONY No. 1 [29]
Jan. 21/22/Feb. 6–26 § Feb. 5/6–27 § Mar. 31–28 § Nov. 13/14/16/

Dec. 5 [Philadelphia Orch., Philadelphia]/6 [ibid.]–30 § Mar. 26–33 § Jan. 11/12–34 § Feb. 20/21/22/23–36 § Nov. 3–37 [BBC Sym, London] § May 3–39 [BBC Sym, London] § Oct. 28–39 § Ap. 24–42 § *Mar. 24/Ap. 11–43* § Oct. 22–44 § *Sept. 21/26* [Ridgefield, Conn.]–*47* § *Dec. 22–51* § *Mar. 29–52*

Symphony No. 2 [17]
Feb. 28/Mar. 1/3/16/24/31–29 § Mar. 13/14/15/–30 § Mar. 26–33 § Jan. 11/12–34 § May 3–39 [BBC Sym, London] § *Nov. 4–39* § Ap. 24–42 § *Dec. 3–44* § *Nov. 5–49*

Symphony No. 3 [Eroica] [52]
Jan. 28/29/Feb. 1–26 § Feb. 1/2 [Philadelphia]–27 § Mar. 7/9/May 3 [Paris]/13 [Rome]/19 [Vienna]/25 [Leipzig]/28 [Berlin]/30 [Brussels]/Jn. 4 [London]–30 § Dec. 15 [Philadelphia]/21/27–30 § Nov. 27–32 and Mar. 6 [Philadelphia]/7 [Washington]/8 [Baltimore]/Ap. 2–33 § Jan. 18/19/Ap. 1/28–34 § Mar. 30–35 § Jn. 4–37 [BBC Sym, London] § *Dec. 3/27* [Baltimore]–*38* and *Jan. 31* [Chicago]/*Feb. 1* [Pittsburgh]/7 [Providence]/May 8 [BBC Sym, London]–*39* § *Oct. 28–39* and *Jn. 13* [Rio de Janeiro]/*20* [Buenos Aires]–*40* § Ap. 26–42 § *Nov. 5–44* § *Sept. 1–45* § *Feb. 19/Ap. 20–49* § *Nov. 26–49* and *Ap. 14–17* [Baltimore]/*27* [Houston]/*May 5* [Pasadena]/*7* [San Francisco]/*10* [Seattle]/*15* [St. Louis]/*19* [Detroit]–*50* § *Dec. 6–53*

Symphony No. 4 [23]
Feb. 4/5/14/16/17–28 § Ap. 1/2/4/5–31 § Ap. 2/15–33 § Jan. 25/26–34 § Jan. 30/31/Feb. 1/22/26 [Hartford]–36 § May 19–38 [BBC Sym, London] § May 8–39 [BBC Sym, London] § *Nov. 4–39* § Ap. 26–42 § *Feb. 3–51*

Symphony No. 5 [21]
Jan. 17–26 § Feb. 1/2 [Philadelphia]–27 § Mar. 4/6/7–31 § Nov. 6–32 and Ap. 9–33 § Jan. 25/26/Mar. 15 [Hartford]–34 § May 23–

38 [BBC Sym, London] § *Oct. 22–38* and May 12–39 [BBC Sym, London] § *Nov. 11–39* and *Jly. 1* [Buenos Aires]/*10* [Rio de Janeiro]–*40* § Ap. 29–42 § *Ap. 18–44* § *May 8–45* § *Mar. 22–52*

Symphony No. 6 [Pastoral] [38]
Mar. 1/2/4/5 [Philadelphia]/6 [Washington]/7 [Baltimore]/8 [Buffalo]/9 [Pittsburgh]/11/17/25–28 § Dec. 11/12/14–30 § Oct. 23/24/Nov. 3/4/17 [Greenwich]–32 § Ap. 9–33 § Feb. 1/2/Mar. 25–34 § Feb. 2/3–35 § Jn. 2 [BBC Sym, London]/8 [BBC Sym, Oxford]–37 § *Jan. 8–38* § May 12–39 [BBC Sym, London] § *Nov. 11–39* and *Jn. 29–40* [Buenos Aires] § *Ap. 12–41* § Ap. 29–42 § *Mar. 5–44* § *Mar. 16–47* § *Mar. 19–49* § *Jan. 12–52* § *Mar. 7–54*

Symphony No. 7 [35]
Oct. 3/4/5/6/Nov. 4 [Philadelphia]–29 and Mar. 9/May 21 [Budapest]/23 [Prague]/26 [Dresden]–30 § Ap. 16–33 § Feb. 1/2/22/23–34 § Ap. 4 [Hartford]/20/Jn. 12 [BBC Sym, London]/14 [ibid.]–35 § Mar. 16 [Boston]/Ap. 1/3/5–36 § *Mar. 14* [Washington]/May 7 [BBC Sym, London]–39 § *Nov. 18–39* and *Feb. 21/Jn. 15* [São Paulo]/*22* [Buenos Aires]/*Jly. 3* [Montevideo]–*40* § Ap. 24–41 [Chicago Sym, Chicago] § May 1–42 § *Nov. 19–44* § Ap. 19–45 [Los Angeles Philharmonic, Los Angeles] § *Oct. 25–47* § *Nov. 10–51*

Symphony No. 8 [18]
Oct. 17/18/19/20–29 § Ap. 23–33 § Feb. 15/16/18–34 § Mar. 5/6/8–36 § *Jan. 20/May 7–39* [BBC Sym, London] § *Nov. 25–39* § May 3–42 § *Oct. 31–43* § *Oct. 22–44* § *Nov. 8–52*

Symphony No. 9 [Choral] [20]
[Rethberg, Homer, Crooks, Gange, Schola Cantorum] Feb. 5/6–27 § [Morgana, Braslau, Crooks, Pinza, Schola Cantorum] Mar. 29/30/Ap. 1–28 § [Rethberg, Matzenauer,

Martinelli, Pinza, Schola Cantorum] *Ap. 28–32* § [Tentoni, Onegin, Althouse, Pinza, Schola Cantorum] Feb. 15/16/18–34 § [Tentoni, Bampton, Kullman, Pinza, Schola Cantorum] Mar. 5/6/8–36 § [Baillie, Jarred, Jones, Williams, BBC Choral Society—Woodgate] Nov. 3–37 [BBC Sym, London] § [Bovy, Thorborg, Peerce, Pinza, Schola Cantorum] *Feb. 6–38* § [Baillie, Balfour, Jones, Williams, BBC Choral Society—Woodgate] May 22–39 [BBC Sym, London] § [Novotna, Thorborg, Peerce, Moscona, chorus under Wilhousky] Dec. 2–39 § [Kirk, Eustis, Johnson, Kipnis, Westminster Choir—Williamson] May 3–42 § [Andreotti, Merriman, Peerce, Alvary, Collegiate Chorale—Shaw] *Sept. 25–45* § [McKnight, Hobson, Horne, Scott, Collegiate Chorale—Shaw] *Ap. 3–48* § [Farrell, Merriman, Peerce, Scott, Robert Shaw Chorale—Shaw] *Mar. 29–52*

BELIEVE ME IF ALL THOSE ENDEARING YOUNG CHARMS [1]
[Gianini] Mar. 1–36 [Broadcast, "General Motors Symphony Orchestra"]

BELLINI
NORMA: ACT I, INTRODUCTION AND DRUIDS' CHORUS [1]
[chorus under Wilhousky] *Dec. 2–45*

BERLIOZ
BENVENUTO CELLINI: OVERTURE [6]
Mar. 30/31/Ap. 1–33 § Ap. 12/13/14–34
THE DAMNATION OF FAUST: SCENE 3, RÁKÓCZY MARCH [7]
Dec. 25/26/28–30 and Jan. 3–31 § Jn. 14 [BBC Sym, London]–37 § *Ap. 5–41* § *Sept. 2–45*
. . . SCENE 7, EXCERPTS [BALLET OF THE SYLPHS, one would assume] [1]
[Harrell, Moscona] *Feb. 16–47*

LES FRANCS-JUGES [1]
Ap. 5–41
HAROLD IN ITALY [8]
[Pollain] Oct. 3/Nov. 1/2/3–29 § [Primrose] *Jan. 2–39* § [Primrose] *Oct. 27–46* § [Cooley] *Feb. 12–49* § [Cooley] *Nov. 29–53*
ROMAN CARNIVAL OVERTURE [5]
Oct. 7/9/11–42 § *Feb. 12–49* § *Jan. 10–53*
ROMEO AND JULIET: DRAMATIC SYMPHONY [entire score, 4]
[Tourel, Gerard, Moscona, Westminster Choir—Williamson] Oct. 7/9/11–42 § [Swarthout, Garris, Moscona, chorus under Wilhousky] *Feb. 9 and 16–47*
. . . PART II, ROMEO ALONE AND GREAT FESTIVITIES AT THE HOUSE OF CAPULET; LOVE SCENE [the citations in programs are vague as to the exact music played, but presumably the number of performances are 2 and 6 respectively]
Feb. 9/10–28 § Nov. 19–38 § *Ap. 5–41* § Nov. 4–45 [with MAB AND ROMEO ALONE, etc.] § Oct. 29–49 [with ROMEO ALONE, etc.]
. . . PART II, QUEEN MAB SCHERZO [28]
Feb. 9/10–28 § Mar. 20/21/22/23/30/May 16 [Munich]/18 [Vienna]/30 [Brussels]–30 § Nov. 16/18/19–32 § May 28–37 [BBC Sym, London] § *Feb. 5–38* § *Jn. 13* [Rio de Janeiro]/*20* [Buenos Aires]/*Jly. 8* [São Paulo]–*40* § *Ap. 5–41* § Feb. 6 [Philadelphia Orch., Philadelphia]/7 [ibid.]/10 [Philadelphia Orch.]–42 § *Mar. 26–44* § *Feb. 4–45* § *Nov. 4–45* § *Feb. 14–48* § *Feb. 12–49* § *Nov. 10–51*

BIZET
L'ARLÉSIENNE: SUITES NOS. 1 AND 2 [1]
Sept. 19–43
CARMEN: SUITE No. 1 [2]
Sept. 19–43 § *Aug. 2–52*

La Jolie Fille de Perth: Suite [1]
Sept. 19–43

BOCCHERINI
Concerto for 'Cello in B-flat
Major [5]
[Wallenstein] Mar. 27/28/29–30 §
[Wallenstein] Mar. 11/13–36
Quartet in D Major [1]
Nov. 19–49
Quintet in E, Op. 13, No. 5:
Minuet (in A) [2]
Ap. 4–43 § Aug. 27–44

BOITO
Mefistofele: Prologue [2]
[Moscona, chorus under Wil-
housky, boys' choir under Petri]
Dec. 2–45 § [Moscona, Robert
Shaw Chorale—Shaw, Columbus
Boys' Choir] Mar. 14–54

BOLZONI
Medieval Castle Serenade [1]
Jly. 18–43
Menuetto in B Major [1]
Jn. 20–43

BORODIN
Prince Igor: Polovtzian Dances
[6]
Feb. 27/28/Mar. 1/2–30 § Mar.
16/17–33
Symphony No. 2 [3]
Feb. 23/24–28 § Feb. 26–38

BOSSI
Intermezzi Goldoniani [4]
Nov. 10/11/13–32 § Sept. 3–44

BRAHMS
Academic Festival Overture [6]
Mar. 28/29/31–35 § Feb. 11–39 §
Jn. 10–43 § Nov. 6–48
Concerto for Piano No. 1 [3]
[Horowitz] Mar. 14/15/17–35
Concerto for Piano No. 2 [6]
[Casadesus] Jan. 30/31/Feb. 2–36
§ [Horowitz] May 6–40 § [Horo-
witz] Feb. 19–45 § [Horowitz]
Oct. 23–48
Concerto for Violin [5]
[Heifetz] Ap. 5/7–33 § [Heifetz]
Feb. 21/22/24–35

Double Concerto for Violin and
'Cello [8]
[Guidi, Wallenstein] Oct. 24/25/
27–29 § [Piastro, Wallenstein]
Feb. 14/15/17–35 § [Mischakoff,
Miller] Oct. 21–39 § [Mischakoff,
Miller] Nov. 13–48
A German Requiem [5]
[Rethberg, Schorr, Schola Can-
torum] Mar. 7/8/10–35 § [Baillie,
Sved, BBC Choral Society—Wood-
gate] Oct. 30–37 [BBC Sym, Lon-
don] § [della Chiesa, Janssen,
Westminster Choir—Williamson]
Jan. 24–43
Gesänge für Frauenchoir
(Gesang aus Fingal, Lied von
Schakespeare, Der Gärtner)
[3]
[chorus of women from the Schola
Cantorum] Mar. 28/29/31–35
Gesang der Parzen [1]
[Robert Shaw Chorale] Nov. 27–
48
Liebeslieder Waltzer [6] [There
are no orchestral parts in this
score.]
[Bos, Luboschutz, small chorus
from the Schola Cantorum] Mar.
28/29/31–35 § [Bartlett, Robert-
son, BBC Singers—Woodgate] Jn.
3–38 [London] § [Leinsdorf,
Kahn, 17 voices under Preston]
Feb. 11–39 § [Luboschutz, Nie-
menoff, 17 voices under Preston]
Dec. 27–42
Serenade No. 1 [3]
Ap. 3/5/7–35
. . . Allegro molto [only] [5]
Mar. 14/15/17–35 § May 6–40 §
Jan. 17–43
. . . Minuets 1 and 2 [only] [3]
Mar. 9–47 § Oct. 23/Nov. 6–48
Serenade No. 2 [5]
Mar. 28/29/31–35 § Jan. 22–38 §
Dec. 27–42
Symphony No. 1 [28]
Nov. 13/14/16/Dec. 5 [Philadel-
phia Orch., Philadelphia]/6 [ibid.]
/16 [Washington]/17 [Balti-
more]–30 § Dec. 20–31 § Feb. 25–
34 § Feb. 14/15/17/Mar. 30–35 §
May 26 [BBC Sym, London]/Jn.

8 [BBC Sym, Oxford]–37 § *Dec.*
25–37 § *May 6/14* [Washington]/
Jn. 19 [Buenos Aires]/*Jly. 9* [Rio
de Janeiro]–*40* § *Jan. 17/Mar. 24–
43* § *Ap. 18–44* § *Oct. 30–48* §
May 17 [Chicago]/*27* [Philadel-
phia]–*50* § *Nov. 3–51* § Sept. 29–
52 [Philharmonia Orch., London]

SYMPHONY NO. 2 [34]
Jan. 26/27/29/30 [Baltimore]/31
[Washington]/Feb. 1 [Philadel-
phia]–28 § Ap. 9/11/12/13/May
12 [Rome]/Jn. 1 [London]–30 §
Mar. 28/29/Ap. 1/28–34 § Feb.
21/22/24–35 § Feb. 15/16–36 §
Feb. 12/Jn. 10 [BBC Sym, Lon-
don]–38 § *Jn. 27* [Buenos Aires]/
Jly. 4 [Montevideo]/8 [São
Paulo]–*40* § *Jan. 3*/Feb. 13 [Cin-
cinnati Sym, Cincinnati]/14
[*ibid.*]–42 § *Mar. 9–47* § *Nov. 6–
48* § *May 13–50* [Denver] § *Feb.
10–51* § Sept. 29–52 [Philhar-
monia Orch., London]

SYMPHONY NO. 3 [25]
Oct. 10/11/13–29 § Mar. 26/27/
28/29–31 § Oct. 6/7/8/9/24 [Phila-
delphia]/25 [Washington]–32 §
Mar. 14/15/17–35 § *Oct. 15–38* §
Jan. 10–39 [Boston] § *Feb. 8–41* §
Dec. 20–42 § *Mar. 3–46* § *Feb.
21–48* § *Nov. 20–48* § Oct. 1 [Phil-
harmonia Orch., London]/*Nov. 1–
52*

SYMPHONY No 4 [25]
Dec. 10/11/13–31 § Jan. 14–34 §
Ap. 3/5/7/20/29 [Providence] Jn.
3 [BBC Sym, London]/5 [ibid.]–
35 § Mar. 14/15/17 [Boston]–36 §
Feb. 11–39 § *Jan. 10–43* § *Oct.
28–45* § *Nov. 27–48* § *Feb. 25/Ap.
25* [New Orleans]/*May 3* [Pasa-
dena]/*May 21* [Cleveland]/*25*
[Washington]–*50* § *Dec. 22–51* §
Oct. 1–52 [Philharmonia Orch.,
London]

TRAGIC OVERTURE [11]
Feb. 21/22/24–35 § Oct. 30–37
[BBC Sym, London] § *Jan. 15–38*
§ *Jan. 3–43* § *Oct. 28–45* § *Mar.
9–47* § *Oct. 30–48* § Sept. 29–52
[Philharmonia Orch., London] §
Nov. 22–53

VARIATIONS ON A THEME OF HAYDN
[40]
Feb. 7–26 § Mar. 27/28–29 § Ap.
16/17/May 3 [Paris]/28 [Berlin]/
Jn. 4 [London]–30 § Nov. 29–31 §
Nov. 10/11/13–32 § Feb. 3/4–34
§ Feb. 14/15/17/Ap. 4 [Hart-
ford]–35 § Mar. 16–36 [Boston] §
Jn. 22–37 [BBC Sym, London] §
Feb. 26/Dec. 13 [Newark]/27
[Baltimore]–38 and *Jan. 31*
[Chicago]/*Feb. 1* [Pittsburgh]/7
[Providence]–*39* § *Jn. 14* [Rio de
Janeiro]/*22* [Buenos Aires]–*40* §
Dec. 20–42 § Ap. 19–45 [Los
Angeles Philharmonic, Los
Angeles]/*Nov. 17–46* § *Feb. 21–
48* § *Nov. 20–48* § *Feb.25/Ap. 19*
[Richmond]/*22* [Atlanta]/*May 1*
[Dallas]/9 [Portland]/23 [Pitts-
burgh]–*50* § Oct. 1–52 [Philhar-
monia Orch., London]

BRAHMS (orch. by Dvořák)
HUNGARIAN DANCES No. 1 [3]
Dec. 27–42 and *Jan. 10–43* § *Nov.
13–48*
. . . Nos. 17, 20, 21 [4]
Mar. 28/29/31–35 § *Jly. 2–44*
BRAHMS (orch. by Rubbra)
VARIATIONS ON A THEME OF HANDEL
[1]
Jan. 7–39

BRUCKNER
SYMPHONY NO. 4 [ROMANTIC] [3]
Nov. 24/25–32 § Feb. 3–34
SYMPHONY NO. 7 [8]
Mar. 4/6/7/8–31 § Jan. 24/25/26/
27–35

BUSCH
VARIATIONS ON A THEME OF MOZART
[2]
Oct. 31/Nov. 1–29

BUSONI
BERCEUSE ÉLÉGIAQUE [8]
Mar. 21/22/30–29 § Oct. 27/28/
30–32 § *Mar. 13–48* § *Dec. 10–49*
RONDO ARLECCHINESCO [11]
[Tedeschi] Mar. 15/16/17/18–28
§ [Raggini] Oct. 27/28/30–32 §

[Nash] May 26–37 [BBC Sym, London] § [Peerce] *Jan. 15–38* § [McKinley] *Jan. 20–46* § [Gallu] *Dec. 10–49*

CASTELNUOVO-TEDESCO

CONCERTO FOR 'CELLO [2]
[Piatigorsky] Jan. 31/Feb. 1–35

OVERTURE TO A FAIRY TALE [1]
Nov. 25–45

THE PROPHETS [2]
[Heifetz] Ap. 12/13–33

TAMING OF THE SHREW: OVERTURE [8]
Dec. 10/11/13–31 § Mar. 23/24/25–33 § *Mar. 30–40* § *Mar. 26–44*

VIOLIN VARIATIONS [4]
[Guidi] Ap. 9/11/12/13–30

CATALANI

LORELEI: DANCE OF THE WATER NYMPHS and LA WALLY: PRELUDE TO ACT IV [3]
Jan. 21–39 § *Mar. 23–47* § *Aug. 2–52*

CHASINS

FLIRTATION IN A CHINESE GARDEN and PARADE [4]
Ap. 8/10/12/18–31

CHERUBINI

ALI BABA: OVERTURE [1]
Dec. 3–49

ANACREON: OVERTURE [19]
Feb. 27/Mar. 22/23–28 § Ap. 19/20–30 § Nov. 22/23/28 [Philadelphia Orch., Philadelphia]/29 [ibid.]/Dec. 1 [ibid.]–30 § Ap. 12/13–33 § Jn. 3–35 [BBC Sym, London] § *Jan. 22–38* § *Jn. 29* [Buenos Aires]/*Jly. 10* [Rio de Janeiro]–40 § *Feb. 4–45* § *Dec. 22–51* § *Mar. 21–53*

FANISKA: OVERTURE [1]
Jan. 21–34

MEDEA: OVERTURE [2]
Dec. 20–31 § *Feb. 18–50*

REQUIEM MASS IN C MINOR [1]
[Robert Shaw Chorale–Hunter conducting] *Feb. 18–50*

QUARTET IN E-FLAT: SCHERZO [1]
Ap. 4–43

SYMPHONY IN D MAJOR [3]
May 28–37 [BBC Sym, London] § *Mar. 23–47* § *Mar. 8–52*

CIMAROSA

IL MATRIMONIO PER RAGGIRO: OVERTURE [1]
Nov. 12–49

IL MATRIMONIO SEGRETO: OVERTURE [1]
Nov. 14–43

COPELAND

EL SALON MEXICO [1]
Mar. 14–42

CORELLI-GEMINIANI

CONCERTO GROSSO No. 12 [LA FOLLIA] [1]
May 26–37 [BBC Sym, London]

CRESTON

CHORIC DANCE No. 2 [4]
Nov. 1–42 and Feb. 13 [Cincinnati Sym, Cincinnati]/14 [ibid.]/Feb. 26 [Philadelphia Orch., Philadelphia]–43

FRONTIERS [1]
Nov. 25–45

DEBUSSY

LA COUR DES LEYS [3]
[chorus of women from the Schola Cantorum] Ap. 16/17/19–36

LA DAMOISELLE ÉLUE [4]
[Sayao, chorus of women from the Schola Cantorum] Ap. 16/17/19–36 § [Novotna, Glatz, chorus of women under Preston] *Ap. 13–40*

IMAGES [SET III] [for orchestra]. PART 2: IBERIA [31]
Feb. 21/22/23/24/Mar. 4 [Philadelphia]/5 [Washington]/6 [Baltimore]/7 [Rochester]/8 [Pittsburgh]/10–29 § Feb. 22/23/24–34 § Ap. 16/17/19–36 § Jn. 14–37 [BBC Sym, London] § *Nov. 2–38* § *Ap. 13/Jn. 25* [Buenos Aires]–40 § Nov. 14 [Philadelphia Orch., Philadelphia]/15 [ibid.]–41 and Jan. 13 [Philadelphia Orch., Washington]–42 § *Nov. 14–43* §

Feb. 11–45 § *Mar. 2–48* § *Mar. 25/Ap. 25* [New Orleans]/*May 3* [Pasadena] 25 [Washington]–*50* § *Feb. 14–53*

MARCHE ÉCOSSAISE [1]
Ap. 13–40

LE MARTYRE DE SAINT-SÉBASTIEN [3]
[chorus of women from the Schola Cantorum] Ap. 16/17/19–36

LA MER [53]
Feb. 7–26 § Feb. 23/24/Mar. 4/5 [Philadelphia]/6 [Washington]/7 [Baltimore]/8 [Buffalo]/9 [Pittsburgh]–28 § Oct. 24/25/27–29 and Ap. 3/4/May 4 [Paris]/10 [Turin]/14 [Florence]/21 [Budapest]/26 [Dresden]/27 [Berlin]/Jn. 2 [London]–30 § Oct. 6/7/8/9/24 [Philadelphia]/25 [Washington]–32 § Jn. 12 [BBC Sym, London]/14 [*ibid.*]–35 § Ap. 16/17/19–36 § *Jan. 8–38* § *Ap. 13/Jn. 20* [Buenos Aires]/*Jly. 3* [Montevideo]/*9* [Rio de Janeiro]–*40* § Feb. 6 [Philadelphia Orch., Philadelphia]/7 [ibid.]/10 [Philadelphia Orch.]–42 § *Ap. 11–43* § *Feb. 11–45* § *Mar. 2–47* § *Nov. 29–47* and *Mar. 27–48* § *Oct. 29–49* § *Ap. 15/17* [Baltimore]/*May 7* [San Francisco]/*15* [St Louis]/*17* [Chicago]/*27* [Philadelphia]–*50* § *Feb. 14–53*

NOCTURNES: No. 1 NUAGES [13] and No. 2 FÊTES [14] [no performance of the set of three]
Dec. 25/26/28–30 and Jan. 3–31 § Mar. 25–33 § Ap. 17/18–35 § Mar. 17/Ap. 16/17/19–36 § *Ap. 13–40* § *Mar. 27–48* [NUAGES omitted] § *Mar. 15–52*

PRELUDE TO THE AFTERNOON OF A FAUN [23]
Mar. 20/21/22/23/30/May 16 [Munich]/18 [Vienna]/30 [Brussels]–30 § Nov. 16/18/19–32 § Ap. 17/18–35 § Mar. 1 [Broadcast, "General Motors Symphony Orchestra"]/Ap. 16/17/19–36 § *Jn. 20–43* § *Feb. 11–45* § *Mar. 27–48* § *Oct. 7–49* [Ridgefield, Conn.] § *Feb. 17–51* § *Feb. 14–53*

DEBUSSY (orch. by Ravel)
DANSE [1]
Ap. 13–40

DIXIE (orch. by Frank Black) [1]
Ap. 19–50 [Richmond]

DONIZETTI
DON PASQUALE: OVERTURE [2]
Jn. 20–43 § *Mar. 13–48*

DUKAS
ARIANE ET BARBE-BLEUE, EXCERPTS [unspecified] [1]
Mar. 2–47

THE SORCERER'S APPRENTICE [15]
Feb. 28/Mar. 1/3/16/17/24–29 § Mar. 16/29–30 § Ap. 1/3/5–36 § *Feb. 12–38* § *Jn. 20–43* § *Mar. 18/Ap. 22* [Atlanta]–*50*

DVOŘÁK
CONCERTO FOR 'CELLO, OP. 104 [1]
[Kurtz] *Jan. 28–45*

OTHELLO: OVERTURE [4]
Mar. 19/20/21/22–31

SCHERZO CAPRICCIOSO [2]
Ap. 20–40 § *Jan. 28–45*

SLAVONIC DANCE No. 6 [2]
Feb. 13/14–36

SYMPHONY No. 5 [FROM THE NEW WORLD] [6]
Mar. 1–31 § *Nov. 5–38* § *Dec. 13–41* § *Mar. 18/Ap. 29* [Austin]–*50* § *Jan. 31–53*

SYMPHONIC VARIATIONS ON AN ORIGINAL THEME, OP. 78 [5]
Dec. 10/11/13–31 § *Dec. 4–48* § *Nov. 17–51*

ELGAR
INTRODUCTION AND ALLEGRO FOR STRINGS [5]
Mar. 26/27/28/29–31 § *Ap. 20–40*

VARIATIONS ON AN ORIGINAL THEME [ENIGMA] [16]
Jan. 26/27/29/30 [Baltimore]/31 [Washington]/Feb. 1 [Philadelphia]/21–28 § Ap. 19/20/Jn. 2 [London]–30 § Jn. 3–35 [BBC Sym, London] § *Feb. 4–39* § *Nov. 18–45* § *Nov. 5–49* § *Feb. 17–51* § *Jan. 5–52*

ENESCO
ROUMANIAN RHAPSODY No. 1 [5]
Nov. 3/4/6–32 § *Dec. 14–40* § *Jan. 13–46*

DE FALLA
EL AMOR BRUJO [6]
[Braslau] Mar. 1/2–28 § [Braslau] Ap. 19/20–34 § [Burzio] *Jan. 28–39* § [RITUAL DANCE OF FIRE and DANCE OF TERROR, only] *Sept. 3–44*

FERNANDEZ
BATUQUE [3]
May 14 [Washington]/*Jly. 8* [São Paulo]/*9* [Rio de Janeiro]–*40*
REISADO DO PASTOREIO: SUITE [1]
May 14–40

FORONI
OVERTURE IN C MINOR [1]
Sept. 2–45

FRANCHETTI
CRISTOFORO COLOMBO: NOCTURNE, ACT II [1]
[Horne] *Dec. 14–40*

FRANCK
LES ÉOLIDES [19]
Oct. 17/18/19/20/Nov. 3–29 and Mar. 7/May 9 [Milan]/30 [Brussels]/Jn. 3 [London]–30 § Mar. 11/13/14/15–36 § *Nov. 2–38* § *Ap. 27/Jn. 19* [Buenos Aires]–*40* § *Jly. 2–44* § *Mar. 5–49* § *Dec. 13–53*
PSYCHÉ [6 performances, none of them of the entire score]
[EXCERPTS] Ap. 1/2/4/5–31 § [PSYCHÉ'S SLUMBER and PSYCHÉ AND EROS] *Jan. 14–39* § [PSYCHÉ AND EROS] *Jan. 5–52*
REDEMPTION: SYMPHONIC INTERLUDE [sometimes called SYMPHONIC PIECE or PRELUDE TO PART II] [11]
Mar. 29/30/Ap. 1–28 § Nov. 26/27/29/Dec. 14 [Philadelphia]/15 [Washington]/16 [Baltimore]–31 § *Mar. 2–47* § *Mar. 15–52*
SYMPHONY IN D MINOR [15]
Dec. 25/26/28–30 and Jan. 3/

Mar. 9 [Philadelphia]/10 [Washington]/11 [Baltimore]–31 § Mar. 12/Ap. 8–33 § Mar. 25/Ap. 19/20/21–34 § *Dec. 14–40* § *Mar. 24–46*

FRANCK (orch. by Pierné)
PRELUDE, CHORALE, AND FUGUE [4]
Oct. 20/21/22/23–32

GARIBALDI'S WAR HYMN [1]
Sept. 9–43

GEMINIANI
CONCERTO GROSSO FOR STRINGS IN C MINOR, OP. 2, No. 2 [3]
Ap. 20/21/22–33
CONCERTO GROSSO FOR STRINGS IN G MINOR, OP. 3, No. 2 [4]
Ap. 12/13/14–34 § Jn. 12–35 [BBC Sym, London]

GERSHWIN
AN AMERICAN IN PARIS [2]
Nov. 14–43 § *Mar. 18–45*
PIANO CONCERTO IN F [1]
[Levant] *Ap. 2–44*
RHAPSODY IN BLUE [1]
[Wilde] *Nov. 1–42*

GILBERT
COMEDY-OVERTURE ON NEGRO THEMES [2]
Feb. 7–43 § Feb. 26–43 [Philadelphia Orch., Philadelphia]

GILLET
LOIN DE BAL [1]
[Special orchestra of Heifetz, Milstein, Primrose, Feuermann, Wallenstein, and others with N.B.C. Symphony personnel] Private benefit concert, Dec. 29–39

GILLIS
SYMPHONY 5½ [SYMPHONY FOR FUN] [1]
Sept. 21–47

GIORDANO
IL RE: DANCE OF THE MOOR [1]
Dec. 10–49
SIBERIA: PRELUDE TO ACT II [1]
Dec. 10–49

GLINKA

LA JOTA ARAGONESA (CAPRICCIO BRILLANTE) [7]
Nov. 7–43 § *Sept. 3–44* § *Nov. 4–45* § *Feb. 28–48* § *Mar. 4/Ap. 25* [New Orleans]/*May 3* [Pasadena]*–50*

KAMARINSKAYA [4]
Jan. 7/9/18–31 § *Dec. 21–40*

GLUCK

IPHIGENIA IN AULIS: OVERTURE [16]
Feb. 28/Mar. 1/3/9 [Pittsburgh]/16/17/24–29 § Mar. 26/27/28/29–31 § F e b . 4–34 § A p . 24–41 [Chicago Sym, Chicago] § *Jan. 28–39* § *Feb. 8–41* § *Nov. 22–52*

ORFEO: ACT II [2]
[Merriman, Philips, chorus under Wilhousky] Ap. 1–45 § [Merriman, Gibson, Robert Shaw Chorale] *Nov. 22–52*

GOLDMARK

RUSTIC WEDDING SYMPHONY [5 performances, none of them of the entire score]
[three movements, otherwise unspecified] Feb. 15/16/25 [Hartford]/[SERENADE only] Mar. 1–36 [Broadcast, "General Motors Symphony Orchestra"] § [IN THE GARDEN and SERENADE] *Sept. 3–44*

GOMEZ

IL GUARANY: OVERTURE [2]
Jn. 14 [Rio de Janeiro]/*Jly. 8* [São Paulo]*–40*

GOOSENS

SINFONIETTA [5]
Mar. 27/28/29/30/Jn. 3 [London]*–30*

GOULD

LINCOLN LEGEND [1]
Nov. 1–42

GRAENER

THE FLUTE OF SAN-SOUCI [SUITE FOR CHAMBER ORCHESTRA] [5]
Dec. 3/4/5/6–31 § *Nov. 5–38*

GRIEG

AUS HOLBERGS ZEIT [SUITE FOR STRING ORCHESTRA] [1]
Ap. 27–40

GRIFFES

THE WHITE PEACOCK [1]
Feb. 7–43

GROFÉ

THE GRAND CANYON SUITE [2]
Feb. 7–43 § *Sept 2–45*

HANDEL

CONCERTO GROSSO NO. 5: MENUETTO [only] [1]
Jn. 20–43

CONCERTO GROSSO NO. 12 [7]
Nov. 14/15/17–29 § Jan. 31/Feb. 1–35 § *Feb. 19–38* § *Nov. 22–47*

SUSANNA: OVERTURE [4]
Mar. 11/13/14/15–36

HANSON

SYMPHONY NO. 2 [3]
Mar. 1/3/5–33

HARRIS

SYMPHONY NO. 3 [1]
Mar. 16–40

HAYDN

QUARTET IN F, OP. 3, NO. 5: SERENADE [2]
Ap. 4–43 § *Aug. 27–44*

SINFONIE CONCERTANTE IN B-FLAT MAJOR FOR SOLO VIOLIN, 'CELLO, OBOE, AND BASSOON WITH ORCHESTRA, OP. 84 [2]
[Mischakoff, Miller, Bloom, Polisi] *Oct. 14–39* § [Mischakoff, Miller, Bloom, Polisi] *Mar. 6–48*

SYMPHONY NO. 31 [HORN SIGNAL] [4]
Mar. 15/16/18–34 § *Oct. 29–38*

SYMPHONY NO. 88 [sometimes called B. & H. No. 13] [12]
Feb. 9/10/19/21/26/Mar. 10 [Pittsburgh]–28 § Nov. 7/8/10–29 § Mar. 15/Ap. 9 [Hartford]–31 § *Feb 19–38*

SYMPHONY NO. 92 [OXFORD] [2]
Jn. 8–37 [BBC Sym, Oxford] § *Mar. 19–44*

SYMPHONY NO. 94 [SURPRISE] [2]
Jn. 20–43 § Jn. 24–53
SYMPHONY NO. 98 [3]
Jan. 22–38 § Mar. 25–45 § Nov.
19–49
SYMPHONY NO. 99 [13]
Mar. 20/21/22/23–30 § Feb. 1–41
§ Jan. 9 [Philadelphia Orch.,
Philadelphia]/10 [ibid.]/13 [Phila-
delphia Orch., Washington]–42 §
Oct. 14/16/18–42 § Jly. 2–44 §
Mar. 12–49
SYMPHONY NO. 101 [CLOCK] [27]
Jan. 14/15/16/30/31–26 § Mar. 9
[Pittsburgh]/17/23/27/28–29 §
Ap. 19/20/May 4 [Paris]/14
[Florence]/16 [Munich]/18
[Vienna]/27 [Berlin]/Jn. 2 [Lon-
don]–30 § Jan. 1/2/4/18–31 § Feb.
4–34 § Ap. 23/24–36 § Ap. 4–42 §
Jan. 13–45
SYMPHONY NO. 104 [London] [1]
Oct. 31–43
TOY SYMPHONY [1]
Feb. 15–41

HÉROLD
ZAMPA OVERTURE [3]
Ap. 4–43 § Aug. 27–44 § Aug. 2–
52

HONEGGER
PASTORALE D'ETE and PACIFIC 231
[always played as a pair for
some reason] [12]
Jan. 26/27/29/30 [Baltimore]/31
[Washington]/Feb. 1 [Philadel-
phia]/4/5/21–28 § Ap. 16/17/
May 6 [Zurich]–30

HUMPERDINCK
HANSEL AND GRETEL: OVERTURE [2]
Jan. 13–46 § Aug. 2–52
THE KING'S CHILDREN: PRELUDE TO
ACT III [1]
Nov. 17–46

D'INDY
ISTAR VARIATIONS [8]
Jan. 7/9/18–31 § Oct. 13/14/15/
16/Nov. 17 [Greenwich]–32

THE INTERNATIONALE (orch. Toscanini) [1]
Nov. 7–43

KABAVELSKY
COLAS BREUGNON: OVERTURE [10]
Ap. 11–43 § Jan. 21–45 § Ap. 7–
46 § Sept. 21–47 § Mar. 4/Ap. 19
[Richmond]/May 1 [Dallas]/9
[Portland]/23 [Pittsburgh]–50 §
Mar. 8–52
SYMPHONY NO. 2, OP. 19 [4]
Nov. 8–42 and Feb. 26 [Philadel-
phia Orch., Philadelphia]–43 §
Mar. 25–45 § Feb. 26–49

KALINNIKOV
SYMPHONY NO. 1 IN C MINOR [1]
Nov. 7–43

KENNAN
NIGHT SOLILOQUY [2]
Feb. 7/26 [Philadelphia Orch.,
Philadelphia]–43

KODÁLY
DANCES OF MAROSSZÉK [4]
Dec. 11/12/14–30 § Feb. 8–41
HÁRY JÁNOS: SUITE [1]
Nov. 29–47
PSALMUS HUNGARICUS [2]
[Gridley, Schola Cantorum, St
Patrick's Boys' Choir] Nov. 20/
22–29
SUMMER EVENING [8]
Ap. 3/4/5/6/May 21 [Budapest]–
30 § Ap. 12/13/14–34

KOZELUČH
QUARTET NO. 2: ANDANTE AND
ALLEGRO [only] [4]
Mar. 11/13/14/15–36

LIADOV
KIKIMORA [4]
Nov. 7–43 § Jan. 13–46 § Dec. 11–
48 § Jly. 26–52

LISZT
FROM THE CRADLE TO THE GRAVE
[Symphonic poem DER WOHL-
FAHRTSTAAT] [1]
Feb. 8–41

HUNGARIAN RHAPSODY NO. 2
Ap. 4–43
MEPHISTO WALTZ and DANSE
MACABRE [Paraphrase of the
DIES IRAE] [played as a pair for
some reason] [2]
[Siloti] Nov. 19/21–30
ORPHEUS: SYMPHONIC POEM [1]
Nov. 26–38

LOEFFLER
MEMORIES OF MY CHILDHOOD [2]
Jan. 7–39 § Nov. 1–42

MANCINELLI
SCENE VENEZIANE [3]
*Jn. 25–44 § Jan. 13–46 § Mar. 13–
48*

MARTUCCI
CONCERTO IN B-FLAT MINOR FOR
PIANO AND ORCHESTRA [2]
[D'Attili] *Jan. 20–46* § [Horszow-
ski] *Jan. 10–53*
CANZONE DEI RICORDI [1]
Mar. 29–41
DANZA [TARANTELLA] [5]
*Jan. 1/2/4–31 § Feb. 19–38 § Feb.
8–41*
NOTTURNO and NOVELETTA [10 and
11]
*Feb. 7/26/Ap. 1/3/5–36 § Oct.
15–38 § Nov. 20* [Philadelphia
Orch., Philadelphia]/21 [ibid.]/24
[Philadelphia Orch.]–42 and *Feb.
13* [Cincinnati Sym, Cincinnati]/
14 [ibid.]–43 § [NOVELETTA only]
Mar. 13–48
SYMPHONY No. 1 [4]
Ap. 20/21/22–33 § Nov. 26–38
SYMPHONY No. 2 [3]
Mar. 22/23–28 § Mar. 30–40

MASSENET
SCÈNES ALSACIENNES [1]
Jly. 18–43

MENDELSSOHN
CONCERTO FOR VIOLIN [6]
[Bolognini] *Ap. 20/21–33* § [Mil-
stein] *Mar. 26/27/29–36* §
[Heifetz] *Ap. 9–44*

HEBRIDES OVERTURE [1]
Nov. 4–45
INCIDENTAL MUSIC TO "A MID-
SUMMER NIGHT'S DREAM"
["entire score"–actually OVER-
TURE and Nos. 1, 5, 7, 10 and
12, since the whole score is
virtually never played in con-
cert] [3]
[Eustis, Kirk, University of Penn-
sylvania Choral Society–Godsell]
Jan. 9 [Philadelphia Orch., Phila-
delphia]/10 [ibid.]–42 § [Philips,
Warner, chorus under Wilhousky]
Nov. 1–47
. . . OVERTURE [etc.] [5]
Feb. 23/24–28 § Jan. 13 [Phila-
delphia Orch., Washington] [Nos.
5 and 7 were also played, q.v.]/
24–42 § *Feb. 10–51*
. . . No. 7, NOCTURNE, followed by
No. 1, SCHERZO [each work
played 35 times]
Jan. 17/Feb. 1–26 § Mar. 15/16/
17/18/25–28 § Ap. 9/11/12/13/
May 3 [Paris]/6 [Zurich]/8
[Milan]/13 [Rome]/14 [Florence]
/19 [Vienna]/23 [Prague]/25
[Leipzig]/26 [Dresden]/27
[Berlin]/Jn. 2 [London]–30 § Jan.
21/Feb. 11 [Broadcast, "General
Motors Symphony Orchestra"]/
Mar. 15 [Hartford]–34 § Jn. 14–
35 [BBC Sym, London] § *Jn. 15*
[São Paulo]/Jly. 1 [Buenos Aires]/
3 [Montevideo]/10 [Rio de Ja-
neiro]–40 § [No. 5, INTERMEZZO,
substituted for No. 1] Jan. 13–42
[Philadelphia Orch., Washington]
§ *Sept 6–47* [Ridgefield, Conn.] §
[No. 1 only] *Ap. 19* [Richmond]/
May 1 [Dallas]/ 9 [Portland]/23
[Pittsburgh]–50 [*This is the
Maestro's favorite "touring ve-
hicle" and it should be noted that
of the thirty-five performances
cited, only thirteen took place in
New York, an unusual balance for
Toscanini's repertory.*]
OCTET FOR STRINGS, OP. 20 [1]
Mar. 30–47
. . . SCHERZO [only] [1]
Mar. 18–45

QUINTET FOR STRINGS, OP. 87 [1]
  Nov. 1–47
SYMPHONY No. 3 [SCOTCH] [1]
  Ap. 5–41
SYMPHONY No. 4 [ITALIAN] [10]
  Oct. 27/28/30–32 and Mar. 4/15
  [Hartford]–33 § Feb. 5–38 § Mar.
  14–42 § Mar. 12–49 § Oct. 7–49
  [Ridgefield, Conn.] § Feb. 28–54
SYMPHONY No. 5 [REFORMATION]
  [13]
  Dec. 3/4/5/6–31 § Mar. 23/24/
  25–33 § Nov. 19–38 § Nov. 8–42
  and Feb. 26–43 [Philadelphia
  Orch., Philadelphia] § Sept. 9–45
  § Mar. 30–47 § Dec. 13–53
THE TALE OF LOVELY MELUSINE:
  OVERTURE [2]
  Nov. 1–47 § Dec. 11–48

MEYERBEER
DINORAH: OVERTURE [1]
  Nov. 12–38

MIGNONE
CONGADA [2]
  Jn. 13 [Rio de Janeiro] § 15 [São
  Paulo]–40
FANTASIA BRASILEIRA [1]
  Nov. 14–43
SYMPHONIC IMPRESSIONS OF FOUR
  OLD BRAZILIAN CHURCHES [1]
  Ap. 2–44

MONTEVERDI
SONATA SOPRA "SANCTA MARIA" [3]
  [Schola Cantorum] Mar. 29/30/
  Ap. 1–28

MOSSOLOFF
IRON FOUNDRY [2]
  Mar. 16/17–33

MOUSSORGSKY
BORIS GODUNOV: INTRODUCTION AND
  POLONAISE FROM ACT III [1]
  Ap. 4–43
KHOVANTCHINA: PRELUDE [2]
  Mar. 12–44 § Dec. 13–53

MOUSSORGSKY (orch. Ravel)
PICTURES AT AN EXHIBITION [21]
  Mar. 13/14/15/May 6 [Zurich]/9

[Milan]/13 [Rome]/Jn. 3 [Lon-
  don]–30 § Feb. 13/14/15/16–36 §
  Jan. 29–38 § Ap. 20/Jly. 1 [Buenos
  Aires]/10 [Rio de Janeiro]–40 §
  Nov. 20 [Philadelphia Orch.,
  Philadelphia]/21 [ibid.]/24 [Phila-
  delphia Orch.]–42 § Feb. 19–45 §
  Feb. 14–48 § Jan. 24–53

MOZART
ADAGIO AND FUGUE FOR STRINGS, K.
  545 [4]
  Oct. 24/25/27/Nov. 2–29
CONCERTO FOR BASSOON No. 1, K.
  191 [1]
  [Sharrow] Nov. 8–47
CONCERTI FOR PIANO IN D MINOR,
  K. 466, and C MAJOR, K. 467
  [2 + 2]
  [Iturbi] Mar. 28/29–34
CONCERTO FOR PIANO IN B-FLAT, K.
  595 [4]
  [Serkin] Feb. 20/21/23–36 § [Hor-
  szowski] Dec. 5–43
DIVERTIMENTO IN B-FLAT, K. 287
  [2]
  Nov. 3–46 § Nov. 8–47
DON GIOVANNI: OVERTURE [1]
  Jan. 27–46
MASONIC FUNERAL MUSIC, K. 477
  [orchestral portion only] [3]
  Nov. 14/15/17–29
MARRIAGE OF FIGARO: OVERTURE [2]
  Dec. 5–43 § Nov. 8–47
A MUSICAL JOKE, K. 522 [1]
  [Special orchestra of Heifetz, Mil-
  stein, Primrose, Feuermann, Wal-
  lenstein, and others with N.B.C.
  Symphony personnel] Private ben-
  efit concert Dec. 29–39
OVERTURE IN THE ITALIAN STYLE,
  K. 318 [4]
  Feb. 4/5/16/17–28
SYMPHONIA CONCERTANTE FOR VIO-
  LIN, VIOLA, AND ORCHESTRA IN
  E-FLAT MAJOR, K. 364 [1]
  [Mischakoff, Cooley] Feb. 15–41
SYMPHONY No. 1, K. 16 [3]
  Mar. 30/31/Ap. 1–33
SYMPHONY No. 28, K. 200 [2]
  Oct. 20/21–32
SYMPHONY No. 29, K. 201 [6]
  Nov. 26/27/Dec. 14 [Philadel-

phia]/15 [Washington]/16 [Balti-more]–31 § *Sept. 3–44*
SYMPHONY No. 35 [HAFFNER] [19]
Feb. 21/22/23/24/Mar. 4 [Phila-delphia]/5 [Washington]/6 [Balti-more]/7 [Rochester]/8 [Pitts-burgh]/10–29 § Nov. 22/23/28 [Philadelphia Orch., Philadelphia] /29 [ibid.]/Dec. 1 [ibid.]–30 § Jn. 14–35 [BBC Sym, London] § *Jan. 7–39* § *Dec. 5–43* § *Nov. 3–46*
SYMPHONY No. 38 [PRAGUE] [9]
Feb. 7–26 § Feb. 27/28/Mar. 1/2 /3 [Philadelphia]/4 [Washington] /5 [Baltimore]/May 10 [Turin]–30
SYMPHONY No. 39, K. 543 [1]
Mar. 6–48
SYMPHONY No. 40, K. 550 [17]
Ap. 16/17/19–31 § Ap. 12/13/14–34 § Ap. 26–36 § Jn. 14–37 [BBC Sym, London] § *Dec. 25–37* § *Jn. 23–40* [Buenos Aires] § Nov. 20 [Philadelphia Orch., Philadelphia] /21 [ibid.]/24 [Philadelphia Orch.] –42 § *Jan. 27–46* § *Dec. 4–48* § *Mar. 11–50* § *Mar. 21–53*
SYMPHONY No. 41 [JUPITER] [11]
Nov. 20/22/23/24–29 and Mar. 16–30 § Mar. 30/31/Ap. 1–33 § Jn. 3–38 [BBC Sym, London] § *Ap. 20–40* § *Feb. 4–45*
DIE ZAUBERFLÖTE: OVERTURE [THE MAGIC FLUTE] [10]
Ap. 1–29 § *Jan. 8*/May 19 [BBC Sym, London]–38 § *Jn. 19–40* [Buenos Aires] § *Feb. 1–41* § *Oct. 31–43* § *Dec. 9–45* § *Nov. 3–46* § *Nov. 8–47* § *Nov. 26–49*

NICOLAI
THE MERRY WIVES OF WINDSOR: OVERTURE [1]
Jly. 18–43

PAËR
IL SARGINO: OVERTURE [4]
Oct. 17/18/19/20–29

PAGANINI
MOTO PERPETUO [10]
Ap. 12/13/14–34 § *Jan. 29–38* § *Feb. 21*/Mar. 16/Jn. 14 [Rio de Janeiro]/*15* [São Paulo]/*22* [Bue-nos Aires]/*Jly. 3* [Montevideo]–40

PIZZETTI
CONCERTO DELL'ESTATE [12]
Feb. 28/Mar. 1/3/16/24–29 § Mar. 3 [Pittsburgh]/4 [Washington]/5 [Baltimore]–30 § Dec. 3/4/5/6–31
INTRODUCTION TO THE AGAMEMNON OF AESCHYLUS [2]
[Schola Cantorum] Ap. 16/17–31
LA PISANELLE: SUITE [4]
Feb. 23/24/Mar. 4/9 [Pittsburgh] –28
RONDO VENEZIANO [9]
Feb. 27/28/Mar. 1/2/3 [Philadel-phia]/May 4 [Paris]/8 [Milan]/14 [Florence]/27 [Berlin]–30

PONCHIELLI
LA GIOCONDA: DANCE OF THE HOURS [3]
Ap. 4–43 § *Oct. 31–44* § *Jly. 26–52*

PROKOFIEV
SYMPHONY No. 1 [CLASSICAL] [9]
Mar. 14/15/23–29 § *Oct. 21–39* § *Jn. 25–44* § *Jan. 13–46* § *Nov. 15–47* § *Mar. 25–50* § *Nov. 10–51*

PUCCINI
LA BOHÈME [1]
[Albanese, McKnight, Peerce, Valentino, Moscona, Cehanovsky, Baccaloni, chorus under Peter Wil-housky and boys' chorus under Edoardo Petri]–*Feb. 3* and *10–46*
MANON LESCAUT: MINUET [ACT I] and INTERMEZZO [ACT III] [1]
Jly. 2–44
. . . PRELUDE TO ACT III [1]
Dec. 10–49

RAFF
SYMPHONY No. 3 [2]
Jan. 7/9–31

RAVEL
BOLERO [16]
Nov. 14/15/17/23–29 and Mar. 3 [Philadelphia]/4 [Washington]/5 [Baltimore]/7/May 4 [Paris]/9

[Milan]/19 [Vienna]/25 [Leipzig] –30 § Dec. 20–31 and Mar. 12–32 § Jan. 14–34 § *Jan. 21–39*

DAPHNIS AND CHLOE: 2ND SUITE [25]
Feb. 16/17/19/26/Mar. 10 [Pittsburgh]/11–28 § Mar. 14/15/23–29 § Mar. 26/27/28/29–31 § Jan. 28–34 § Mar. 26/27/29–36 § May 26–37 [BBC Sym, London] § *Nov. 26 –38* and *Jan. 10–39* [Boston] § *Nov. 19–49* and *Ap. 19* [Richmond]/*May 1* [Dallas]/9 [Portland]/23 [Pittsburgh]–50

LA VALSE [6]
Ap. 27/*May 14* [Washington]/*Jn. 14* [Rio de Janeiro]/27 [Buenos Aires]–40 § *Nov. 21–43* § *Feb. 19– 45*

RESPIGHI

BALLATA DELLE GNOMIDI [3]
Mar. 23/24/25–33

THE FOUNTAINS OF ROME [13]
Mar. 13/14/15/16–30 § *Feb. 4*/ *Mar. 14* [Washington]–39 § *Jn. 19* [Buenos Aires]/*Jly. 4* [Montevideo]/9 [Rio de Janeiro]–40 § Ap. 24–41 [Chicago Sym, Chicago] § *Mar. 23–47* § *Feb. 17–51* § *Dec. 22–51*

THE PINES OF ROME [20]
Jan. 14/15/16/17/30/31–26 § Feb. 4/5/9/10/21/26–28 § Nov. 29–31 § Mar. 12–33 § Ap. 23/24–36 § *Mar. 19–44* § Jan. 13–45 § *Mar. 22 –52* § *Mar. 14–53*

ROMAN FESTIVALS [21]
Feb. 21/22/23/24/Mar. 4 [Philadelphia]/5 [Washington]/6 [Baltimore]/7 [Rochester]/9 [Pittsburgh]/10/17–29 § Oct. 17/18/19 /20/Nov. 3–29 and May 12 [Rome]–30 § *Mar. 30–40* § Nov. 14 [Philadelphia Orch., Philadelphia] /15 [ibid.]–41 § *Dec. 10–49*

RIETI

SINFONIA TRIPARTITA [1]
Nov. 25–45

RIMSKY-KORSAKOV

SNOW MAIDEN: SUITE [4]
Ap. 8/10/12/18–31

ROGER-DUCCASSE

SARABANDE [8]
[Schola Cantorum] Jan. 28/29–26 § [Schola Cantorum] Oct. 31/Nov. 1–29 § [Schola Cantorum] Mar. 15 /16/18–34 § [chorus under Wilhousky] *Ap. 7–46*

ROSSINI

THE BARBER OF SEVILLE: OVERTURE [19]
Mar. 1/2/4/5 [Philadelphia]/6 [Washington]/7 [Baltimore]/8 [Buffalo]/9 [Pittsburgh]/11/17/25 –28 § Mar. 15/Ap. 9 [Hartford]– 31 § *Mar. 14–39* [Washington] § *Jn. 15* [São Paulo]/22 [Buenos Aires]–40 § *Nov. 21–43* § *Oct. 31– 44* § *Mar. 21–54*

LA CENERENTOLA: OVERTURE [8]
Oct. 22–38 and *Jan. 31* [Chicago]– 39 § *Jn. 13* [Rio de Janeiro] § *Jly. 1* [Buenos Aires]–40 § *Ap. 27* [Houston]/*May 5* [Pasadena]/*10* [Seattle]/*19* [Detroit]–50 [This is another favorite work for tours. Apparently Toscanini felt it was best to give unfamiliar audiences light, melodic works, rather than overtax them with the weightier classics.]

LA GAZZA LADRA: OVERTURE [2]
Ap. 12–41 § *Jn. 25–44*

THE ITALIAN WOMAN IN ALGIERS: OVERTURE [24]
Oct. 10/11/13/Nov. 4 [Philadelphia]–29 and Mar. 7/16/May 8 [Milan]/12 [Rome]/21 [Budapest] /23 [Prague]/Jn.1 [London]–30 § Feb. 2/3/Ap. 4 [Hartford]/29 [Providence]–35 § Mar. 14/15/19 [Boston]–36 § Jn. 2 [BBC Sym, London]/8 [BBC Sym, Oxford]– 37 § *Sept. 6–47* [Ridgefield, Conn.] § *Ap. 14/17* [Baltimore]/*May 7* [San Francisco]/*17* [Chicago]–50 [Another "touring vehicle."]

SEMIRAMIDE: OVERTURE [12]
Oct. 13/14/15/16/Nov. 17 [Greenwich]–32 § Jan. 21–34 § Mar. 25 [Broadcast, "General Motors Symphony Orchestra"]/Jn. 12–35 [BBC Sym, London] § *Feb. 5–38* § Ap.

19–45 [Los Angeles Philharmonic, Los Angeles] § *Mar. 13–48* § *Nov. 17–51*
THE SIEGE OF CORINTH: OVERTURE [2]
Jan. 7/9–31
IL SIGNOR BRUSCHINO: OVERTURE [7]
Mar. 20/21/22/23–30 § *Ap. 5–41* § *Nov. 8–42* § *Nov. 11–45*
THE SILKEN LADDER: OVERTURE [10]
Jan. 14/Ap. 19/20/21–34 § *Jan. 29 /Jn. 3* [BBC Sym, London]–38 § *Mar. 5–49* § *Ap. 22* [Atlanta]/*May 15* [St. Louis]/*27* [Philadelphia]–*50*
SONATA NO. 3 FOR TWO VIOLINS, 'CELLO, AND BASS [played by orchestra] [1]
Nov. 15–52
WILLIAM TELL: OVERTURE [12]
Mar. 21/22/30–29 § *Jan. 28–39* § *Mar. 16/Jly. 8* [São Paulo]–*40* § *Sept. 9–43* § *Ap. 29* [Austin]/*May 13* [Denver]/*21* [Cleveland]–*50* § *Mar. 15–52* § *Jan. 17–53*
. . . PASSO A SEI [SEXTET], ACT I and DANCE OF THE SOLDIERS, ACT III [5 + 2]
Nov. 19–38 § *Feb. 21–40* § [PASSO A SEI only] *Ap. 4–43* § *Jan. 5–52* § *Jan. 31–53*

ROUSSEL
THE SPIDER'S FEAST [9]
Dec. 25/26/28–30 and Jan. 3–31 § Ap. 19/20/21–34 §*Feb. 19–38* § *Ap. 7–46*
SYMPHONY NO. 4 [2]
Feb. 13/14–36

RUBINSTEIN
(orch. Mueller-Berghaus)
VALSE CAPRICE [1]
Dec. 21–40

DESABATA
GETHSEMANE [7]
Jan. 21/22/24/Feb. 6–26 § Mar. 30/31/Ap. 1–33
JUVENTUS [4]
Feb. 16/17/19/Mar. 10 [Pittsburgh]–28

SAINT-SAËNS
CONCERTO FOR 'CELLO [1]
[Schulz] Feb. 27–28
DANSE MACABRE [10]
Feb. 25 [Hartford]/Mar. 1 [Broadcast, "General Motors Symphony Orchestra"]–36 *Jan. 8–38* § *Jn. 28 –40* [Buenos Aires] § *Oct. 7–49* [Ridgefield, Conn.] § *Mar. 25/Ap. 22* [Atlanta]/*29* [Austin]/*May 13* [Denver]/*21* [Cleveland]–*50*
SYMPHONY NO. 3 [with organ] [11]
Mar. 15/16/18/24–28 § Feb. 26/27/28/Mar. 8–31 § Jan. 27/28–34 § *Nov. 15–52*

SAMMARTINI
SYMPHONY NO. 3 [3]
Jan. 1/2/4–31

SCARLATTI (orch. Tommasini)
THE GOOD-HUMORED LADIES [8]
Mar. 15/16/18/24–28 § *Feb. 5/Jn. 10* [BBC Sym, London]–38 § *Jan. 10–39* [Boston] § *Mar. 24–46*

SCHELLING
IMPRESSIONS FROM AN ARTIST'S LIFE [4]
[Schelling] Mar. 14/15–29 § [Schelling] Oct. 20/21–32

SCHUBERT
SYMPHONY NO. 2 [3]
Nov. 12–38 § *Mar. 23–40* § *Mar. 26–44*
SYMPHONY NO. 5 [1]
Mar. 14–53
SYMPHONY NO. 8 [UNFINISHED] [17]
Jan. 24–26 § Nov. 19/21/Dec. 15 [Philadelphia]/16 [Washington]/ 17 [Baltimore]/21/27–30 § *Oct. 14 –39* § *Jan. 24–42* § *Mar. 5–49* § *Mar. 11/Ap. 22* [Atlanta]/*29* [Austin]/*May 13* [Denver]/*21* [Cleveland]/*27* [Philadelphia]–*50*
SYMPHONY NO. 9 [sometimes called No. 7] [22]
Mar. 21/22/30–29 § Mar. 9 [Philadelphia]/10 [Washington]/11 [Baltimore]–31 § Nov. 16/18/19/ 20–32 § Jan. 31/Feb. 1–35 § Ap. 26–36 § *Jan. 1/Jn. 3* [BBC Sym,

London]–38 § *Jn. 14* [Rio de
Janeiro]/*25* [Buenos Aires]–*40* §
Nov. 14 [Philadelphia Orch., Phil-
adelphia]/15 [ibid.]–41 § *Nov. 11
–45* § *Feb. 23–47* § *Feb. 7–53*

SCHUBERT (orch. Brahms)
ELLEN'S SECOND SONG [THE LADY
OF THE LAKE] [3]
[Schola Cantorum] Mar. 28/29/31
–35

SCHUBERT (orch. Joachim)
SYMPHONY IN C MAJOR [from the
SONATA or GRAND DUO FOR
PIANO, FOUR HANDS, OP. 140–
in all probability the lost GAS-
TEIN SYMPHONY, i.e., No. 7] [1]
Feb. 15–41

SCHUBERT ("paraphrased" and
otherwise reconstructed by Liszt)
WANDERER FANTASY [2]
[Siloti] Nov. 19/21–30

SCHUMANN
CONCERTO FOR 'CELLO, OP. 129 [3]
[Schulz] Ap. 1–29 § [Wallenstein]
Mar. 23/24–33
MANFRED OVERTURE [13]
Oct. 3/4/5/6–29 § Mar. 26/27/29–
36 § *Nov. 19–38* § Feb. 13 [Cin-
cinnati Sym, Cincinnati/]14 [*ibid.*]
/26 [Philadelphia Orch., Philadel-
phia]–43 § *Nov. 10–46* § *Jan. 3–
53*
SYMPHONY No. 2 [9]
Oct. 13/14/15/16–32 § Jan. 21–34
§ Mar. 11/13–36 § *Mar. 29–41* §
Mar. 17–46
SYMPHONY No. 3 [RHENISH] [10]
Ap. 3/4/5/6/May 8 [Milan]–30 §
Nov. 29–31 § *Jan. 29–38* § *Mar. 16
40* § *Mar. 18–45* § *Nov. 12–49*
SYMPHONY No. 4 [4]
Feb. 26/27/28/Mar. 1–31

SHOSTAKOVICH
SYMPHONY No. 1 [7]
Ap. 8/10/12/18–31 § Jn. 4–37
[BBC Sym, London] § *Jan. 14–39*
§ *Mar. 12–44*

SYMPHONY No. 7 [LENINGRAD] [4]
Jly. 19/Oct. 14/16/18–42

SIBELIUS
EN SAGA [13]
Jan. 1/2/4–31 § Nov. 3/4/6–32 §
Mar. 26/27/29–36 § Jn. 14–37
[BBC Sym, London] § *Feb. 18–39*
§ *Feb. 26–49* § *Mar. 15–52*
FINLANDIA [5]
Oct. 31/Nov. 1–29 § *Feb. 18–39* §
Dec. 7–40 § *Jly. 26–52*
POHJOLA'S DAUGHTER and LEMMIN-
KÄINEN'S HOMECOMING [1]
Dec. 7–40
THE SWAN OF TUONELLA [16]
Jan. 14/15/16–26 § Oct. 13/14/15
/16/Nov. 17 [Greenwich]–32 §
Feb. 13/14/Ap. 23/24–36 § *Feb.
18–39* § *Dec. 7–40* § *Aug. 27–44* §
Jan. 13–45
SYMPHONY No. 2 [4]
Jan. 15/Jn. 10 [BBC Sym, Lon-
don]–38 § *Feb. 18–39* § *Dec. 7–40*
SYMPHONY No. 4 [6]
Mar. 19/20/21/22–31 § Feb. 24–
34 § *Ap. 27–40*

SIEGMEISTER
WESTERN SUITE [1]
Nov. 25–45

SINIGAGLIA
LE BARUFFE CHIOZZOTTE [8]
Jan. 26/27/29/30 [Baltimore]/31
[Washington]/Feb. 1 [Philadel-
phia]/14–28 § *Feb. 23–47*
PIEDMONT SUITE: OVER FIELDS AND
WOODS and RUSTIC DANCE [1]
Ap. 12–41

SMETANA
THE BARTERED BRIDE: OVERTURE
[10]
Ap. 8/10/12/18–31 § Feb. 22/23/
24/Mar. 15 [Hartford]–34 § *Nov.
26–38* § *Nov. 17–46*
THE MOLDAU [26]
Ap. 3/4/12/13/May 23 [Prague]–
30 § Ap. 1/2/4/5–31 § Mar. 16–36
[Boston] § *Feb. 26*/May 19 [BBC
Sym, London]–38 § *Jn. 13* [Rio de

Janeiro]/29 [Buenos Aires]/*Jly. 3* [Montevideo]–40 § *Dec.   13–41* § *Mar. 26–44* § *Sept. 9–45* § *Sept. 21 –47* § *Mar. 11/Ap. 27* [Houston]/ *May 5* [Pasadena]/*10* [Seattle]/*19* [Detroit]/*25*   [Washington]–*50* § *Mar. 14–53*

SMITH (orch. Toscanini)

THE STAR-SPANGLED BANNER [Undoubtedly Toscanini played national anthems at a number of his concerts, but since they are not "normal" symphonic works, I have listed only the two—ironically "The Star-Spangled Banner" and "The Internationale" —which exist in Toscanini arrangements.]

May 14–40 [Washington] § Oct. 7 /9/11–42 [augmented by Tourel, Gerald, Moscona, Westminster Choir—Williamson] § *Ap. 25–43* § *Sept. 9–43* § *Sept. 2–45*

SONZOGNO

IL NEGRO and TANGO FOR ORCHESTRA [2]
[Wallenstein—in IL NEGRO only] Ap. 17/18–35

SOUSA

EL CAPITAN [1]
Aug. 27–44
SEMPER FIDELIS [1]
Aug. 27–44
THE STARS AND STRIPES FOREVER [2]
Ap. 4–43 § May 25–44 [combined NBC and P-SNY]

STRAUSS, J.

ON THE BEAUTIFUL BLUE DANUBE [1]
Dec. 6–41
TRITSCH-TRATSCH [2]
Feb. 15–41 § *Sept. 6–47* [Ridgefield, Conn.]
VOICES OF SPRING [4]
Feb. 15–41 § *Jly. 18–43* § *Jan. 13– 46* § *Sept. 6–47* [Ridgefield, Conn.]

STRAUSS, R.

DEATH AND TRANSFIGURATION [30]
Mar. 15/16/17/18–28 § Mar. 20/ 21/22/23/30/May 16 [Munich]/ 18 [Vienna]/28 [Berlin]/Jn. 3 [London]–30 § Jan. 18–31 § Feb. 22/23/24–34 § Mar. 17 [Boston]/ Ap. 1/3/5–36 § Jn. 2–37 [BBC Sym, London] § *Jan. 1–38* § *Jn. 15* [São Paulo]/*25* [Buenos Aires]–*40* § Jan. 9 [Philadelphia Orch., Philadelphia]/10 [ibid.]/13 [Philadelphia Orch., Washington]–42 § *Nov. 17–46* § *Mar. 8–52*
DON JUAN [17]
Dec. 20–31 § Oct. 27/28/30–32 § Jan. 21–34 § Ap. 29–35 [Providence] § *Oct.   14–39* § *May   14* [Washington]/*Jn.   20*   [Buenos Aires]–*40* § *Feb. 14–48* § *Mar. 25 /Ap. 14/17* [Baltimore]/*May 7* [San Francisco]/*15* [St. Louis]/*17* [Chicago]–*50* § *Feb. 28–54*
DON QUIXOTE [9]
[Wallenstein, Pollain] Oct. 3/4/5/ 6–29 § [Wallenstein, Pollain] Ap. 19–31 § [Feuermann, Cooley] *Oct. 22–38* § [Feuermann, Shore] May 23–38 [BBC Sym, London] § [Miller, Cooley] *Dec. 11–48* § [Miller, Cooley] *Nov. 22–53*
EIN HELDENLEBEN [14]
Nov. 7/8/10–29 § Nov. 22/23/28 [Philadelphia Orch., Philadelphia] /29 [ibid.]/Dec. 1 [ibid.]–30 § Mar. 1/3/4/5/15 [Hartford]–33 § *Feb. 1–41*
SALOME: SALOME'S DANCE [DANCE OF THE SEVEN VEILS] [5]
Jan. 24/25/26/27–35 § *Jan. 14–39*
TILL EULENSPIEGEL [17]
Mar. 22/23/24–28 § Mar. 27/28/ 29/May 14 [Florence]/30 [Brussels]–30 § Nov.   10/11/13–32 § *Feb. 21/Mar. 16/Jn. 22* [Buenos Aires]–*40* § *Mar. 17–46* § *Mar. 5– 49* § *Nov. 1–52*
ZUEIGNUNG [1]
[Gianini] Mar. 1–36 [Broadcast, "General Motors Symphony Orchestra"]

STRAVINSKY

FIREWORKS [4]
Oct. 24/25/27/Nov. 23–29
PETROUCHKA: SUITE [apparently the music of the fair from the first and fourth scenes] [8]
Jan. 21/22/24 Feb. 6–26 § Mar. 15/16/18–34 § Dec. 21–40

STRONG

DIE NACHT: SUITE FOR ORCHESTRA [1]
Oct. 21–39

VON SUPPÉ

POET AND PEASANT OVERTURE [1]
Jly. 18–43

TANSMAN

QUATRE DANSES POLONAISES [6]
Oct. 6/7/8/9/24 [Philadelphia]/ 25 [Washington]–32

TCHAIKOVSKY

CONCERTO FOR PIANO No. 1 [2]
[Horowitz] Ap. 19–41 § [Horowitz] Ap. 25–43
EUGENE ONEGIN: WALTZES [1]
Aug. 27–44
MANFRED SYMPHONY [usually called a symphonic poem] [9]
Mar. 16/17/19–33 § Dec. 21–40 § Jan. 21–45 § Nov. 10–46 § Feb. 28 –48 § Dec. 3–49 § Jan. 10–53
NUTCRACKER BALLET: SUITE No. 1 [4]
Ap. 6–40 § Ap. 25–43 § Jn. 25–44 § Nov. 17–51
ROMEO AND JULIET: OVERTURE-FANTASIA [16]
Jan. 14/27/Mar. 15 [Hartford]–34 § Mar. 11/13/14/15–36 § Oct. 15 –38 § Ap. 6/Jn. 27 [Buenos Aires] –40 § Ap. 7–46 § Nov. 12–49 and May 5 [Pasadena]/10 [Seattle]/19 [Detroit]–50 § Mar. 21–53
SYMPHONY No. 6 [PATHÉTIQUE] [16]
Oct. 29/Dec. 31 [Newark]–38 § Ap. 6–40 § Ap. 19–41/Feb. 6 [Philadelphia Orch., Philadelphia] /7 [ibid.]/10 [Philadelphia Orch.] –42 § Ap. 25–43 § Ap. 18–44 §

Nov. 15–47 § Mar. 4/Ap. 19 [Richmond]/May 1 [Dallas]/9 [Portland]/23 [Pittsburgh]–50 § Mar. 21–54
THE TEMPEST: OVERTURE-FANTASIA [4]
Ap. 5/7/8–33 § Mar. 12–44
THE VOYEVODA: OVERTURE [1]
Ap. 19–41

THOMAS

MIGNON OVERTURE [3]
Mar. 14–42 § Oct. 7–49 [Ridgefield, Conn.] § Jly. 26–52

TOMMASINI

THE CARNIVAL OF VENICE [VARIATIONS IN THE STYLE OF PAGANINI] [11]
Oct. 10/11/13/Nov. 2/4 [Philadelphia]–29 and May 9 [Milan]/ 12 [Rome]–30 § May 28–37 [BBC Sym, London] § Jan. 15–38 § Mar. 29–41 § Mar. 13–48
PRELUDE, FANFARE, AND FUGUE [3]
Mar. 21/22/30–29
SERENATA: CHIARO DI LUNA [5]
Jan. 1/2/4–31 § Jan. 27/28–34
TUSCAN LANDSCAPES [2]
Jan. 28/29–26

VAUGHAN WILLIAMS

FANTASIA FOR DOUBLE STRING ORCHESTRA ON A THEME OF THOMAS TALLIS [3]
May 19–38 [BBC Sym, London] § Oct. 15–38 § Nov. 18–45
SYMPHONY No. 2 [LONDON] [1]
Dec. 9–45

VERDI

AÏDA [1]
[Nelli, Gustafson, Tucker, Valdengo, Stitch-Randall, Scott, Harbour, Assandri, Robert Shaw Chorale] Mar. 26 and Ap. 2–49
. . . CIELI AZZIRRI [1]
[Gianini] Mar. 1–36 [Broadcast, "General Motors Symphony Orchestra"]
. . ."OVERTURE" [a MS score, never

previously heard in public] [1]
Mar. 30–40

UN BALLO IN MASCHERA [1]
[Peerce, Merrill, Nelli, Turner, Haskins, Cehanovsky, Moscona, Scott, Rossi, Robert Shaw Chorale] *Jan. 17* and *24–54*
. . . ERI TU, CHE MACCHIARI [2]
[Valentino] *Jly. 25–43* § [Valentino] *Oct. 31–44*

DON CARLOS: O DON FATALE [1]
[Merriman] *Jly. 25–43*

FALSTAFF [1]
[Nelli, Merrill, Elmo, Stitch-Randall, Valdengo, Carelli, Rossi, Scott, Guarrara, Robert Shaw Chorale] *Ap. 1* and *8–50*

LA FORZA DEL DESTINO: OVERTURE [3]
Jan. 31–43 § *Jan. 27–46* § *Nov. 8–52*
. . . PACE, PACE, MIO DIO [2]
[Rethberg] *Mar. 24–35* [Broadcast, "General Motors Symphony Orchestra"] § [Ribla] *Jly. 25–43*

HYMN OF THE NATIONS [2]
[della Chiesa, Peerce, Moscona, Westminster Choir—Williamson] *Jan. 31–43* § [Milanov, Peerce, Moscona, All City High School Chorus under Peter Wilhousky] *May 25–44* [combined NBC and P-SNY]

I LOMBARDI: TRIO; QUI POSA IL FIANCO . . . QUAL VOLUTTA [1]
[della Chiesa, Peerce, Moscona] *Jan. 31–43*

LUISA MILLER: OVERTURE [1]
Jly. 25–43
. . . QUANDO LE SERE AL PLACIDO [1]
[Peerce] *Jly. 25–43*

NABUCODONOSOR [NABUCCO]—CHORUS [presumably VA PENSIERO SULL'ALI DORATE] [2]
[Westminster Choir] *Jan. 31–43* § [Westminster Choir] *Oct. 31–44*

OTELLO [1]
[Nelli, Merriman, Vinay, Valdengo, Assandri, Chabay, Newman, Moscona, chorus under Wilhousky, boys' chorus under Petri] *Dec. 6* and *13–47*

. . . AVE MARIA [1]
[Rethberg] *Mar. 24–35* [Broadcast, "General Motors Symphony Orchestra"]
. . . BALLABILLI [dances] [3]
Jan. 31–43 § *Jan. 27–46* § *Mar. 13–48*

QUARTET IN E MINOR [2]
Mar. 17–36 [Boston] § *Jan. 27–46*

REQUIEM [8]
[Rethberg, Matzenauer, Chamlee, Pinza, Schola Cantorum] *Jan. 15/16–31* § [Milanov, Castagna, Kullmann, Moscona, Schola Cantorum] *Mar. 4* and [Milanov, Thorborg, Roswaenge, Moscona, BBC Choral Society—Woodgate] *May 27/30–38* [BBC Sym, London] § [Milanov, Castagna, Bjoerling, Moscona, Schola Cantorum] *Nov. 23–40* § [Nelli, Merriman, McGrath, Scott, Collegiate Chorale—Shaw] *Ap. 26–48* § [Nelli, Barbieri, DiStefano, Sepi, Robert Shaw Chorale—Hunter] *Jan. 27–51*

RIGOLETTO: ACT III [2]
[Ribla, Merriman, Peerce, Valentino, Moscona] *Jly. 25–43* § [Milanov, Merriman, Peerce, Warren, Moscona] *May 25–44* [combined NBC and P-SNY]
. . . QUARTET: BELLA FIGLIA DELL'-AMORE [1]
[Ribla, Merriman, Peerce, Valentino] *Oct. 31–44*

THE SICILIAN VESPERS: OVERTURE [5]
Ap. 17/18/29 [Providence]–35 § *Jan. 24–42* § *Oct. 31–44*

TE DEUM [9]
[Schola Cantorum] *Ap. 16/17–31* § [BBC Choral Society—Woodgate] *May 27/30–38* [BBC Sym, London] § [Westminster Choir] *Nov. 23–40* § [chorus under Wilhousky] *Dec. 2–45* § [Collegiate Chorale—Shaw] *Ap. 26–48* § [Robert Shaw Chorale—Hunter] *Feb. 27–51* § [Robert Shaw Chorale—Shaw] *Mar. 14–54*

LA TRAVIATA [1]
[Albanese, Peerce, Merrill, Ceha-

novsky, chorus under Wilhousky]
Dec. 1 and *8–46*
. . . PRELUDES [1 + 3]
[Acts I and III] Feb. 11–34
[Broadcast, "General Motors Symphony Orchestra"] § [Act III] *Jan. 31–43* § [ibid.] *Oct. 31–44*

VIEUXTEMPS
BALLADE and POLONAISE [4]
Dec. 14–40 § Feb. 6 [Philadelphia Orch., Philadelphia]/7 [ibid.]/10 [Philadelphia Orch.]–42

VIOTTI
CONCERTO FOR VIOLIN IN A MINOR, No. 22 [2]
[Piastro] Nov. 24/25–32

VIVALDI
CONCERTO [presumably No. 5] IN A MAJOR [3]
Mar. 15/16/18–34
CONCERTO [presumably No. 11] IN D MINOR [7]
Jan. 21/22/30/31–26 § Jn. 4–37 [BBC Sym, London] § *Dec. 25–37* § *Mar. 14–54*
CONCERTO FOR VIOLIN IN A MINOR WITH STRINGS AND ORGAN [presumably Pincherle No. 12] [3]
[Guidi] Mar. 22/23/24–28
CONCERTO IN B-FLAT FOR VIOLIN AND STRINGS [presumably Pincherle No. 405] [1]
[Mischakoff] *Nov. 22–47*
THE SEASONS: SPRING [4]
[Guidi] Feb. 9/10/19/26–28
. . . WINTER [2]
[presumably Piastro] Feb. 13/14–36

VIVALDI (arr. Bach)
CONCERTO FOR FOUR PIANOS [4]
[Carreras, Sheridan, Kurthy, Marshall] Oct. 13/14/15/16–32

WAGENAAR, B.
SYMPHONY No. 2 [3]
Nov. 10/11/13–32

WAGNER
A FAUST OVERTURE [18]
Mar. 14/15/23–29 § Mar. 27/28/May 6 [Zurich]/9 [Milan]–30 § Mar. 1/3/4/5/15 [Hartford]–33 § Ap. 15–34 § Jn. 5–35 [BBC Sym, London] Jn. 16–37 [BBC Sym, London] § *Mar. 5–38* § *Mar. 29–41* § *Oct. 27–46*
THE FLYING DUTCHMAN [23]
Mar. 15/Ap. 8/10/12/18–31 § Nov. 26/27/29–31 § Dec. 14 [Philadelphia]/15 [Washington]/16 [Baltimore]/Nov. 2–32 § Ap. 20/21/22–33 § Mar. 15/16/18–34 § Mar. 16–36 [Boston] § *Feb. 26–38* § *Feb. 25–39* § Nov. 30–42 § *Mar. 31–46*
DIE GÖTTERDÄMMERUNG: DAWN AND SIEGFRIED'S RHINE JOURNEY [concert version by Toscanini] [30]
Oct. 10/11/13/Nov. 2/4 [Philadelphia]/24–29 § Jan. 11/17–31 § Oct. 20/21/22/23–32 and Mar. 19/Ap. 12/13/15–33 § Jn. 16–37 [BBC Sym, London] § [program listings are unclear but the Dawn music may have been omitted from the following three performances] *Mar. 5–38* § *Feb. 25/Mar. 14* [Washington]–39 § [special version with the whole of the Siegfried-Brunhilde duet and additional material, see entry below: Traubel, Melchior] *Feb. 22–41* § *Nov. 30–42* § May 25–44 [combined NBC and P-SNY] § *Jan. 6–46* § *Nov. 24–46* § *Mar. 20–48* § *Feb. 26–49* § *Dec. 17–49* § *Nov. 24–51* § *Ap. 4–54*
. . . SIEGFRIED'S DEATH AND FUNERAL MUSIC [concert version by Toscanini] [29]
Jan. 14/15/16/30/31/Feb. 1–26 § Feb. 27/Mar. 25/31–28 § Nov. 20/22/24–29 and Ap. 3/4 [in memory of Cosima Wagner]–30 § Dec. 8 [Philadelphia Orch., Philadelphia]/18–30 § Ap. 29–34 § Ap. 21/Jn. 3 [BBC Sym, London]/5 [ibid.]–35 § Ap. 23/24–36 § *Dec. 3–38* § *Jan. 10–39* [Boston] § Feb.

22–41 § Jan. 13–45 § *Dec. 17–49* §
Dec. 29–51 § *Mar. 7–53*
. . . IMMOLATION SCENE and OR-
   CHESTRAL FINALE [3]
[Kappel] Ap. 29–34 § [Traubel]
Feb. 22–41 § [Traubel] *Nov. 30–
42*
LOHENGRIN: PRELUDE [19]
   Feb. 19/Mar. 31–28 § Dec. 8
[Philadelphia Orch., Philadelphia]
/18–30 and Jan. 11/17/Ap. 9
[Hartford]–31 § Mar. 19/25/Ap.
22–33 § Ap. 22–34 § Ap. 21–35 §
Jn. 16–37 [BBC Sym, London] §
Mar. 5–38 § *Jn. 25–40* [Buenos
Aires] § *Feb. 22–41* § *Mar. 24–43*
§ *Dec. 29–51* § *Ap. 4–54*
LOHENGRIN: PRELUDE TO ACT III
   [Humperdinck ending] [12]
Mar. 15–31 § Mar. 19/Ap. 22–33 §
Ap. 22–34 § Ap. 21–35 § Mar. 1–
36 [Broadcast, "General Motors
Symphony Orchestra"] § Jn. 16–37
[BBC Sym, London] § *Mar. 5–38*
§ *Jn. 25–40* [Buenos Aires] § *Mar.
24–43* § *Mar. 20–48* § *Mar. 7–53*
DIE MEISTERSINGER: PRELUDE [54]
   [Highest frequency of any work
   in the listing.]
Feb. 14/Mar. 31–28 § Mar. 9
[Pittsburgh]/Ap. 1–29 § Nov. 14/
15/17/23–29 and Mar. 22 [end of
children's series, special appear-
ance of Toscanini]/May 4 [Paris]/
Jn. 4 [London]–30 § Dec. 18–30 §
Jan. 11/17/Mar. 22/Ap. 9 [Hart-
ford]–31 § Ap. 5/7/8–33 § Ap. 29
–34 § Ap. 4 [Hartford]/21–35 §
Ap. 29–36 § May 28–37 [BBC
Sym, London] § *Jan. 22–38* § *Dec.
13* [Newark]/27 [Baltimore]–38
and *Jan. 7/31* [Chicago]/*Feb. 1*
[Pittsburgh]/7 [Providence]–39 §
Oct. 21–39 and *Jn. 13* [Rio de
Janeiro]/*19* [Buenos Aires]/*Jly. 1*
[ibid.]/*4* [Montevideo]/*Jly. 10*
[Rio de Janeiro]–*40* § *Mar. 14–42*
§ Nov. 30–42 § Feb. 13 [Cincin-
nati Sym, Cincinnati]/14 [ibid.]/
26 [Philadelphia Orch., Philadel-
phia]/*Mar. 24–43* § *Feb. 4*/Ap. 19
–45 [Los Angeles Philharmonic,

Los Angeles] § *Jan. 6–46* § *Mar.
18/Ap. 25* [New Orleans]/29
[Austin]/*May 3* [Pasadena]/25
[Washington]–*50* § *Feb. 7–53*/Ap.
4–54 [This was Toscanini's last
performance of any work in New
York.]
. . . PRELUDE TO ACT III [Humper-
dinck ending] [5]
Ap. 16/17–30 § *Nov. 19–38* § *Nov.
28–43* § *Nov. 24–51*
PARSIFAL: PRELUDE and GOOD FRI-
   DAY SPELL [23 and 32]
[SPELL only] Feb. 19/Mar. 22/23/
24–28 § Mar. 27/28/31–29 § Ap.
16/17–30 § [PRELUDE only] Ap. 1/
2/4/5–31 § Ap. 28–32 § Ap. 12/13
/15–33 § [ACT III excerpts un-
specified; Clemens, Bonelli, Metropolitan Opera Chorus] Ap. 22–34
§ Ap. 21/Jn. 5 [BBC Sym, Lon-
don]–35 § [PRELUDE only] *Mar. 5–
38* § [SPELL only] *Nov. 12–38* §
[SPELL only] *Oct. 21–39* § *Feb. 21
–40* § [both plus PRELUDE ACT II,
KLINGSOR'S MAGIC GARDEN, PRE-
LUDE ACT III, and FINALE] *Mar.
23*/*Jn. 13* [Rio de Janeiro]/*19*
[Buenos Aires]–*40* § *Ap. 12–41* §
[SPELL only] *Dec. 6–41* § *Ap. 4–
42* § *Ap. 9–44* § *Ap. 6–47* § *Dec.
17–49* and [SPELL only] *Ap. 27*
[Houston]/*May 5* [Pasadena]/*10*
[Seattle]/*19* [Detroit]–*50*
RIENZI OVERTURE [1]
   Dec. 3–38
SIEGFRIED: FOREST MURMURS [28]
   Ap. 16/17/19/20–30 and Mar.
15–31 § Mar. 19/Ap. 22–33 §
Ap. 15–34 § Mar. 24–35 [Broad-
cast, "General Motors Symphony
Orchestra"] § Jn. 16–37 [BBC
Sym, London] § *Dec. 3/13*
[Newark]/27 [Baltimore]–38 and
Jan. 10 [Boston]/*31* [Chicago]/
Feb. 1 [Pittsburgh]/9 [Provi-
dence]–39 § *Jn. 23* [Buenos Aires]
/*Jly. 9* [Rio de Janerio]–*40* §
Nov. 30–42 § *Aug. 27–44* § *Mar.
20–48* § *Oct. 7–49* [Ridgefield,
Conn.] and Ap. 25 [New Orleans]/

May 3 [Pasadena]/*25* [Washington]–*50* § *Dec. 20–51* § *Ap. 4–54*

SIEGFRIED IDYLL [20]

Feb. 27–28 § Dec. 8 [Philadelphia Orch., Philadelphia]/18–30 § Ap. 9–31 [Hartford] § Nov. 2/20–32 § Feb. 11 [Broadcast, "General Motors Symphony Orchestra"]/Ap. 15/21–34 § Ap. 29–36 § Jn. 16–37 [BBC Sym, London] § *Feb. 12–38* § *Jn. 23* [Buenos Aires]–*40* § *Ap. 24–41* [Chicago Sym, Chicago] § Nov. 30–42 § *Jan. 6–46* § *Sept. 6–47* [Ridgefield, Conn.] § *Jly. 26–52* § *Mar. 7–53*

TANNHÄUSER: OVERTURE [original Dresden version] [26]

Feb. 27/Mar. 1/2/4 [Philadelphia]/5 [Washington]/6 [Baltimore]/7 [Rochester]/8 [Pittsburgh]/11/25/31–28 § Feb. 21/22/23/24/Mar. 10/31–29 § Ap. 9–31 [Hartford] § Feb. 25–36 [Hartford] § *Mar. 5–38* § *Mar. 14–39* [Washington] § *Jn. 23* [Buenos Aires]/*Jly. 8* [São Paulo]–*40* § *Ap. 24–41* [Chicago Sym, Chicago] § May 25–44 [combined NBC and P-SNY] § *Dec. 4–48*

. . . OVERTURE WITH THE VENUSBERG BACCHANAL [Paris version] [30]

Feb. 27/28/Mar. 1/2/3 [Philadelphia]/4 [Washington]/5 [Baltimore]/May 19 [Vienna]/25 [Leipzig]–30 § Dec. 8 [Philadelphia Orch., Philadelphia]/18–30 and Mar. 22–31 § Mar. 6 [Philadelphia]/7 [Washington]/8 [Baltimore]–32 § Nov. 2/20–32 § Ap. 22–34 § Feb. 2/3–35 § Jn. 16–37 [BBC Sym, London] § *Feb. 25–39* § Nov. 20 [Philadelphia Orch., Philadelphia]/21 [ibid.]–24 [Philadelphia Orch.]–42 § *Nov. 28–43* § *Mar. 20–48* § *Ap. 20–49* § *Nov. 8–52* § *Ap. 4–54*

. . . VENUSBERG BACCHANAL [only] [4]

May 10 [Turin]/Jn. 1 [London]–30 § Dec. 21–30 and Jan. 11–31

. . . PRELUDE TO ACT III [original version] [4]

Mar. 5–31 § *Feb. 25–39* § *Jan. 6–46* § *Nov. 29–53*

. . . DICH TEURE HALLE [2]

[Lehmann] Feb. 4–34 [Broadcast, "General Motors Symphony Orchestra"] § [Traubel] *Feb. 22–41*

TRISTAN UND ISOLDE: PRELUDE and ISOLDE'S LOVE-DEATH [45 + 44]

Jan. 28/29/Feb. 7–26 § Feb. 14/27/Mar. 5 [Philadelphia]/6 [Washington]/7 [Baltimore]/8 [Buffalo]/10 [Pittsburgh]–28 § Mar. 16/29/Ap. 9/11/May 3 [Paris]/21 [Budapest]/23 [Prague]/26 [Dresden]/Jn. 2 [London]–30 § Dec. 8 [Philadelphia Orch., Philadelphia]/18–30 § Nov. 2/27 [LOVE-DEATH sung by Alsen]–32 and Mar. 6 [Philadelphia]/7 [Washington]/8 [Baltimore]–33 § Jan. 27/[PRELUDE only] 28–34 § [LOVE-DEATH AND TRANSFIGURATION is the program citation, but I assume only the usual music was played] Ap. 21–35 § Ap. 29–36 § *Mar. 5–38* § *Feb. 25–39* § *Jn. 23* [Buenos Aires]/*29* [ibid.]/*Jly. 4* [Montevideo]/*8* [São Paulo]–*40* § [PRELUDE only, operatic ending] *Feb. 22–41* § Nov. 30–42 [LOVE-DEATH sung by Traubel] and *Feb. 13* [Cincinnati Sym, Cincinnati]/*14* [ibid.]/*Mar. 24–43* § *Nov. 28–43* § May 25–44 [combined NBC and P-SNY]/Ap. 19–45 [Los Angeles Philharmonic, Los Angeles] § *Dec. 29–51* § *Mar. 7–53*

. . . ACT II "LOVE SCENE" [no idea of extent of excerpt] [1]

[Kappel, Telva, Althouse] Ap. 15–34

DIE WALKÜRE: ACT I, SCENE 3 [final entrance of Sieglinde to end of act] [6]

[Alsen, Althouse] Nov. 2/27–32 § [Kappel, Althouse] Ap. 29–34 § [Traubel, Melchoir] *Feb. 22–41* § [Bampton, Svanholm] *Ap. 6–47* § [Bampton, Svanholm] *Ap. 20–49*

. . . PRELUDE TO ACT III [modified for concert, THE RIDE OF THE VALKYRIES] [18]

Nov. 20/22/24–29 § Mar. 15–31 §
Feb. 2/3–35 § Ap. 29–36 § Jn.
16–37 [BBC Sym, London] §
Mar. 5–38 § *Feb. 25–39* § *Jn. 29–*
40 [Buenos Aires] § *Nov. 28–43* §
[operatic text with choral parts,
All City High School Chorus
under Peter Wilhousky] May 25–
44 [combined NBC and P-SNY] §
Mar. 20–48 § *Ap. 20–49* § *Dec.*
17–49 § *Dec. 29–51* § *Mar. 7–53*

WALDTEUFEL
THE SKATERS WALTZ [2]
Jn. 25–44 § *Oct. 7–49* [Ridgefield,
Conn.]

WEBER
EURYANTHE: OVERTURE [9]
Jan. 14/15/16/Feb. 6–26 § Ap.
23/24–36 § *Feb. 12–38* § Jan. 13–
45 § *Nov. 3–51*
DER FREISCHÜTZ: OVERTURE [5]
Mar. 1–36 [Broadcast, "General
Motors Symphony Orchestra"] §
Feb. 25 [Hartford]/Mar. 16
[Boston]–36 § *Feb. 19–45* § *Jn. 5–*
52
OBERON: OVERTURE [16]
Feb. 26/27/28/Mar. 1/9 [Phila-
delphia]/10 [Washington]/11
[Baltimore]–31 § Ap. 1/3/5–36 §
Dec. 13 [Newark]/27 [Baltimore]–
38 § *Jn. 27–40* [Buenos Aires] §
Mar. 19–44 § *Aug. 2–52* § *Feb.*
28–54
THE RULER OF THE SPIRITS: OVER-
TURE [4]

Mar. 13/14/15/May 26 [Dres-
den]–30

WEBER (orch. Berlioz)
INVITATION TO THE DANCE [17]
Dec. 10/11/13–31 § *Feb. 19*/May
19 [BBC Sym, London]–38 § *Jan.*
3 [Chicago]/*Feb. 1* [Pittsburgh]/
4/7 [Providence]–*39* § *Jn. 15* [Rio
de Janeiro]/*Jly. 1* [Buenos Aires]/
3 [Montivideo]/*10* [Rio de Ja-
neiro]–*40* § Ap. 24–41 [Chicago
Sym, Chicago] § Ap. 19–45 [Los
Angeles Philharmonic, Los
Angeles]/*Mar. 12–49* § *Dec. 13–53*

WELPRIK
DANCES AND SONGS OF THE GHETTO
[2]
Mar. 16/17–33

WETZLER
SYMPHONIC DANCE: THE BASQUE
VENUS [3]
Nov. 14/15/17–29

WILLIAMS
SYMPHONY No. 7 [DANZARINUS
TUCADORES DE CROTALOS] [1]
Jn. 29–40 [Buenos Aires]

WOLF-FERRARI
THE CURIOUS LADIES: OVERTURE [2]
Nov. 18–45 § *Nov. 29–47*
THE SECRET OF SUZANNE: OVERTURE
[5]
Dec. 11/12/14–30 and Jan. 18–
31 § *Jan. 20–46*

Appendix Two: *A Note on Equipment*

The sound produced by a record when we play it cannot be any better than the best sound which the reproducing apparatus is itself capable of producing. The common term "high fidelity" suggests that there is, in a Pickwickian sense, "low fidelity." Actually, sound is either faithful to the original or not; it is either fidelity or non-fidelity. (Infidelity also has its effect on reproduction, but it is not a problem of electroacoustics.) "Low fidelity" or "medium fidelity" recordings depart from the original by the limitation of frequency range and/or the introduction of tonal distortion, incorrect balance, etc. A high fidelity recording reproduced on high fidelity equipment will yield excellent sound, providing the recording and equipment are actually of first quality and *are being used properly*. A high fidelity recording played on a machine of less than high fidelity standards, may not sound bad, but whatever defects the machine has will be heard in the recording. Similarly, a recording of less than the highest fidelity will be ruthlessly exposed by high fidelity equipment, although, if it is a good recording, it will not sound disagreeable. A "low fidelity" machine makes everything sound the same, and thus disks which I here condemn as offering poor sound, may seem limited, completely lacking in presence, but not unpleasant, on "low fidelity" reproducers, and the most brilliant recordings here listed, played over the same equipment, will appear to have the same kind of sound. That is why, in the pre-high fidelity era record companies (which also made home reproducing-equipment) could turn out and sell millions of copies of poor records; only a small number of consumers had equipment which showed up their faults. With the public demand for high fidelity, records and the equipment to play them on had to be raised to a higher standard in order to sell.

I am not particularly interested in what these records might sound like reproduced over a multi-speaker system in the Royal Festival Hall or any other concert room, nor am I interested in the sound which they yield on small, "ultra low-fidelity" home-type machines, played (as they so often are) so that ff comes out as a mild, choked-up sound, and anything under mf is inaudible. "Music-lovers" who are interested only in securing dulcet background noises that will not interfere with their own brilliant talk, might, had the opportunity been offered them, have been crunching popcorn during the Sermon on the Mount. Music, as Artur Schnabel brilliantly set forth in a Harvard lecture shortly before his death, is defenseless. The philistine is free at all times to do his worst, unless a militant public restrains his hand, and the manner in which one treats music is a matter of personal morality, similar to the manner in which one treats a child or any defenseless thing.

The evaluations given in Chapter Three above were made on the basis of the sound produced by two high fidelity machines. The first of these was made for me by E.M.G. Handmade Gramophones, London, and made use of two Whiteley speakers (one 10 inch, one 12 inch) mounted in corner baffles to provide a sense of non-directional sound from a broad source. This is essential for good presence in orchestral recordings, since an orchestra is the broadest sound source there is, and the effect of hearing it come from a hole in the wall or from within a small cabinet is completely artificial. F. G. G. Davey's steep-cut filter was incorporated and proved a very desirable accessory.

The second machine was of somewhat larger size and offered greater flexibility in control. The records were played with the B.J. arm mounted with the Garrard 301 transcription table. The Garrard 301 is an excellent design, beautifully realized in production, and I have the highest regard for its performance. In the B.J. arm I used a Decca (London) ffrr H-type (magenta) head with a modified, diamond-tipped armature of my own design. For comparison I also made use of a G.E. cartridge in a Fairchild 280 arm, which proved to be superior to the B.J., but unfortunately did not permit the mounting of the Decca head.

Eventually two amplifiers were used, the Leak TL 10/Point-One amplifier, pre-amplifier combination and the Pye HF 25/25A amplifier and pre-amplifier. Both proved to be excellent, athough the superior power handling capacity and negligible transient distortion of the Pye (and certain other features of its design) gave it an advantage over the admirable, but smaller, Leak. Three speaker systems were used: a Barker single-cone unit on a corner baffle, a twelve-inch Tannoy dual concentric in a Klipsch-horn corner mounting, and the identical type of speaker in the Pye "Concerto" bass-reflex cabinet. The latter unit, as modified by myself with more effective acoustical insulation, proved to be my choice. The Tannoy dual concentric, particularly in its fifteen-inch form, is probably the standard of the world for speakers of its type, or at least I so regard it.

It must be added that equally good sound could have been obtained from a number of other combinations of high quality components. The reader, however, may have a certain interest in what I used, and he is entitled to know.*

* It should be noted that these remarks are unsolicited. All the equipment mentioned was selected, bought, and paid for by myself. Similarly one should note that although the RCA Victor Company did supply me with certain records as "review copies," the majority of the recordings discussed were also bought and paid for. The reader may assume that I take both the equipment and the recordings on their actual merits, as I am capable of judging them, uncorrupted by any commercial interest.

APPENDIX THREE: *Chronology of Toscanini's Life*

1867	Toscanini born, March 25, in Parma, Italy.
1876/85	Student at the Royal School of Music, Parma. Graduates at eighteen with highest honors in 'cello, piano, and composition.
1886	'Cellist and assistant chorus master with Rossi's opera company in Brazil. Professional debut as a conductor in *Aïda*, June 25, in Rio de Janeiro. Italian debut in *Edmea* of Catalani at Turin, November 4.
1886/98	Barnstorming in various Italian opera houses. Premieres: *I Pagliacci*, 1892; *La Bohème*, 1896; first Italian performance of *Die Götterdämmerung*, 1895; etc.
1896	Debut as a symphonic conductor, Turin, March 20.
1897	Marries Carla de Martini in Milan, June 21.
1898/1903 1906/08	Musical Director of La Scala, Milan.
1908/15	Conductor at the Metropolitan Opera House, New York. First North American appearances at age forty-one.
1913	First New York appearance as symphonic conductor, April 13.
1915/19	Living in semi-retirement in Milan.
1920/21	North American tour with La Scala Orchestra.
1921/29	Musical Director of La Scala, Milan.
1926/27	Appears as guest conductor of the New York Philharmonic during two seasons.
1927/36	Conductor of the Philharmonic-Symphony Orchestra of New York, sharing large portions of the season with Mengelberg (1927-30), Kleiber (1930-32), Walter (1931-34), Klemperer (1934-36), Rodzinski (1934-35), Beecham (1935-36), and others.
1930	European tour with the Philharmonic-Symphony Orchestra of New York.
1930/31	Conducts two seasons at Bayreuth.
1931	Attacked by Fascists, Bologna, May 14.
1934/37	Conducts at Salzburg Festival.
1935/39	London concerts with the B.B.C. Symphony.
1937/54	Conductor of the National Broadcasting Company Symphony Orchestra, engaged and trained for him by Rodzinski. Shares orchestra with Rodzinski (1937-38), Stokowski (1941-44), Cantelli (1949-54), and others.

1938/39	Conductor of Lucerne Festival.
1940	Tours South America with the N.B.C. Symphony.
1950	Tours the United States with the N.B.C. Symphony.
1954	Retires as conductor of the N.B.C. Symphony, April 4; leads the orchestra for the last time, June 5.

Appendix Four: *The Toscanini Recordings Listed by Composers*

For reference and index purposes I here list all Toscanini recordings released in the United States (or Britain) through April, 1956. Persons wishing to read my comments on any individual recording will find them in Chapter 3 in chronological order under the year cited for the disk. The exceptions to this rule are the V-Disks, which were not available commercially, and are listed as a group on pp. 128-30. V-Disk recordings are here identified by a star before the year.

By my count, 262 Toscanini recordings were released in the period covered by this listing, representing 186 separate works of music. The difference between these two figures represents seventy-six duplications of a previously recorded work.

Only authorized recordings are given here. Air checks and pirated disks, never available through normal commercial channels, being excluded for obvious reasons.

The names of assisting artists are given in backets.

Composer and Work	Year(s) of Recording(s)
BACH	
SUITE NO. 3: AIR [AIR ON THE G STRING]	1946
BARBER	
QUARTET, OP. 11: ADAGIO FOR STRINGS	1942
BEETHOVEN	
CONCERTO FOR PIANO NO. 1 [Dorfmann]	1945
CONCERTO FOR PIANO NO. 3 [Rubinstein]	1944
CONCERTO FOR VIOLIN [Heifetz]	1940
CORIOLAN OVERTURE	1945
THE CREATURES OF PROMETHEUS: OVERTURE	1944
EGMONT OVERTURE [#1]	1939
[#2]	1953
FIDELIO [Bampton, Steber, Peerce, etc.]	1944
: ARIA: KOMM, O HOFFNUNG [Bampton]	1944
LEONORE OVERTURE NO. 1 [#1]	1939
[#2]	★1944
LEONORE OVERTURE NO. 2	1939
LEONORE OVERTURE NO. 3 [#1]	1939
[#2]	1945
MISSA SOLEMNIS [Marshall, Merriman, Conley, Hines, Shaw Chorale]	1953
OVERTURE FOR THE CONSECRATION OF THE HOUSE	1946
QUARTET NO. 16 (OP. 135): LENTO AND VIVACE (Ar. for orch.)	1938

246

Composer and Work	Year(s) of Recording(s)
SEPTET, OP. 20 (Ar. for orch.)	1951
SYMPHONY NO. 1: FINALE	1921
SYMPHONY NO. 1: [#1]	1937
[#2]	1951
SYMPHONY NO. 2	1949
SYMPHONY NO. 3: [EROICA] [#1]	1939
[#2]	1949
SYMPHONY NO. 4: [#1]	1939
[#2]	1951
SYMPHONY NO. 5: FINALE	1920
SYMPHONY NO. 5: [#1]	1939
[#2]	1952
SYMPHONY NO. 6: [PASTORAL] [#1]	1937
[#2]	1952
SYMPHONY NO. 7: [#1]	1936
[#2]	1951
SYMPHONY NO. 8: [#1]	1941
[#2]	1952
SYMPHONY NO. 9: [CHORAL] [Farrell, Merriman, Peerce, Scott, Robert Shaw Chorale]	1952

BERLIOZ

THE DAMNATION OF FAUST: RÁKÓCZY MARCH [#1]	1920
[#2]	1945
HAROLD IN ITALY [Cooley]	1953
ROMAN CARNIVAL OVERTURE	1953
ROMEO AND JULIET, DRAMATIC SYMPHONY: PART II	1946
ROMEO ALONE; GREAT FESTIVITIES AT THE HOUSE OF CAPULET; LOVE SCENE	
: QUEEN MAB SCHERZO	1951

BIZET

L'ARLÉSIENNE: SUITE NO. 1 : NO. 4: CARILLON	★1943
: SUITE NO. 2 : NO. 4: FARANDOLE	1921
CARMEN: SUITE NO. 1	1952
: PRELUDE TO ACT IV [ARAGONAISE]	1921
: MARCH OF THE TOREADORS	★1943

BOCCHERINI

QUINTET, OP. 13, NO. 5: MINUET	★1943

BOITO

MEFISTOFELE: PROLOGUE [Moscona, Columbus Boys' Choir, Shaw Chorale]	1954

BRAHMS

CONCERTO FOR PIANO NO. 2 [Horowitz]	1940
HUNGARIAN DANCES (Orch. by Dvořák): NO. 1 [#1]	★1943
[#2]	1953
Nos. 17, 20, 21	1953
SYMPHONY NO. 1 [#1]	1941
[#2]	1951
SYMPHONY NO. 2	1952
SYMPHONY NO. 3	1952

Composer and Work	Year(s) of Recording(s)
SYMPHONY No. 4	1951
TRAGIC OVERTURE	1937
VARIATIONS ON A THEME OF HAYDN [#1]	1936
[#2]	1952
CASTELNUOVO-TEDESCO	
OVERTURE TO A FAIRY TALE	★1945
CATALANI	
LA WALLY: PRELUDE TO ACT IV	1952
LORELEI: DANCE OF THE WATER NYMPHS	1952
CHERUBINI	
SYMPHONY IN D	1952
DEBUSSY	
IMAGES, THIRD SET: No. 2: IBERIA	1950
LA MER	1950
PRELUDE TO THE AFTERNOON OF A FAUN	★1945
DONIZETTI	
DON PASQUALE: OVERTURE [#1]	1921
[#2]	1951
DUKAS	
ARIANE ET BARBE-BLEU, EXCERPTS	★1947
THE SORCERER'S APPRENTICE [#1]	1929
[#2]	1950
DVOŘÁK	
SYMPHONY No. 5 [FROM THE NEW WORLD]	1953
ELGAR	
VARIATIONS ON AN ORIGINAL THEME [ENIGMA]	1951
: No. 7 TROYTE	★1945
FRANCK	
PSYCHÉ: No. 4 PSYCHÉ AND EROS	1952
GALILEI (Orch. by Respighi)	
GAGLIARDA	1920
GARIBALDI'S WAR HYMN	★1943
GERSHWIN	
AN AMERICAN IN PARIS	1945
GILLIS	
SYMPHONY No. 5½ [SYMPHONY FOR FUN]	★1947
GLINKA	
JOTA ARGONESA	★1943
KAMARINSKAYA	1940
GLUCK	
ORFEO: ACT II [Merriman, Gibson, Robert Shaw Chorale]	1952
: DANCE OF THE SPIRITS [#1]	1929
[#2]	1946

Composer and Work	Year(s) of Recording(s)
GROFÉ	
GRAND CANYON SUITE	1945
: ON THE TRAIL AND CLOUDBURST	★1943
HAYDN	
SYMPHONY No. 88	1938
SYMPHONY No. 94 [SURPRISE]	1953
SYMPHONY No. 98	1945
SYMPHONY No. 101 [CLOCK] [#1]	1929
[#2]	1947
HÉROLD	
ZAMPA OVERTURE [#1]	★1943
[#2]	1952
HUMPERDINCK	
HANSEL AND GRETEL: PRELUDE	1952
KABALEVSKY	
COLAS BREUGNON: OVERTURE [#1]	★1945
[#2]	1946
LIADOV	
KIKIMORA	1952
MARTUCCI	
NOVELETTA	★1948
MASSENET	
SUITE No. 4 [SCÈNES PITTORESQUES]: No. 4 FÊTE BOHÈME	1921
MENDELSSOHN	
INCIDENTAL MUSIC TO "A MIDSUMMER NIGHT'S DREAM":	
No. 1 SCHERZO [#1]	1921
[#2]	1926
[#3]	1929
[#4]	1946
[#5]	1947
No. 7 NOCTURNE [#1]	1926
[#2]	1947
No. 10 WEDDING MARCH [#1]	1921
[#2]	1947
OVERTURE, No. 5 INTERMEZZO, No. 12 FINALE [chorus of women]	1947
OCTET FOR STRINGS, OP. 20	1947
SCHERZO	1945
SYMPHONY No. 4 [ITALIAN]	1954
SYMPHONY No. 5 [REFORMATION]	1953
MOUSSORGSKY (Orch. by Ravel)	
PICTURES AT AN EXHIBITION	1953
MOZART	
CONCERTO FOR BASSOON No. 1 [Sharrow]	1947
DIVERTIMENTO No. 15 [K. 287]	1947

Composer and Work	Year(s) of Recording(s)
THE MAGIC FLUTE: OVERTURE	1938
SYMPHONY No. 35 [HAFFNER] [#1]	1929
[#2]	1946
SYMPHONY No. 39: MINUETTO AND FINALE	1920
SYMPHONY No. 40: FIRST MOVEMENT	★1946
SYMPHONY No. 40: [#1]	1938/39
[#2]	1950
SYMPHONY No. 41 [JUPITER]	1945/46

PAGANINI
| MOTO PERPETUO | 1939 |

PIZETTI
| LA PISANELLE: LE QUAI DU PORT DE FAMAGOUSTE | 1920 |

PONCHIELLI
| LA GIOCONDA: DANCE OF THE HOURS [#1] | ★1943 |
| [#2] | 1952 |

PROKOFIEV
| SYMPHONY No. 1 [CLASSICAL] [#1] | ★1944 |
| [#2] | 1951 |

PUCCINI
LA BOHÈME [Albanese, McKnight, Peerce, Valentino, etc.]	1946
: FINALE, ACT I; MUSETTA'S WALTZ SONG, FINALE, ACT II	
(taken from the same performance)	★1946

RAVEL
| DAPHNIS AND CHLOE: SUITE No. 2 | 1949 |

RESPIGHI
THE FOUNTAINS OF ROME	1951
THE PINES OF ROME	1953
ROMAN FESTIVALS	1949

ROSSINI
THE BARBER OF SEVILLE: OVERTURE [#1]	1929
[#2]	1945
LA CENERENTOLA: OVERTURE	1945
LA GAZZA LADRA: OVERTURE [#1]	★1941
[#2]	1945
THE ITALIAN WOMAN IN ALGIERS: OVERTURE	1936
THE SILKEN LADDER: OVERTURE	1938
SEMIRAMIDE: OVERTURE [#1]	1936
[#2]	1951
IL SIGNOR BRUSCHINO: OVERTURE [#1]	★1945
[#2]	1945
WILLIAM TELL: OVERTURE [#1]	1939
[#2]	1953
: ACT I, PASSO A SEI [#1]	★1943
[#2]	1945

SAINT-SAËNS
| DANSE MACABRE | 1950 |
| SYMPHONY No. 3 | 1952 |

Composer and Work	Year(s) of Recording(s)
SCHUBERT	
SYMPHONY No. 5	1953
SYMPHONY No. 8 [UNFINISHED]	1950
SYMPHONY No. 9 [THE GREAT C MAJOR] [#1]	1947
[#2]	1953
SCHUMANN	
MANFRED OVERTURE	1947
SIBELIUS	
FINLANDIA	1952
THE SWAN OF TUONELA	★1945
SMETANA	
MA VLAST: No. 2, VLTAVA [THE MOLDAU] [#1]	★1941
[#2]	1950
SOUSA	
THE STARS AND STRIPES FOREVER [#1]	★1943
[#2]	1945
STRAUSS, J., JR.	
ON THE BEAUTIFUL BLUE DANUBE [#1]	★1941
[#2]	1942
TRITSCH-TRATSCH POLKA	1941
STRAUSS, R.	
DEATH AND TRANSFIGURATION	1952
DON JUAN	1951
TILL EULENSPIEGEL	1952
VON SUPPÉ	
POET AND PEASANT OVERTURE	1943
TCHAIKOVSKY	
CONCERTO FOR PIANO No. 1 [Horowitz]	1941
MANFRED SYMPHONY	1949
NUTCRACKER BALLET: SUITE [#1]	★1943
[#2]	1951
ROMEO AND JULIET: OVERTURE-FANTASIA	1946
SYMPHONY No. 6 [PATHÉTIQUE]	1947
THOMAS	
MIGNON: OVERTURE [#1]	1942
[#2]	1952
VAUGHAN WILLIAMS	
FANTASIA FOR DOUBLE STRING ORCHESTRA ON A THEME OF THOMAS TALLIS	★1945
VERDI	
AÏDA [Nelli, Gustafson, Tucker, Valdengo, etc.] (release pending)	1949
A MASKED BALL [Nelli, Turner, Peerce, Merrill, etc.]	1954
DON CARLOS: O DON FATALE [Merriman]	★1943
FALSTAFF [Nelli, Merriman, Elmo, Valdengo, etc.]	1950

Composer and Work	Year(s) of Recording(s)
La Forza del Destino: Overture [#1]	1945
[#2]	★1946
[#3]	1952
Otello [Nelli, Merriman, Vinay, Valdengo, etc.]	1947
: Willow Song and Ave Maria (same performance)	★1947
Te Deum [Shaw Chorale]	1954
Requiem Mass [Nelli, Barbieri, Di Stefano, Siepi, Shaw Chorale]	1951
Rigoletto: Quartet [Ribla, Merriman, Peerce, Valentino]	★1943
La Traviata [Albanese, Peerce, Merrill, etc.]	1946
: Preludes to Acts I and III [#1]	1929
[#2]	1941

WAGNER

A Faust Overture	1946
Die Götterdämmerung:	
Dawn and Siegfried's Rhine Journey (Ar. Toscanini) [#1]	1936
[#2]	1941
[#3]	1949
: Siegfried's Death and Funeral Music (Ar. Toscanini) [#1]	1941
[#2]	1952
: Immolation Scene [Traubel]	1941
: Orchestral Finale (contained in Immolation Scene)	★1941
Lohengrin: Prelude to Act I [#1]	1936
[#2]	1941
[#3]	1951
: Prelude to Act III [#1]	1936
[#2]	1951
Die Meistersinger: Prelude to Act I [#1]	1946
[#2]	1951
: Prelude to Act III	1951
Parsifal: Prelude and Good Friday Spell	1949
Siegfried Idyll [#1]	1936
[#2]	1946
[#3]	1952
Siegfried: Forest Murmurs	1951
Tristan und Isolde: Prelude	1952
: Liebestod [#1]	1942
[#2]	★1943
[#3]	1952
Die Walküre: Ride of the Valkyries [#1]	1946
[#2]	1952

WALDTEUFEL

The Skaters Waltz	1945

WEBER

Euryanthe: Overture	1951
Der Freischütz: Overture [#1]	1945
[#2]	1952
Invitation to the Dance (Orch. by Berlioz) [#1]	1938
[#2]	1951
Oberon: Overture	1952

WOLF-FERRARI

The Secret of Suzanne: Overture	1921